PIECES
❖OF MY❖
HEART

*Writings Inspired by
Animals and Nature*

JIM WILLIS

*Foreword by Marc Bekoff
Illustrations by Christine J. Head*

Praise for *Pieces of My Heart*

"Jim Willis has a keen understanding of the intricate relationships we humans have with animals. His stories and poems resonate on many levels – and keep readers coming back for more. This is a superb collection of works."
Janet Tobiassen DVM, About.com Guide to Veterinary Medicine

"Jim Willis is making a difference in the lives of animals every day. This comes through loud and clear in Pieces of My Heart. *Compassionate, spiritual, emotional, heart-wrenching, and insightful, this book will move you in ways you never thought possible. It's an inspirational journey that stays on your mind long after you finish reading. Do animals matter? They do to Jim Willis. And after you read* Pieces of My Heart *animals will matter to you, too."*
Vernon Weir, Development Director, American Sanctuary Association

"Everything Jim Willis writes comes from the heart. His prose has impact and a depth of understanding and compassion that I admire greatly. Pieces of My Heart *is a must for anyone who cares for the safety and well-being of all animals."*
Kerry Parmenter, Founder & Managing Director, Planet Pet Downunder, Sydney, Australia

*"*Pieces of My Heart *by Jim Willis is uniquely his 'other way' of seeing life and humanity. Some stories would be agonizingly sad were it not for the hope and belief that he holds out to the reader. The collection is best taken in small pieces, each one carefully and thoughtfully savored. If life is a piece of cake, this collection is the icing."*
Barbara J. Andrews, Managing Editor, TheDogPlace.com; author, *World of the Akita* and other breed-specific books; columnist, *ShowSight* magazine, and freelance dog sport journalist

"The writings of Jim Willis have inspired me to keep Animal Home operating. His prose, 'The Animals' Savior' has been the opening statement on our Dog Rescue page for a long time. His essay 'How Could You?' is so powerful that I get tears in my eyes just thinking about it. If people could only apply his writings to

all animals, including the human animal, this earth would be heaven."
Herb Rabe, President, AnimalHome.com

"In Pieces of My Heart, Jim Willis has opened a window into the heart, mind, and soul of a man who is brother to the creatures he writes about; a man who shares every nuance of their fragile lives; a man who selflessly acts on his beliefs. As you read, you'll laugh, you'll cry, you'll be profoundly moved, and you'll hear pieces of your own heart strumming in response. Listen..."
Franny Syufy, Writer-Editor for Cats at About.com

"Jim Willis makes a connection with the hearts and souls of animals that all humans should strive for. His writings read as if the creatures he so passionately cares for penned them. He powerfully reinforces the concept and importance of the human-animal bond, and that bond is evident in nearly everything he writes. Pieces of My Heart comes closer to speaking the minds of our non-human animal brethren and speaking up for Creation than anything else you'll ever read."
Dick Weavil, Publisher, AnimalTalk newsletter

"Jim's writings have made me laugh and cry. His understanding of God's creatures and the respect we should have for them is inspiring."
Peggy Haynes, Director, Pet Rescue North, Inc., Jacksonville, Florida

"Touching, poignant, humorous, and honest...all words that describe Pieces of My Heart. *With a clear perspective, Jim Willis offers his readers inspirational stories and unlimited compassion.* Pieces of My Heart *is a memorable and gentle work of heartfelt emotion. This work encourages a deep introspection on life, as well as an honest look at the world's most dangerous predator, man, and our dealings with animals. It inspires us, poetically and movingly, to look closer at our actions and to take responsibility for them. I strongly recommend this book to anyone who has loved, cared for, rescued, or has had even the slightest concern for the well-being of the animals we share our world with."*
Stacy Mantle, Author of Conquering the Food Chain: Living Amongst Animals (Without Becoming One)

I am sometimes asked, "Why do you spend so much of your time and money talking about kindness to animals when there is so much cruelty to men?" I answer: "I am working at the roots."
~ GEORGE T. ANGELL
❖

PIECES
❖OF MY❖
HEART

*Writings Inspired by
Animals and Nature*

❖

JIM WILLIS

A publication of
Jim Willis and The Tiergarten Sanctuary Trust
USA & Europe
tiergartenjim@yahoo.com

Published in the USA by:

INFI∞ITY
PUBLISHING.COM

519 West Lancaster Avenue
Haverford, PA 19041-1413
Info@infinitypublishing.com
www.infinitypublishing.com
www.buybooksontheweb.com
Phone 610-520-2500
Toll-free 877-BUY BOOK
Fax 610-519-0261

Sales of this book support the efforts of The Tiergarten Sanctuary Trust, founded by the Author. We encourage ordering directly from the publisher.

❖The Author has made a special arrangement with the publisher whereby animal, conservation/environmental, and advocacy organizations may order *Pieces of My Heart* in quantity at a substantial discount for resale in order to benefit their fundraising. Please refer to the last page of the book for details, visit the *Pieces of My Heart* website at *www.crean.com/jimwillis*, or call the publisher for more information.

❖ *Illustrations Copyright Christine J. Head*
❖ *Text design and layout by Michelle Crean*
❖ *Photography by Peggy Strain*
❖ *Cover design by Doreen J. Sanfelici*

Printed in the United States of America on recycled paper.
ISBN 0-7414-1015-X

Dedicated to my parents, Valentina and Earl Willis,
who gave me some of the greatest examples of my life
and taught me to love words.
To my wife, Nicole, who makes everything possible
and is my unsung heroine.
To my wife's parents, Jutta and Hermann Valentin,
who loved me as their son.
And to the beautiful human and animal spirits who have
accompanied us on our journey through this life
and sometimes run on ahead.

Never doubt that a small group of thoughtful,
committed citizens can change the world.
Indeed, it is the only thing that ever has.
~ MARGARET MEAD
❖

❖ Table of Contents ❖

MINDING ANIMALS: GRACE, COMPASSION, PLAY, AND LOVE
by Marc Bekoff

Jim Willis tirelessly and selflessly works for nonhuman animal beings (hereafter animals). Anyone who has read his essays knows just how much he respects and loves *all* animals, small and large, skinny and fat, tailed or tailless, black, white, or mottled. Jim also writes about the need for connection, deep and reciprocal interconnections among *all* animals. I couldn't agree more.

As someone who has studied animal behavior for more than three decades, I can attest to how important ethological studies are, not only for learning about the amazing beings with whom we share Earth, sky, and water, but also for learning about who we are, our place in nature, our humanness. In my studies I ask, "What is it like to be another individual?" and I try to place myself in their paws, in their hearts and minds, to learn as much as I can about *their* worlds. We can be best understood in relationship to others. Animals are surely an important "way of knowing," sources of deep wisdom, humility, grace, compassion, and love.

Studying animal behavior, especially their emotional – passionate – natures and their individual personalities also informs discussion of evolutionary continuity, following up on Charles Darwin's ideas that differences among many animals are differences in degree, not differences in kind. It is very clear that learning about other animal beings – how they spend their time, who they interact with, where they do what they do and how, their intellectual and cognitive abilities (cognitive ethology), and their deep emotional lives – is essential for gaining a full appreciation of human spirituality and what it is to be human. Tool-use, language-use, self-awareness and self-consciousness, culture, art, and rationality no longer can reliably be used to draw species boundaries that separate humans from other animal beings. Such speciesistic claims that only humans use tools or language, are self-aware, have culture, are artists, or use reason are no longer defensible given the enormous growth in our knowledge of our animal kin with whom we share this planet.

Skeptical dismissals that animals are nothing other than non-sentient automatons are dead-ends. Skeptics need to share the burden of proof with those who claim that some animals have highly evolved passionate natures and that they have deep feelings about the worlds in which they live. While one cannot prove without doubt that some animals have rich emotional lives, it also is impossible to prove that they do not. Keeping open hearts and minds is the only way to head into the future.

In my research I try to identify and empathize with the animals who I study. A few years ago I developed the idea of "minding animals." Basically, the phrase "minding animals" means two things. First, "minding animals" refers to caring for other animal beings, respecting them for who they are, appreciating their own world views, and wondering what and how they're feeling and why. The second meaning refers to the fact that many animals have very active and thoughtful minds. I call myself a deep ethologist. I, as the "see-er," try to become the "seen." I become coyote, I become penguin (I also become tree, and often I become rock). I name my animal friends and try to step into their sensory and motor worlds to discover what it might be like to be a given individual, how they sense their surroundings and how they move about and behave in certain situations.

In my work I also stress that it is through social cooperation that groups (communities) are built from individuals agreeing to work in harmony with other individuals. In my view, cooperation is not merely always a by-product of tempering aggressive and selfish tendencies (combating Richard Dawkins's selfish genes), and attempts at reconciliation. Rather, cooperation and fairness can evolve on their own because they are important in the formation and maintenance of social relationships. This view, in which nature is sanitized, contrasts with those who see aggression, cheating, selfishness, and perhaps amorality as driving the evolution of sociality. The combative Hobbesian world in which individuals are constantly at one another's throats is not the natural state of affairs, nature is not always red in tooth and claw, and altruism is not always simply selfishness disguised. It is important to consider the possibility that it feels good to be nice to others, to cooperate with them and to treat them fairly, to forgive them for their mistakes and shortcomings, to love them.

I also am deeply concerned with the nature and asymmetry of human-animal interactions from theoretical and practical perspectives, specifically the anthropocentric use of animals that usually is justified by some form of a utilitarian calculus in which human benefits are traded off against costs to the animal. I also am deeply concerned about the ways in which humans attempt to live with – manage, control, dominate – wild nature, especially as we go about "redecorating" nature for our own benefits.

I am a patient and compassionate activist who believes that "getting my hands dirty," getting out there and showing people about the horrible things we do to far too many animals, is the best way to make long-lasting changes in their hearts and heads. Indifference is deadly. My activism centers on getting people to think and to tell me why they think, feel, and act the ways they do.

As an unwavering dreamer and optimist, I often feel victimized by hope. Nonetheless, it is my passionate dream that changes in attitude and heart will ultimately bring forth harmony in the relationships between animals and humans, for non-human animals will forever be competing with humans, their dominant, big-brained, mammalian kin. Without a doubt, the animals are likely to lose most of these encounters as humans continue to try to redecorate nature for their own selfish ends.

Activism for animals has helped me tap into my own spirituality for there are numerous costs to activism – harassment, intimidation, humiliation, and frustration – that often become personal. I have felt the effects of attempts to silence my questions about the reintroduction of Canadian lynx into Colorado (*www.bouldernews.com/opinion/columnists/bekmarc.html*) as well as my questioning why dogs had to be killed in physiology courses in medical school in order for students to learn about life (*www.bouldernews.com/opinion/columnists/bekoff.html*). (I left a graduate medical program because I did not want to kill cats or dogs as part of my education "in the name of science." I did not want to kill animals to learn about life and gave up a life-long dream.) Such assaults made me dig deeply into my heart in my efforts to understand and to explain to others why I was doing what I was doing, whether it was organizing protests to save animals or partaking in candlelight vigils and prayer services for animals who had been killed. Suffice it to say, compassionate people who push the envelope can easily engender the wrath of small minds. (I was once called a "flake" by some of my colleagues for my position on animal rights. I was flattered and wondered why they were taking the time to engage a flake! Surely they have better things to do with their valuable time.)

One worldview that drives me is that I believe that every individual counts and that every individual makes a difference. As Margaret Mead noted: "Never doubt that a small group of thoughtful, committed citizens can change the world. Indeed, it is the only thing that ever has." Creative proactive solutions drenched in deep humility, compassion, caring, respect, and love need to be developed to deal with the broad range of problems with which we are currently confronted. Activism often underlies their formulation and implementation.

I am an optimist, a hopeful human being. I never say "never." I ache with the pains of other beings and also feel pangs when I see inanimate landscapes being destroyed. Surely we do not want to be remembered as the generation that killed nature. Now is the time for everyone to work for universal planetary peace. There is no alternative to world peace and we must sow seeds without hesitation to accomplish this urgent goal. It is essential that we do better than our ancestors. No one could argue that a world with significantly less – no – cruelty and with boundless compassion, respect, grace, humility, spirituality, peace, and love would not be a better world in which to live and to raise our children and theirs with grace and humility. We are all citizens of Earth, members of a global community in which intimate reciprocal and beneficent peaceful relationships are mandatory. We have compelling responsibilities for making Earth a better and more peaceful habitat for all beings. Time is not on our side. We must reflect and step lightly as we "redecorate nature."

I yearn for a seamless tapestry of oneness, a warm blanket, a soul-scape of deep and reciprocal friendships in which all individuals count, a single community in which individuals are at one with all others, in which the see-er and the seen are one, a community in which it feels good and makes individuals happy to be kind to others. My own dreams and spirituality are based on a deep and passionate drive for reconciliation, a seamless unity – a wholeness and oneness – motivated by trust, compassion, respect, grace, humility, and love. I continually plead for developing heart-felt and holistic science that allows for fun, joy, and play along with interdisciplinary talk about kindness, compassion, respect, grace, humility, spirituality, peace, and love. Science need not be suspicious of things it cannot fully understand. Animals trust us.

Our companion's hearts, like our hearts, are very fragile, so we must be very gentle with them. Their and our heartbeats are synchronous and nourish one another's spirit and soul. We can never be too nice or too generous with our love for our dear and trusting companions, who are so full of forgiveness and grace and are deeply pure of heart. Indeed, by honoring our companions' trust in us and love for us we can view our own spirituality in a mirror in which all life is clearly reflected and boundlessly interconnected.

Our companions can make us more human and humane if we open ourselves up to the depths of their presence and the essence of their very being. So, what can we do? Here are a few suggestions:

Let us make every effort to understand and to appreciate the essence of our companions;

Let us drench ourselves in their spirit and soul;

Let us praise them openly and thank them graciously and gracefully for who they are as we embrace their lessons in compassion, devotion, respect, spirituality, and love. Their lives and ours will be richer, more fulfilled, complete, and radiant. Love will abound and the awe-inspiring universe as a whole will become a better place – a soul-scape – in which to live in harmony with all of our kin, other life, and inanimate landscapes.

Let us never defile that trust. Let us *never* avert our eyes or our other senses, or our hearts from the eyes and voices of all other beings, our kin, our friends, who urgently beg for and truly need our immediate, uncompromising, and unconditional aid and love. We are obliged not to do so. We certainly can do much more than we have done.

In the end, in my humble opinion, it boils down to love. The power of love must not be underestimated as we try to reconnect with nature and other animals. We must love the universe and all of its inhabitants – animate and inanimate.

In the grand scheme of things, individuals receive what they give. If love is poured out in abundance then it will be returned in abundance, and there is no fear of exhausting the potent self-reinforcing feeling that serves as a powerful stimulant for generating compassion, respect, and love for all life. It is important to recognize that each and every individual plays an essential role and that each individual's spirit and love are intertwined with the spirit and love of others. These emergent interrelationships, which transcend individuals' embodied selves, foster a sense of oneness and can work in harmony to make this a better and more compassionate world for all beings.

So, as I have argued before and will continue to argue, when animals and other wild nature lose, we all lose. We must stroll with our kin and not leave them in our tumultuous wake of rampant, self-serving destruction. Holism and universal compassion and love need to replace impersonal, cold, and objective reductionism that alienates and disembodies individuals, and dispenses with, or fragments their hearts, their spirits, and their souls.

We must also play more and enjoy life whenever we can. I really mean this! Even when times are tough it is important to be "light." I've studied animal play for more than thirty years and I've come to view play as being characterized by what I call the "Five S's of Play," its Spirit, Symmetry, Synchrony, Sacredness, and Soulfulness. The Spirit of play is laid bare for all to see as animals prodigally run about, wrestle, and knock one another over. The Symmetry and Synchrony of play are reflected in the harmony of the mutual agreements to trust one another – individuals share intentions to cooperate with one another to prevent play from spilling over into fighting. This trust is Sacred. Finally, there is a deepness to animal play in that the players are so immersed in play that they are the play. Play is thus a Soulful activity, perhaps the essence of an individual's being in the moment as they play from deep in their hearts. As Aquinas noted, play is about being, there are no why's in play. By playing more – by following the lead of the animals who we love as they romp about with one another – we'll be able to face the troubled world more squarely. By playing more we will be able harness the energy needed to make more concerted efforts to heal a wounded world. Play is serious business; play allows us to rekindle the flame of compassion, respect, and love.

We can indeed love animals more and not love people less. We need to be motivated by love and not by fear of what it will mean if we come to love animals for who they are. Animals are not less than human. They are who they are and need to be understood in their own worlds.

It is essential that we do better than our ancestors and we surely have the resources to do so. The big question is whether we will choose to make the proactive commitment to making this a better world – a more compassionate world in which deep interrelationships abound and are nourished by respect, compassion, grace, humility, spirituality, and love – a world in which love is plentiful and shared – before it's too late. I hope so. Jim Willis's work is clearly a step in the right direction. Jim's heart is in the right place and I sincerely hope that everyone will follow his selfless lead.

———

Dr. Marc Bekoff teaches biology at the University of Colorado, Boulder. He is the author or editor of many books including the Encyclopedia of Animal Rights and Animal Welfare; Strolling with Our Kin: Speaking For and Respecting Voiceless Animals, *and* The Smile of a Dolphin: Remarkable Accounts of Animal Emotions. *His latest book,* Minding Animals: Awareness, Emotions, and Heart *will be published in April 2002 (Oxford University Press, from which some of this essay is taken) and his book with Dr. Jane Goodall titled* The Ten Trusts: What We Must Do to Care for the Animals We Love *will be published in October 2002 (Harper Collins). He and Dr. Goodall recently co-founded Ethologists for the Ethical Treatment of Animals/Citizens for ResponsibleAnimal Behavior Studies,www.ethologicalethics.org.*

————

If you talk with the animals they will talk with you and you will know each other. If you do not talk to them, you will not know them, and what you do not know, you will fear. What one fears one destroys.
~ CHIEF DAN GEORGE
❖

PREFACE

When I was a child my parents wouldn't allow me to have a dog or cat, due to finances and their physical handicaps. I made do with turtles, fish and the much over-rated "sea monkeys." My parents answered my frequent complaints about not having a "real pet" by assuring me that when I grew up I could have as many animals as I liked. (I grew up to exceed their expectations.) I befriended every animal I met, including a dead pigeon I found frozen on the ground one winter day when I was about six. My mother met me at the front door and forbid me to bring in the dead bird "to get warm." I cried and threw a fit on the front porch until most of the neighborhood was at their windows.

My mother thought she was doing me a favor when I was fourteen by talking a city animal shelter director into accepting me as a volunteer. I worked there every weekend and school holiday for two years and it left a permanent impression on me. Every week I fell hopelessly in love with one or more animals. Time and again I heard the gas chamber chugging in the back room and then saw the bodies of my animal friends loaded into a freezer until they could be carted away to the city dump. (How incredibly cruel that the gas chamber is still used in some American shelters today!) I met the public and heard all their lame excuses for betraying the pets who loved them and I couldn't understand how they could bear to part with the pets I loved fiercely for those few days until most of them went to that ominous back room. I don't know where I found the emotional strength to survive that experience at such a young age, but I vowed that someday, no matter what else I might do in life, I would do what I could to help animals. Writing about animals and animal issues has become my adult version of crying and throwing a fit.

Since that time, I have rescued animals and placed them in good homes. Over a decade ago in Germany, my wife and I founded and funded a multi-species, all-breed rescue effort, now The Tiergarten Sanctuary Trust. That effort has amounted to a drop in a bucket compared to the tremendous need, especially during an interim five years in America, where puppy and kitten mills crank out litter after litter, where pet shops sell their overpriced and poorly bred fluffy wares, where much of the public refuses to spay or neuter their pets, and where governments and the media turn a blind eye to the silent holocaust that results.

Early in 2001, I wrote the essay from a dog's point of view, "How Could You?" It has been much published and people around the world have written to tell me its truths made them cry. A Michigan philanthropist paid his local newspaper seven thousand dollars to publish it as a full-page advertisement and one of their columnists followed up on the public's reaction. I hope it has made some of the public think about the consequences of their actions and to consider carefully before adding a pet to their lives. Although I sent "HCY?" to many national animal organizations, few chose to publish it. Someone in the publications department of one of the largest organizations declined to use it with "we intend our publication to be a safe haven for animal lovers."

I don't think we *can* remain in our safe havens, when by doing so we ignore the plight of animals, when many animals have no haven at all. My essay and the grassroots effort to publish it that resulted became one of the reasons to write *Pieces of My Heart*. Since the animals cannot speak for themselves, since nature cannot defend itself, I will add my voice to those who speak for them. Those who know me know that I prefer the label "animal advocate," because I won't accept any division between "animal welfare" and "animal rights" – the animals are dependent upon us to cooperate well and everything we do for them is a part of the whole.

My wife Nicole and I have for many years shared our lives with over three dozen rescued animals. We often took the special needs animals, the elderly, those with medical and behavior problems, and those refused by other rescues or threatened with death for such normal canine behavior as biting. Our love changed and healed them, and their love bettered and blessed us. It has been a rewarding experience with moments of heartbreak and laughter. We've had the privilege of cooperating with dedicated people who work hard to help animals, many of them under-appreciated volunteers. This involvement takes its toll on all of us, emotionally and financially, but a lick from a dog or the purr of a cat who wouldn't still be in this world if it weren't for our efforts makes it all worthwhile.

Pieces of My Heart is much like me – sometimes funny, sometimes spiritual, sometimes irreverent (I happen to believe our

Creator has a sense of humor, otherwise we would be dust by now), sometimes handicapped by humanness yet always appreciative of the human-animal bond, often angry about what the "status quo" represents for animals and our environment, sometimes comforting, sometimes in need of comfort, always committed, and sometimes suggesting that I should be "committed." Any errors in the writing are mine, helped by constant interruptions from the animals who own me. (Special thanks is due my lap-cat and muse, "Danube.")

Some of my writings deal with grief and loss. Nicole and I lost all of our parents, some lifelong friends, and some of our best animal friends over the past few years. We understand how much it hurts to lose a loved one, human or animal. Regarding the latter, it is frustrating that those of us who know the love of animals and their power to change lives, and suffer the void when they leave us, or remember all those we could not save, must find a way to communicate with a public who doesn't give a damn about animals. We have to work together in order to convince the public to care. I hope everyone who loves animals will become more involved in efforts to help them and I have included resources and suggestions for doing so at the end of this book. It is because of all of you who are currently helping animals and protecting our environment that I refuse to give up hope for a more responsible, compassionate future. There have been enough positive developments to give us reasons for hope and together we will make this world a better place, even if we have to endure the barbs and insults of the uncaring and their epitaphs for "animal rights crazies" and "tree huggers"...we will win because we fight for what our Creator intended.

I have chosen to publish my book with two print-on-demand publishers in the US and the UK, because they have agreed to grant animal and environmental groups the same discount as booksellers, thus allowing the groups to use this book as a fundraiser. You will find more information about that arrangement at the end of the book.

I wish I could acknowledge all the people who have inspired, educated, supported or assisted me in my efforts. There is almost nothing I've done in life that wasn't helped by someone and any acknowledgment list could run to several pages and I would still inadvertently omit someone whose kindness mattered. Those who have been a part of my life and my efforts know who they are and they should know they are appreciated, not the least of whom have been my animal friends. I consider them all proof that the Creator knows what He is doing. However, I would be remiss if I didn't express particular thanks to, past and present, my wife Nicole, our parents, our animals, Vera Kienic, Naomi Jorgensen, Eileen Shackelton, Viola Evans, Annemarie and Christine Michel, Genevieve Purcell, Ruth and Chuck Bechman, Lois and John Staub, the Grosso family, Dan Willis, Jim and Dorothy and Valerie Willis, the Mraz family, the Dunn family, the Buchmann family, the Mathias family, Elvira and Gerhard Rösch, Luise Eckhard, Käthe and Gerry Albrecht, Christine and Tilman Schwen, Heinz Scholl, Sarah Griffith, John Fisher, Mary and Caty McCall-Braun, Franny Syufy, Margaret Rovenski-Rau, Christine Head, Michelle and Pat Crean, PC and Bob Hanes, Doreen and Bruce Sanfelici, Dion Campbell, Marsha and Gary Koschik, Gail Sutton, Susan Intessimone, Anne Paullin, Terry Fillows, Renee Christina, Esther Schwartz, Paula and Scott Sykes, Robin Ware, Judy Hough, Carol and Larry Carter, Peggy and Ben Strain, Shirley Georgetti, Pam Wintermantel, Sheila McGregor, Deb Orpen, Anne Kreider, Lisa Mesmer, Norma Joiner, Joan Bishop, Lisa Woods, Yvonne Johnson, Mary and Roger Hames, Terry Stevens, Martha and Frank Fetsko, Dr. Janet Tobiassen Crosby, Dick Weavil, Dr. Jane Goodall, His Holiness the Dalai Lama, Terry Harnwell and John Parkin of The African Conservation Foundation; Nancy Gallagher and friends from "The Daily Drool;" Sylvie McGee and Basset-L; Canine-L; the Ohio Valley Rescue list; The Brooke County WV Animal Welfare League; Vernon Weir and The American Sanctuary Association; Animal Friends of Pittsburgh; all the veterinarians who have cared for our animals, all the volunteer fosters and relayers who have assisted our rescue efforts, and all those who have published my writings, especially Infinity Publishing.com in the USA and AuthorsOnline in the UK.

I am greatly honored by having a foreword to my book contributed by Dr. Marc Bekoff, a scientist with a heart, an animal advocate who appreciates animals' spiritual worth, and the author of respected works on themes and feelings I touch on in my book.

On behalf of the animals, I thank my readers for everything you have done and will do for them and our world. I hope you will appreciate these *Pieces of My Heart*.

– *Jim Willis*

Outside of a dog, a book is a man's best friend.
Inside of a dog, it's too dark to read.
~ GROUCHO MARX
❖

THE ANIMALS' SAVIOR

I looked at all the caged animals in the shelter...
the cast-offs of human society.
I saw in their eyes love and hope, fear and dread,
sadness and betrayal.
And I was angry.
"God," I said, "this is terrible! Why don't you do something?"
God was silent for a moment and then He spoke softly.
"I have done something," He replied.
"I created *you*."

WE ARE THEIR HEROES

If you worry that you have not made a difference,
you have,
for only those who do not worry about it have not.
If you feel overwhelmed, if the weight of problems
is too heavy to bear,
remember it is a shared burden
and the strength of numbers can accomplish much.

If you think society and government are blind,
it only serves to remind that we need to change
one mind at a time, one law after another.
We effect change by cooperation, not by isolation.

If you consider that we cannot save them all,
and what difference does one make?,
you ought to know the joy of the one who is saved.
Mourn those we cannot save, it is a eulogy to their being.
Do not let their loss be in vain.

Be kind to yourself, remember your needs
and those of your family and friends of every species.
If you give everything, what will you have left for yourself,
or for them?
Strive to be happy and healthy. You are needed.
Achieving balance in life is a lifelong struggle.
We who help those who do not have all that they need
should be among the most grateful for what we have.

Be proud of your accomplishments, not your opinions.
The quality of your efforts is more important than the quantity.
Forgive your own deficiencies –
sometimes your caring is sufficient.
Everyone can do something, it is up to you to do the thing you can.
A kind word and a gentle touch can change a life.

If anger wells up within you, because people are the problem,
remember your humanity and that people are also the solution.
Concentrate on specific needs, pay attention to the individual –
they make up the whole.
See beyond the unlovable, the unattractive,
the impure and the wounded –
see that their spirit is as deserving as the rest. Help them heal.
Their eyes are windows to their soul
and the mirror of your sincerity.

All species, all beings, share this Earth in a chain of life.
Care more about what makes us alike than what separates us.
Policies, rules and regulations are not infallible.
Apply them judiciously, interpret them wisely.
No decision based purely on money is ever the right one.

Listen to your heart. Sometimes we have to do that which
we are most afraid of.
Be true to yourself and your beliefs.
Family may abandon you,
friends may disappoint you, strangers will ridicule you.
People shun what they do not understand.
Help them to understand – kindly, softly, gently.

Those who do not respect all life are to be pitied.
Often the wrongdoer is as in need of help as his victims.
Forgive, then teach by example.
Educate yourself or you cannot hope to teach others.
No action based in hatred is ever right
and anger drowns out wisdom.

Yours may be a voice crying in the wilderness,
make it a voice to be respected.
Listen more than you talk, be courteous and reliable.
Learn to ask for help. Never waiver from the truth.
Know that it takes a lot of strength to cry
And with every defeat, we learn.

All Creation celebrates that which is in its own best interest.
The Children are our hope – nurture them.
Nature is our legacy – protect it.
The Animals are our brethren – learn from them.

Your rewards will not be material, but they will be meaningful,
and the courage of your convictions can survive anything.
We are small boats cast adrift on a cruel sea,
but someday the tide will turn toward a safe harbor.
No matter how dark the storm clouds,
or deep the pain of heartbreak – never forget:
We are their heroes.

*It was quite incomprehensible to me...why in my evening prayers I should
pray for human beings only. So when my mother had prayed with me
and had kissed me goodnight, I used to add silently a prayer that I had
composed myself for all living creatures. It ran thus:
'O, heavenly Father, protect and bless all things that have breath; guard
them from all evil, and let them sleep in peace.'*
~ ALBERT SCHWEITZER

On Growing Up with a View of Walden Pond

I was born in the late Fifties and grew up in a middle-class neighborhood on the outskirts of the city with a wonderful view of the Pittsburgh cityscape from our front porch. During his lunch break my dad would sometimes go up to the rooftop observation deck of the skyscraper where he worked and my brother and I would set up a small telescope on our front porch so we could wave at each other.

My mother was a homemaker, as were the mothers of most of my friends. Most of my friends had parents still married to each other. I remember adults occasionally referring to some women as "divorcees"...women who bore watching. It wasn't until later that I realized that most of them were divorced because it was their ex-husbands who had warranted watching.

We had a woman who cleaned for us occasionally and she did the heavy chores that my physically handicapped mother couldn't manage. She was a well-padded, jovial, black woman named Mrs. Blue and I rushed home from school whenever she was there so I could play (badly) on my accordion her favorite song, "Red Roses for a Blue Lady." I used to kiss her goodbye on the front porch before she walked to the bus stop. One day some neighborhood kids saw me kissing her and they called me "nigger lover" for a while at school.

I had black friends at school, but it took me a few years to figure out why they didn't live in my neighborhood, or to appreciate that I had the most accepting, non-prejudiced parents on the block. I knew I had the most intelligent and well-read parents on the block, and sometimes the most naïve mother. My mother even had some lesbian friends and up until the day she died, I doubt she ever wondered why two of those women had been "roommates" for fifty years. (She later refused to accept that her godson is permanently gay and after fifteen years still regarded his lifestyle as a "phase" he was going through.) She just plain loved everyone for who she thought they were, and every year she used to leave a birthday card in the aluminum milkbox on the porch for the milkman.

It was a typical American childhood for the time. We walked to school and walked home for lunch. We were always losing our milk money or spending it on penny candy. We had to wear "rubbers" over our shoes when it rained. Sometimes my dad drove us out to the airport to watch propeller planes take off and land. Because the airport was located far removed from the city and we drove past farmland and orchards to get there, I considered it a trip to the country. For the first time since then, after living abroad for many years, I have occasion to go that way frequently and it is now a small city of shopping centers and hotels floating on a sea of concrete. In my childhood, the country was something to be coveted and I would daydream about what I would do if I lived on a farm, as many of the characters in my books did. My only remotely agrarian experience up to that point had been helping my Italian grandfather in his garden. I certainly never dreamed that I would later fly across the Atlantic more than fifty times in planes without propellers.

We had a black and white television with a small picture tube and "rabbit ears." I used to watch "Chiller Theater" on Saturday afternoons, alone in the living room, with one eye on the movie and the other eye on the coat closet in the hallway...ready to bolt at the first sign of the living dead. I had a vivid imagination fed by what I saw on television and by the shopping bag full of books I would bring home weekly from the Carnegie Library. Someday, I vowed, I would go to those places and although I have been to some of them, they weren't as exotic as they were in my childhood fantasies. Kids don't usually incorporate into their fantasies lost luggage, taxi drivers who overcharge, hotel mattresses with bed bugs and mosquitoes that leave welts. The elephants, donkeys and camels in my dreams were all happy and fly-free.

My parents were both physically handicapped, victims of polio, as were many of their friends. They lent me out to do chores for their childless friends, which I did happily. I had to be near death in order to miss a day of school – not only was education the credo of my parents, I had a father who walked on crutches to the bus stop and went to work every day, even when he had pneumonia. I was an excellent student despite a rocky beginning. I got in trouble my first day at school for punching a boy in the stomach. After my mother had delivered me in a taxi to school, he had imitated the way she walked on crutches, with a leg brace, and I walloped him. I don't think I ever told her the reason.

When I was in the third grade I contracted a rare infection in my right hip joint that left me unable to walk within twenty-four hours and I was put into traction at Children's Hospital for weeks, and then sent home in a wheelchair to recuperate. I finally felt like I belonged and my wheelchair was a symbol of fraternity with some of my favorite adopted aunts and uncles. It took me an inordinate amount of time to walk again.

Life changed for me forever in the summer of my ninth year, when I was sent away to our church's camp in the Laurel Mountains of Pennsylvania. I spent every summer there from then until college, first as a camper and then as a staff member. The experience of being in the mountains and in the presence of wildlife did more to shape my loves and commitments than anything else in my life.

I remember mountain laurel and wild rhododendron in bloom, and fog and ferns so thick that you couldn't see where you were going and you didn't care. I remember wading in cold mountain streams until my feet were numb and swimming in a sub-zero swimming hole called "Devil's Hollow," until my lips were blue, my teeth were chattering and a part of my anatomy I was learning to be proud of all but disappeared. I had devoured, reread, and practically memorized the book *My Side of the Mountain*, and for all my tramps through the woods, I never once came upon a hollow tree of sufficient proportions that I thought I could spend the winter in, as had the boy in the book.

I remember hiding in the underbrush during a game of "capture the flag" and having a family of skunks walk by, inches from my nose. When a newborn deer fawn was discovered stuck to a newly asphalted road, a pen was built for "Tar Baby," and I was allowed to bottle feed and help raise her. A few summers later, when I rescued a blind groundhog named "Pete," a friendly snapping turtle named "Freddy," a one-eyed kitten named "Scamper," a thief of a young raccoon named "Rip-Off," a guinea pig in need of boarding for the summer, an orphaned robin, and someone's lost parakeet, the camp director let me turn an unused room under the dining hall into a wildlife "zoo." He probably had cause to rethink his decision when I next raised a clutch of Canada

Geese eggs in an incubator and then refused to allow anyone other than my best friend into the zoo. The camp had a riding program at a nearby hack stable. I went on every trail ride I could and I was horse crazy. During school months I read every horse story in the library and I dreamed of horses. In my thirteenth summer, I was allowed to stay at the barn in between trail rides one day, with my favorite horse and a willowy blonde girl who worked there and who was probably five years my senior. She let me help her clean tack and oil leather. I fell in love that day, although I'm sure it says something that I still remember the horse's name, but not the girl's. It was my good fortune that it took me less time to find a good woman to share my life with, but it took me three decades since that day in the barn before I had the horse I dreamed of.

I don't remember nearly as much about the school months of my childhood as I remember about the summers. The excitement would begin building a month before I packed my footlocker and it wouldn't wear off until I was back home, rooted to a classroom desk and tortured by the Indian Summer blazing outside the window without me. I not only belonged to the mountains, but the mountains belonged to me.

For most of my adult years since college, I have been able to live in rural areas, not always as close to the woods as I would have liked, but at least they were in view. As I write this, there is a groundhog outside my window now, taunting me, daring me to come out and play. He's been there all summer, growing fat, and I chuckle whenever I surprise him and watch his plump butt disappearing into his burrow.

I avoid the city. The few times I've been in a city center during the day, I've felt my throat constrict until I could escape. I will admit that the city holds some fascination at night, for its culture and entertainment, for its multicolored lights reflected in water. But it's not so charming that it can hold my interest the way a portly groundhog can.

I have been in some of the oldest and most magnificent cathedrals of Europe, and visited some modern architectural masterpieces. I'll grant that especially the antiquated buildings leave me in awe of what man was able to accomplish, but no building has ever made me cry and I've never seen a building as awe-inspiring as a tree. I have stood on Alaska's Kenai Peninsula at sunset and was so overwhelmed by the colors that tears ran down my cheeks. I've stood on the shore of the Beaufort Sea in the Arctic and felt an unearthly stillness that extended from me to the horizon in the distance. I've been on the coastal road that winds around Cape Breton, Nova Scotia, with the trees in autumn splendor, with a double rainbow crossed over the ocean, with a feeling that I was in the presence of God. I've walked the beach at the North Sea during a wind so strong that you could lean back into it, unable to fall. I've stood at the foot of the highest waterfall in Maryland, alone on a rock after a flood, when the sun came out for the first time in days and the mist rose from every tree and fern and rock, and I knew that it looked no different than it had on the first day of Creation. No, you may have your steel and glass and the hum of the city if they please you, but the allure is wasted on me.

I recently saw a satellite photo of the United States at night. It showed two broad, unbroken belts of light running along both coasts, and a few globs of light in the middle. Most of the rest of the country was dark, meaning it is sparsely populated. I thought of all the times I've heard someone say they couldn't find work or affordable housing, or that they were unhappy about the crime, drugs, gang warfare, pollution, congestion and rudeness that can accompany city life. I wondered why the discontented didn't move to the darkened areas. That may sound as insensitive as Marie Antoinette's "let them eat cake," but I mean it for reasons of sensitivity. Wouldn't life in the country, near the woods, bring them as much joy as it has brought me? I hoped the reason they stayed put where they are was not because a Mrs. Blue would not be welcomed in some communities and that their children couldn't kiss her goodbye on the front porch.

After my mother died, I removed my watch and put it into a drawer. I was tired of being ruled by a timepiece when I had just had the most severe reminder that life is too short. I was also disappointed that some people judged others by the brand of watch they wear – is a Timex any less valuable than a Rolex if it keeps good time, and is the person who wears it any less so? Of course not.

Today, I own one suit, the black one I bought for my mother's funeral five years ago. Funerals are the only occasion for which I wear it and I've already worn it too many times. I still have some neckties, but almost nothing will induce me to wear one. My uniform of the day is T-shirts in summer, flannel shirts in winter, and blue jeans. The time when I had an important-sounding job title, wore designer clothes, drove a sports car and attended parties with people who had royal titles in front of their names seems so long ago. Not a single party, not even the wedding of the Duke and Duchess of York, was as much fun as walking in the woods with a dog, or rolling on the ground with a pack of them, and my dogs and I love my little pick-up truck.

I'm rarely in the company of young people, but when I am, I notice many of them wear an unhappy, confused look. In their quest for individuality they wear not very attractive clothes with designer names, earrings and piercings, hairstyles and colors my mother wouldn't have approved of, until they all end up looking the same. I know I sound superannuated myself when I worry about the state of youth. I feel sorry for the children who grow up on prescribed medications and those who turn to illegal ones later. I'm sorry modern society has managed to turn everything into a drug – television, music, cell phones, computers and e-mail, shopping.

I don't feel good when I talk to some of the parents, the fathers who worry about the state of the economy and the security of their jobs. The mothers who chauffeur the kids around to competitive sports they probably don't want to play, to activities that won't mean much to them later in life. Everyone is busy, they aren't communicating, and at the end of the day they return to the homes in suburbia they can barely afford and collapse from exhaustion. The family dog is usually bored out of his mind until they deliver him to an animal shelter believing that he'll go to a good home "in the country."

I'd like to take them somewhere. I'd like to load them all into buses and deliver them to the woods. I'd like them to know how it feels to stumble through fog and ferns so thick you can't see where you are going and to not care where you are going. I'd like to see the looks on their faces after they plunge into the water of Devil's Hollow. I think it would do most of them a lot of good to return to a simpler life.

It might be considered blasphemy to write of a return to a simpler life, or a move to the country and woods, without quoting

the chief apostle of such, Thoreau, and preferably from his classic
Walden on his years at Walden Pond:

*"I went to the woods because I wished to live deliberately, to
front only the essential facts of life, and see if I could not learn
what it had to teach, and not, when I came to die, discover that I
had not lived. I did not wish to live what was not life, living is so
dear; nor did I wish to practise resignation, unless it was quite
necessary. I wanted to live deep and suck out all the marrow of
life, to live so sturdily and Spartan-like as to put to rout all that
was not life, to cut a broad swath and shave close, to drive life into
a corner, and reduce it to its lowest terms, and, if it proved to be
mean, why then to get the whole and genuine meanness of it, and
publish its meanness to the world; or if it were sublime, to know it
by experience, and to be able to give a true account of it in my
next excursion."*

Over the years, leaf by leaf, ripple by ripple, and polished
stone by stone, I have created a Walden Pond in my mind. It is the
place I go to write, to think, to sort through feelings. Literally and
figuratively, it is where I belong. I've wept there and I've laughed.
I've watched swallows glide over the water's surface, drinking on
the wing, and heard the cry of the loon.

Following the tragedies at the World Trade Center and the
Pentagon, I spent a lot of time at my inner Walden Pond, and the
rest of the time in my genuine rural existence. On the night of
September 11th, I lay on the grass on a hill and cried. I stared at the
unbroken expanse of starry night and was able to pick out the only
two constellations I've ever been able to identify – the big and
little dippers – and I believed the rest of the stars to be the
innocent souls lost that day. There were more than I had ever seen
at one time. I know it may be some of the world's most valuable
real estate, but I hope on the site of the World Trade Center they
will plant a most beautiful wood, with a pond, as a memorial.

As I approach middle age, I don't know how broad a swath
I've cut yet. As for shaving close, I'm rather lazy about shaving at
all. I know I haven't driven life into a corner – I can barely corner
the chipmunks that the cats bring in and release alive in the house.
I've seen some, sometimes too much, of the meanness of life. Still
I regard life as sublime and the closer it is lived to the woods, the
more sublime it becomes. Perhaps one day I will meet you there,
and after a brief greeting and inquiry about each other's health,

we'll go our separate ways and about the business of doing nothing. Nothing at all except being...being in the woods.

If a man aspires toward a righteous life,
his first act of abstinence is from injury to animals.
~ LEO TOLSTOY
❖

In a world older and more complete than ours they move finished and
complete, gifted with extensions of the senses we have lost or never
attained, living by voices we will never hear.
They are not brethren, they are not underlings, they are other nations,
caught with ourselves in the net of life and time, fellow prisoners of the
splendour and travail of the earth.
~ HENRY BESTON
❖

FOREST LESSONS

I know a place untouched by sorrow,
where leafy bowers wave,
where Man has seldom left his mark,
where memories dwell in caves.
There in verdant pleasures I lose myself
and ponder thoughts reserved
for quiet times of deep reflection,
where true feelings are preserved.
I often take my dog along,
she always knows the way
to woodland treasures hidden deep,
where for hours we might stay...
a soaring cathedral of ancient pines,
jeweled windows of a foliage canopy,
an altar built of hickory boughs,
offerings of violets and wild sweet pea.
I contemplate the solitude,
vow to leave my life behind,
recall a primeval innocence,
the joys of a simpler time.
Too soon the dusk approaches,
and we must take our leave,
with backward glances we forge on,
rejuvenated and relieved –
of burdensome, worrisome thoughts,
of clocks and everyday concerns,
but we'll return soon one day
and of more forest lessons learn.

YOU WEREN'T THE ONE I WANTED

I wanted white and you were black,
I wanted obedient and that you lacked.
I wanted pure and you were mixed,
You wanted her, I had you fixed!
I wanted long hair, yours was curly,
I wanted sweet and I got surly.
I wanted a girl, I got a boy,
I wanted to play, you shunned toys.
I wanted housetrained, that you weren't,
My carpet you ruined, my lawn you burnt.
I wanted tall, you were compressed,
I wanted happy, you were depressed.
I wanted clever and you were not,
You ran away, but you were caught!
I wanted young and you were aged,
I tried crating, you hated cages.
I wanted healthy, you loved the vet,
You were the most impossible I'd ever met!
I wanted this and you weren't that,
I wanted slim and you got fat.
I cried the last time I kissed
that muzzle I didn't know I'd miss.
You were as stubborn as a brick wall,
but you were the one I wanted after all.

THE MEANING OF M.U.T.T.

Dudley wasn't sure how many weeks he'd been in the animal shelter, but it seemed like forever. Each day was the same as the one before and he spent most of his time sitting on the wooden palette in his pen, staring at the wall and waiting for dinner. His life with his former owners, brief though it was, hadn't been great – he wasn't loved or wanted – but even that was better than this, he thought.

He occupied himself by watching a fly on the wall until he heard some of the other dogs barking a greeting to the old bloodhound Humphrey, as he made his morning rounds. Behind his back the others called him "Harrumphrey," because of his habit of "*harrumph!*-ing" whenever anything displeased him, which was most of the time.

Humphrey was the mascot of the shelter, allowed to roam the building as he pleased, and he slept overnight in the office. He'd lost a hind leg years ago when a nearsighted hunter couldn't tell the difference between a bloodhound and a deer, so the shelter staff didn't have to worry about him wandering very far.

Humphrey paused in front of Dudley's pen and inspected the young mixed terrier, which made Dudley even more uncomfortable. He hung his head a little lower and avoided Humphrey's stare.

"You boy...look alive!" Humphrey ordered. "It's opening time and the people will be coming."

"Alive?" Dudley sighed. "Alive for what? Nobody's going to want me. Not even my mama wanted me. They said I was found in a dumpster when I was a puppy."

Humphrey pondered that for a moment.

"Of course you were," he drawled. "Put you there for safekeeping, she did. No place safer than a dumpster – solid steel. Nothin' could have happened to you there, I promise you that."

"My former owners didn't want me either," Dudley explained. "Said they didn't have time for a dog. Said I ate too much. Said I cost too much. Said I didn't match their furniture.

Said they wanted a human baby instead."

"*Harrumph!*" grunted Humphrey. "Some humans are too stupid to take care of themselves, let alone cohabitate with a superior being. It was their loss, I assure you. Why, look at you! You're a fine specimen of a...well, anyone can see that you're obviously a....um..."

"A mutt," said Dudley resignedly. "Go ahead and say it, everyone else does. My former people called me a mutt, everyone that comes down this aisle points and says 'oh, he's just a mutt,' and then they go look at the purebreds on the other side. I'm not even sure what a mutt is, but I know I am one."

"Just a mutt!" Humphrey sputtered. "Why I'll have you know there's nothing better than a mutt! Mutts are healthy, intelligent and brave. Haven't you noticed that the bluebloods on that side are usually only here for a few days, while some of you mutts are here for weeks and months?"

"Yeah," said Dudley, "because nobody wants us."

"Balderdash!" Humphrey roared. "It's because we can hardly stand to part with you! Mutts are some of the most cherished members of the canine community."

"If we're so great, what *is* a mutt?" Dudley asked suspiciously.

"A mutt?...I can scarcely believe you don't know. A mutt is, well, it's an old...newfangled term meaning, let's see, how should I put this?...it's short for, uh...hmmm...yes! It stands for 'Magnificent Under-Touted Terrier' ... M.U.T.T."

"Manigifent under-tooted terrier?! What's that?" Dudley asked, perking up his ears.

"MAGNIFICENT under-TOWted terrier. Touted means 'praised and appreciated,'" Humphrey replied confidently.

"Really? Is that true?" Dudley asked.

"Absolutely. It's even written in the Good Book... Neuteronomy chapter 3, verse 16, I think."

"Well, I'll be..." Dudley shook his head in wonder. "You mean that big boy in the next pen is a M.U.T.T., too?"

"One of the rarest. That's a Lithuanian Liver-Spotted Lop Ear."

"My! And that longhaired girl over there is also a M.U.T.T.?"

"You've got a good eye – she's a, um...Moroccan Multi-colored Mongrel."

"Whoa...that does sound unusual. And what about him?" Dudley asked, pointing to a little dog who almost defied description.

"Him? Why he's a....a Chinese Curly-Q-tailed Cur."

"Goodness! Do they know they are M.U.T.T.'s?" Dudley asked.

"I'm sure they do," Humphrey said, lowering his voice. "But one of the distinguishing features of a M.U.T.T. is modesty – you don't want to brag all over the place and make the pedigreed dogs feel bad."

"I see," Dudley said and shook his shaggy head.

"Now then...it takes more than M.U.T.T. status to get out of here and into the right home. Do you do any tricks?"

"Not really. I can have a 'conniption fit' – at least that's what my former owners used to call it."

"You don't want to overdo it now. A modicum of restraint is called for," Humphrey cautioned.

"Gee, you certainly use a lot of big words," Dudley said.

"My former owner was a librarian. May she rest in peace," Humphrey said as his voice trailed off.

"Oh...I'm sorry."

"Never you mind...I'm as content as a hound can be," Humphrey assured him, trying not to look too hard at the concrete and wire that made up his world, where lace curtains and a comfortable couch used to be.

"You need to put your best paw forward, show your best qualities. You are brave aren't you?"

"Oh yes! I once killed a rat that was as big as a house!" Dudley boasted.

Humphrey squinted his eyes a bit.

"And you are honest aren't you?"

"Absolutely!" Dudley assured him. "...err, actually it was most likely a really big mouse."

"...and sincere?" Humphrey pressed him.

"Quite. Um...the mouse was suffering the effects of poison," Dudley admitted.

"Then that's that," Humphrey concluded. "I hear some humans headed this way...chin up, chest out, show 'em what you've got."

And with that Humphrey marched off toward the office.

The human couple hesitated in the doorway of the kennel for a moment...so many dogs to choose from. They started down the aisle, reading the cards attached to the pens, stopping to let dogs sniff their hands and to give them a scratch under the chin. They seemed kindhearted.

"Look dear," the woman said. "Isn't that one handsome?"

"Too big," the man answered. "He'd eat us out of house and home. I like the look of that one there," he said, pointing to one of the purebreds.

"She is pretty, but too much grooming required," the woman said. "What's this little guy here?" she asked.

"Him? That appears to be a genuine mutt."

Dudley's ears pricked up in an instant. They were talking about him!

"Yes!" he barked as he jumped off his palette and ran to the front of the pen. "I'm a M.U.T.T., and a magnificent one, too! I'm intelligent and loyal – and I'm brave – I once killed a rat as big as a...nevermind...I'm not afraid of anything. Arf! If a burglar ever breaks into your house, I'll bite him on the ankle! Woof! Why, I'm so valuable that my mama put me in a dumpster for safekeeping."

"He's a spunky little guy, isn't he?" the woman commented.

"And look at this," Dudley barked, standing up to get their attention. "I can jump and spin in circles, and chase my tail, and rollover, and dance on my hind legs, and beg...and show my belly...and...," until he toppled over from the effort.

"What was that?!" the man asked.

"I believe that's what my grandmother would have called a 'conniption fit,'" the woman laughed. "Oh, isn't he precious? He's just the sort of energetic dog we want. What do you think?"

"I think we've got ourselves a genuine mutt," the man answered with a smile.

Dudley beamed with joy as his new humans filled out the paperwork in the shelter office. He danced when they put a new red collar and leash on him, and he helped carry his leash in his mouth on their way to the parking lot.

Humphrey watched as the humans picked up the little mutt and gently loaded him into their car, and as Dudley jumped around on the back seat and then gave a goodbye "Arf!" as the car drove away. He turned and walked back down the kennel aisle, stopping to wipe at his eyes with a paw.

"Goshdarn cat allergies!" he muttered. "I've got the weepy-sneezies again."

The other animals looked at him with understanding and they, too, pretended to have an allergy attack. Even the cats.

Animals are reliable, many full of love,
true in their affections, predictable in their actions, grateful and loyal.
Difficult standards for people to live up to.
~ ALFRED A. MONTAPERT
❖

In order to really enjoy a dog,
one doesn't merely try to train him to be semi-human.
The point of it is to open oneself to the possibility
of becoming partly a dog.
~ EDWARD HOAGLAND
❖

"The Basset Chronicles" *were written to amuse myself and our many friends in the world of Basset Hound Rescue, especially subscribers to an e-list "The Daily Drool." The undisputed queen of the chronicles is our solid sable-colored Basset "Alexis." (Sable is not a usual or recognized Basset color, but then again, there isn't much that is "usual" about "Alexis.")*

We adopted her royal sableness when her former owner claimed she had developed a medical condition that prevented her from keeping "Alexis." Although the woman said she could hardly stand the thought of giving up "Alexis," after we adopted her we never once heard from the woman. Knowing and loving "Alexis" as we do, we're sure her former owner fled the country. We're not quite sure "Alexis" is even a dog...she might be an alien from another planet.

Other characters in the chronicles include our German Basset Hounds "Winnie" and "Flash," and the Bassets we rescued in America, "Gabriel," "Gallagher," "Hyacinth," and the diaper-wearing "Daphne," who we adopted at the age of thirteen. Also included are various and sundry of the other animals who make our life interesting.

THE BASSET CHRONICLES:
The Reality of Relaying "Roscoe"

I had offered to be one of the relayers of "Roscoe," a rescued Basset Hound being driven by volunteers to his new home in another state. I departed early Sunday morning to meet up with his first relayer in a Taco Bell parking lot. She and his foster mom from West Virginia were already there when I arrived and Roscoe greeted me like an old friend. He is a nicely marked tri-color and his wonderful temperament didn't indicate his first three years of neglect. We humans traded the requisite half hour's worth of stories about how great our dogs are, illustrated with photos.

"By the way, how is he in the car?" I asked as the two women prepared to depart.

"Just fine!" they answered in unison and sped away teary eyed. Were they crying or laughing?

I'd been warned that Roscoe gets carsick, that he hadn't been fed since the previous evening, and that he'd had a dose of Dramamine before they started out. I decided against giving him any of the dog biscuits I'd brought with me. He regarded me calmly from the passenger side of my truck cab

I pulled out onto the interstate and reached cruising speed. Roscoe began to investigate the truck cab. He nosed and pawed all the storage receptacles, ashtray, and various parts of my anatomy. He was obviously hungry. I glanced back and forth between the road and Roscoe.

"Roscoe, spit that out! That's an air freshener, for crying out loud!"

I steered with my left hand and tried to remove anything that resembled food with my right. Roscoe drooled, long slings of drool, copious ropes of drool.

Roscoe sat back down and sized me up. All of the sudden, a look of rapture crossed his face. Not only was I his new best friend, but I had a truck, and for Roscoe from West Virginia, that made us kindred spirits. Even though he'd been neutered a few days earlier, he apparently had a sudden surge of hormones. He flung himself on me, slurping my glasses askew, his front paws locked around my neck in a chokehold. Then his hind paw flipped my travel cup of scalding hot coffee into my lap.

"AAAGHHH!!"

Flashing blue lights behind me.

"No, officer, I have *not* been drinking," I protested nervously. "This blast...blessed dog just dumped a cup of hot coffee on me at seventy-five miles per hour. You don't say? Fifty-five miles per hour, huh? Well, that's certainly good to know!"

I negotiated three lanes of traffic on the Pittsburgh Parkway. My route was not intentional – in fact, we were traveling in the wrong direction – but Roscoe had chosen that exit with a well-timed poke of his muzzle through the spokes of the steering wheel. I alternated lanes at high speed, trying to get back to the proper route and noted some signage in bright orange. "Beware of D.U.I. drivers," said one. "Beware of aggressive drivers," said the next.

"What a ridiculous state of affairs," I muttered to myself.

Just then, Roscoe flopped over for a bellyrub in a state of excitement and as I reached for the gear shift knob, I instead grabbed a part of Roscoe that he is evidently very proud of. Roscoe was even more surprised at such familiarity from someone he'd known less than an hour. In my surprise I jerked the wheel hard to the right and forced off the road a van filled with churchgoers. I slowed long enough for them to brandish Bibles at me and mouth what I presumed to be some very un-Christian sentiments.

Flashing blue lights behind me, again.

"NO, officer, I am *not* drunk. No, I haven't been shot! The dog and I had an earlier altercation over a jelly-filled donut and he won."

I found my way back to the interstate and was overcome by thirst. I took the next exit and pulled into a McDonald's drive-through.

"Oh, how cute," the woman at the pick-up window cooed. "Would the wittle doggie wike a fwench-fwy?"

"NO – carsick – no food!" I managed to stammer while wrestling a suddenly alert Roscoe. Then, using my groin as a springboard, Roscoe lunged for the drive-up window and succeeded in getting his front half through it. Since I still had two of what Roscoe had recently lost to surgery, I was more preoccupied with my pain than I was in halting his maraudings through the window. Roscoe got his slobbery mouth around the woman's microphone.

"BLABBA-WOOFA-BARFA-SLURPA-AROOOO!" Roscoe delivered into the microphone and it arrived at about 100 decibels in the dining area of the restaurant, accompanied by the screams of children.

"Oh dear. Oh my!" the woman turned back toward me with an alarmed expression. "That's going to be difficult to clean up."

"What?" I asked, still gasping for breath.

"Happy Meals...frightened children throwing Happy Meals."

"Look – I'll leave you to your McDisaster...just gimme a Coke with extra ice please."

I edged onto the interstate again and checked the time. Late again, as usual. I was concentrating on trying to make up some time, weaving in and out around slower moving vehicles. My thigh still burned from the hot coffee and I felt a headache coming on.

"Dr. Roscoe," who must have sensed my pain, decided on a course of treatment and my lap was suddenly awash with ice-cold cola.

"EEEK!" I shrieked and swerved. "EEEK!" the woman in the car next to me shrieked. Roscoe, with his superior hearing, probably noted several more EEEK!s in other cars behind us. Maybe his keen hound nose even detected other embarrassments.

Those old familiar, flashing blue lights.

"No, officer – as I have been telling your colleagues all morning long, I have NOT been drinking!"

As the officer wrote out yet another ticket, I recalled that Roscoe's former owner had threatened to shoot him and I was suddenly feeling a teensy bit more forgiving of the man.

We met the cheerful family of three who would be relaying Roscoe on the next leg of his journey in an Arby's parking lot. I got out of my truck, a sight to behold. My hair was glued in spikes by drool, multi-colored stains spread across my shirt, and the front of my pants made me look like the poster boy for "Attends." People had left the Titanic's lifeboats looking better groomed than I was. I took Roscoe out through the passenger side door and he greeted his new victims with glee. The couple kept shielding their young daughter behind them as we talked.

"Let's see, I think we have everything now, rabies tag, medical records, directions," the wife said.

"You didn't happen to pack a wetsuit did you?" I asked innocently.

She gave me another odd look.

"How is he in the car?" she asked.

"Him? Um, he's ah...definitely a one-of-a-kind dog!" I managed as truthfully as I could.

"Do you know if there's a bar around here?" I asked them. They exchanged glances and gave me a look of pity.

I made it home without further incident and my wife met me at the door.

"How was your relay, dear?" she asked.

"Damp. Very damp and expensive, too. In fact, I think I may be facing some jail time."

Nothing flusters my wife.

"Does the interior of the truck look as bad as you do?" she asked.

"Worse," I replied. "Sea World has fewer surprises."

"Honestly. Why didn't you put him in a crate in the covered bed of the truck?" she suggested.

"A crate? In the back? Are you nuts? – it's cold back there! Never mind. I'm going to take a nap now. I'm exhausted and I feel an attack of mildew coming on."

I hugged my pillow and thought of Roscoe, probably warm and dry in his new home by now. I realized I missed the big lug, but at least everything was finally right in his drool-covered world.

Dogs feel very strongly that they should always go with you in the car, in case the need should arise for them to bark violently at nothing right in your ear.
~ DAVE BARRY
❖

THE PIECES OF MY HEART
(ON FOSTERING)

Our paths will cross for only a short time,
but while you are in my care I will be devoted to you.
If memories of your former life are painful, I will help erase them.
No longer will you hunger and I will help to heal your wounds.
If your former life was good,
I will promise you an even better future.

One day our time together will come to an end
and you will go off to your new home, healthy, happy and healed.
As a parting gift, I will give you a piece of my heart
to remember me by.
I may shed a tear...not for my loss, but for your gain.

Perhaps our paths may cross again for a fleeting instant
and I will be comforted by the aura of love that surrounds you.
There will always be a bond between us,
though we walk separate paths through this life.

After we reach our heavenly reward our paths may cross again.
You may try to return the piece of my heart
with thanks for all that I did for you.
I will tell you to keep it and thank you
for showing me that I could be better
than I thought I could be,
and that I learned in giving came the greatest gifts.

The pieces of our hearts are like grains of sand.
They are pulled along a current beyond our control
until they come together and form a safe haven.

I, like you, came to understand what it meant to be saved.

❖

CANTICLE OF CATS

Open books should be laid on,
mice are everywhere,
lick a paw, after you fall,
paper bags make a lair.

Legs are made for tripping,
warn only with a hiss,
few humans can resist
a head bump and a kiss.

Good grooming is important,
continually sleek the fur,
wash complicated places,
and finish with a purr.

Sleep is a cat's vocation,
look for available laps,
humans may miss appointments,
for fear of disturbing your naps.

Catnip makes you silly,
birds are forbidden prey,
plants on a sunny windowsill
are only in the way.

Claws are useful instruments,
you must work to keep them sharp,
avoid anything upholstered,
or your human will surely carp.

Cats are regal creatures,
noble...aristocratic, too,
to do a human's bidding
will always be beneath you.

Some humans claim they hate cats,
it pains us to admit,
we tolerate and sympathize
with any such idiot.

Every ending has a tail,
and you should have one, too,
the myth about "nine lives,"
may not live as long as you.

Authors like cats because they are such quiet, lovable, wise creatures,
and cats like authors for the same reasons.
~ ROBERTSON DAVIES

A cat isn't fussy — just so long as you remember that he likes his milk in
the shallow rose-patterned saucer and his fish on the blue plate.
From which he will take it and eat it off the floor.
~ ARTHUR BRIDGES

BELOVED OF BAST

It was a perfect sunny afternoon for a catnap and the old farm cat lay sleepily in a pile of straw near the barn door. The sun warmed her tabby coat and she stretched and flexed her claws and yawned pinkly. The bees droned in their pursuit of pollen, birds twittered in the trees and lulled the cat called "Mother" into a deep sleep. She dreamed of stalking mice in the dark corners of the barn, and her whiskers twitched and teeth chattered in anticipation – although if the truth be told, her mousing days were long over and her ribs showed from hunger. She curled up more tightly as if to protect the kittens who had been so much a part of her life for over a dozen years. It was her hundred children, and their children, and theirs, that caused her to be called "Mother," and it had been many generations since anyone remembered her given name.

A gentle breeze played against her fur and her slow breathing rasped back and forth in the rhythm of deepest sleep. She did not hear the stealthy pawsteps as they approached and she was only awakened when a shadow passed in front of her and blocked the sun.

"Mew?!" she awoke with a start and blinked heavily at the silhouette of a large cat before her. She sat up stiffly and squinted into the sun as a small gasp escaped her.

Before her sat the most beautiful cat she had ever seen, with a pelt like burnished gold, stripes of tawny brown, large sapphire colored eyes, and tall ears with tufts. Around her neck she wore a chain of gold from which an amulet hung and from her brick red nose to the dark wild markings around her tail, she was the image of feline beauty.

Mother was too stunned to speak. The golden cat turned her gaze from Mother and surveyed the surroundings, and then she spoke.

"Blessed cat called 'Mother,' you are old and tired, and I have come to take you home. I have known of you for many years and of your trials and tribulations. As of today, that will all be forgotten and you will dwell in my temple, where you will want for nothing. My servants will care for you. You will have a couch in the sun, fresh fish, and the love and respect of all."

Mother struggled to find her voice, not quite understanding if this was a dream or not.

"And who may I ask are you, and where in the world did you come from?!" Mother finally managed to stutter.

The beautiful cat smiled slyly.

"I am Bast and I am from another time and place. I dwell in the Temple of Bubastis near the River Nile – which is rather nice, as temples go – and I am the chosen of Ra, the sun god, the protectress of mothers and children, the goddess of fertility...and several other things which I don't recall at the moment."

"What would you want with me and why would I want to leave here?" Mother asked. "This is my home."

Bast looked at the barn door hanging on one hinge, the pile of manure nearby, the junked and rusted vehicles of Man, and she sniffed.

"Home? It's not much of a home, is it?"

Mother followed the golden cat's gaze around her world and hung her head.

"I know it isn't much to an outsider, but it's all I've ever known."

"Dear cat," Bast said softly. "Leave this place. Your children are mostly gone now, run over on the road, dead from starvation, riddled with disease and suffering, their young stolen by hawks, shaken by dogs, tormented by human boys – and the few who remain healthy are breeding out of control. All of you barely manage to scratch out an existence. The Man and Woman here don't appreciate you. When is the last time they held you, or stroked you, or tended to your wounds, or buried your dead and mourned the loss? They throw you a few crumbs on occasion, but even on the coldest nights you must burrow into the straw for warmth. Come with me to my home, where you can warm your old bones on a hearth, where you will never again know the gnawing of hunger."

Mother blinked and the truth somehow made the world she called home seem barren and dilapidated. She swallowed hard before answering.

"Your Most Beautifulness, I can't deny that what you say is true, but I am needed here. Who will make sure the kittens don't stray into the fields and lose their way, or fall into the stream? What if a rat should appear, or a coyote – who would warn my family? What if the Man should fall ill or die? – maybe the Woman would need comforting."

Bast looked at her and narrowed her eyes to slits. She was more accustomed to commanding than conversing.

"Dearest Mother. You have earned a better place. You have nursed kittens until your breasts ached. You have watched the young you worried over die. The Humans are fools! They are blind to beauty and hardhearted. If they truly loved you, would you sleep here in the straw alone, without so much as a kind word or a caress? Come away with me to my temple of gold and live for all eternity in paradise."

Mother slowly shook her head "no."

"I am sorry, Most Gracious Cat, but I cannot. This is my home, such as it is. I forgave the Man and Woman long ago. I belong here to these hills – these are my trees, my stream, my barnyard. My children and their children and their children need me. Please don't think me ungrateful, but I am, in my own way, happy."

Bast swished her tail. Not being obeyed was a new experience for her, but in deference to such honesty and loyalty, foolish though she thought it, she spoke kindly.

"It is clear, Dear Mother, that I cannot change your mind, but neither can I leave without rewarding you in some way. Surely there is something you want for yourself?"

Mother pondered a moment. She'd never had very much, that was true, but she also didn't have much of an idea of what else a cat could have, or would want.

"Well, I suppose I'd like to keep my claws – I've heard some cats have theirs chopped off by humans and I can't imagine life without my claws."

It was Bast's turn to shake her head. Was there ever a cat less demanding than this one called Mother?

"Keep your claws you shall Mother. But there should be more...let me think. Yes! All tabby cats will wear the mark of my amulet around their necks to commemorate this meeting. Still, that's not much. Let me think some more.

"I have it! From now on, all cats, if only so faintly, will wear the mark of 'M' on their forehead, in honor of the cat called

Mother. Hmmm...that still doesn't seem like much."

Bast closed her eyes and twitched her tufted ears. She lashed her tail back and forth in thought, and stamped her paw with impatience.

"I know!" she announced and licked her paw in satisfaction. "From this day forward, even after you leave this earthly 'home' of yours, your spirit will always be present. At the edge of the forest and field, Man will see a brown tabby cat from the corner of his eye. As he rides in his motorcar, he will spy you by the side of the road. As he turns the corner on a dark night in the city, there you will be. Under lamplight, against fence posts, in the alleys, on doorsteps, you will be there as a constant reminder to Man of what he has foolishly ignored – the simple, quiet, loyal and forgiving heart of a brown tabby cat. That, Most Honored Mother, beloved of Bast, will be my gift to you."

With that pronouncement she shook gold dust from her luxurious fur and strode imperiously out of sight. Mother nestled into her straw and began licking her paws. She hadn't any understanding of what had transpired and wondered if it had been some sort of waking dream. The sun shone, the bees droned, and the birds resumed their twittering. Mother slept soundly away.

The days passed one after the other and all was as it was before, or so it seemed.

It was nearly dusk one day, a short time later, when the Man returned home from the fields. He leaned heavily on the back door frame of the house as he removed his work boots and allowed them to drop with a thud. The Woman was occupied with setting the table for their supper and a fire blazed in the grate.

"I thought you said you found the old mother cat dead yesterday?" he said to his wife.

"I did, indeed," the Woman replied. "I set her out this morning with the trash."

"Odd. I just thought I saw her next to the woodpile as I came in," he said.

"Funny you should say that. I was walking up from the mailbox this morning and I could've sworn I saw her at the edge of the field."

In her temple, in a land and time far away, Bast smiled.

"Free Kittuns"

The sign on the mailbox post was hand-lettered on cardboard and read "FREE KITTUNS." It appeared there two or three times a year, sometimes spelled this way, sometimes that, but the message was always the same.

In a corner of the farmhouse back porch was a cardboard box with a dirty towel inside, on which huddled a bouquet of kittens of different colors, mewing and blinking and waiting for their mama to return from hunting in the fields. The mother cat managed to show them enough interest for the first several weeks, but after having two or three litters per year, she was worn out and her milk barely lasted long enough for her babies to survive.

One by one, people showed up over the next several days and each took a kitten. Before they left the woman who lived there always said the same thing, "You make sure you give that one a good home – I've become very attached to that one."

One by one the kittens and their new people drove down the long driveway and past the sign on the mailbox post, "FREE KITTUNS."

The ginger girl kitten was the first to be picked. Her four-year-old owner loved her very much, but the little girl accidentally injured the kitten's shoulder by picking her up the wrong way. She couldn't be blamed really – no adult had shown her the proper way to handle a kitten. She had named the kitten "Ginger" and was very sad a few weeks later when her older brother and his friends were playing in the living room and someone sat on the kitten.

The solid white boy kitten with blue eyes was the next to leave with a couple who announced even before they went down the porch steps that his name would be "Snowy." Unfortunately, he never learned his name and everyone had paid so little attention to him that nobody realized he was deaf. On his first excursion outside he was run over in the driveway by a mail truck.

The pretty gray and white girl kitten went to live on a nearby farm as a "mouser." Her people called her "the cat," and like her mother and grandmother before her she had many, many "free kittuns," but they sapped her energy. She became ill and died before her current litter of kittens was weaned.

Another brother was a beautiful red tabby. His owner loved him so much that she took him around to meet everyone in the family and her friends, and their cats, and everyone agreed that "Erik" was a handsome boy. Except his owner didn't bother to have him vaccinated. It took all the money in her bank account to pay a veterinarian to treat him when he became sick, but the doctor just shook his head one day and said "I'm sorry."

The solid black boy kitten grew up to be a fine example of a tomcat. The man who adopted him moved shortly thereafter and left "Tommy" where he was, roaming the neighborhood, defending his territory, and fathering many kittens until a bully of a dog cornered him.

The black and white girl kitten got a wonderful home. She was named "Pyewacket." She got the best of food, the best of care until she was nearly five years old. Then her owner met a man who didn't like cats, but she married him anyway. Pyewacket was taken to an animal shelter where there were already a hundred cats. Then one day, there were none.

A pretty woman driving a van took the last two kittens, a gray boy and a brown tiger-striped girl. She promised they would always stay together. She sold them for fifteen dollars each to a laboratory. To this day, they are still together...in a jar of alcohol.

For whatever reason – because Heaven is in a different time zone, or because not even cat souls can be trusted to travel in a straight line without meandering – all the young-again kittens arrived at Heaven's gate simultaneously. They batted and licked each other in glee, romped for awhile, and then solemnly marched through the gate, right past a sign lettered in gold: "YOU ARE FINALLY FREE, KITTENS."

If man could be crossed with a cat, it would improve man,
but deteriorate the cat.
~ MARK TWAIN
❖

HER ROYAL SABLENESS "ALEXIS"

THE BASSET CHRONICLES:
A Basset Full of Bounty

It was Thanksgiving morning and most of the animals were napping following their breakfast. Of the Bassets, Winnie and Flash were snoozing on their living room pillows, Daphne was wandering aimlessly in the yard, and Alexis was prowling room-by-room looking for cats in need of chasing or dust-bunnies to be hunted. She waddled past me in the kitchen singing "A tisket, a tasket, I'm the most beautiful Basset..." when she spied the turkey I was stuffing on the kitchen countertop.

"Eek! Ack! Ohmygosh! He's skinned that ancient Basset!" she shrieked, referring to the aged Daphne.

"Alexis, don't be ridiculous! It's a bird. This is what humans eat on Thanksgiving. It's for our guests and now I'm stuffing it," I explained.

"With what?" she asked.

"The stuffing is made from stale bread crumbs, broth, herbs and spices. If you all are good today, maybe you'll get some stuffing in your dinner."

"I shall count the minutes until I can have some old bread crumbs you've shoved up a bird's behind," she replied.

"Nice talk. Besides, you know we don't eat dogs in America."

"Yeah, well what are these 'hot dogs' I've heard about?" she asked suspiciously.

"They are just called hot dogs – they are made out of pig lips, sheep entrails, cow eyelids and other wholesome meat byproducts," I said.

"Yummy," Alexis said, probably earnestly.

"Alexis, try to be on your best behavior today and stay out of my hair. This is the day we are supposed to count our blessings and be thankful. Maybe you should reflect on what you are thankful for."

"Hmm. Well, I'm thankful that I'm the most beautiful Basset in the world. That I'm the only sable Basset in the world. That I'm the smartest Basset in the world. That..."

"Enough! You are impossibly arrogant. Why don't you go take a nap with Winnie and Flash?"

"The Sauerkraut Twins? No thanks."

"Oh, they aren't so bad – they are just very proud of their German heritage."

"Proud? Whatever I say, Flash just replies 'Hmmmph!' and whatever I suggest, Winnie says 'Das ist nicht za vay vee do it in Deutschland.' I'm sick of it."

"Then go out in the yard with Daphne," I suggested.

"Right. That dog never stops pacing and she can't see worth a darn. Every time I fall asleep in the sun she trips over me, or she barks nonstop at nothing."

"I don't think she barks at nothing," I said. "Perhaps she sees a hunter or stranger, maybe she thinks it's an intruder."

"Intruder? Ha! Daphne wouldn't know an intruder if one stood up in the middle of her food bowl. And another thing, how come she gets all this extra treatment? Diapers, special food, her own blanket, etc.? Not to mention all your terms of endearment like 'Daddy's little pumpkin'."

"She is my little pumpkin and considering her age she deserves a bit of special treatment. Now go away and let me get on with the rest of this dinner."

Alexis left sulking through the dog door and from the kitchen window I watched her dive into leaf piles, run rings around sleeping dogs before dunking her head in the water bucket and running back inside to take the choicest spot on the couch. I shook my head as I sponged up her trail. I continued with the dinner preparations.

I was ready to put the pumpkin pie into the oven when Alexis woke up from her nap and wandered sleepily into the kitchen.

"Whazat?" she asked and yawned.

"Pumpkin pie for dessert," I replied.

A look of horror crossed her face.

"*Aaaah!* Murderer! Run for your lives...he's put the old girl into a pie!"

Her outburst woke Flash. "Hmmmph!" he grunted and put his head down again. Winnie blinked and muttered "Das ist nicht za vay vee do it in Deutschland," and drifted off to sleep again. Daphne continued her endless patrol of the yard.

I heard the dog door swoosh behind me and turned to see Alexis and a scrap of blue and white go through it.

"Alexis! Gimme that goshdarn dish towel!" I yelled and set out after her. Thankfully, of course.

No one appreciates
the very special genius of your conversation
as the dog does.
~ CHRISTOPHER MORLEY
❖

A dog teaches a boy fidelity, perseverance,
and to turn around three times before lying down.
~ ROBERT BENCHLEY
❖

The greatest pleasure of a dog is that you may make a fool of yourself
with him, and not only will he not scold you,
but he will make a fool of himself, too.
~ SAMUEL BUTLER
❖

'IF' FOR DOGS

If you can stay off of the couch when others can't
and are blaming it on you,
If you can keep from counter-cruising,
or at least have the sense to blame them, too,
If you can wait and not be tired of waiting
for your owner late from work again,
and not mess your crate, or if not crated,
have the sense to use the den.

If you can run a little faster than your master,
If you can drink and pee with aim,
If you can meet cats without disaster,
and from eating them refrain;
If you can try to hit non-doglovers
with flings of food and drool,
or bury the things your human needs,
especially car keys, gloves and tools.

If you can make one heap of all your toys,
or strew them about on the stairs,
or place them discreetly under cushions,
while your owner is blissfully unawares;
If you can coerce the neighbor kids
to feed you more treats than allowed,
or convince the dogsitter to serve you dinner
and of your unexplained weight gain be proud.

If you can walk through crowds without a muzzle,
or "break wind" and implicate a human,
If neither squirrels nor roadkills divert you,
and you can ignore the UPS man,
If you can stand to car-ride with your owner,
and despite the driving, not throw-up,
then you are ahead of most creatures,
and – which is more – you are a Dog, my pup!

❖

A HERD OF BEES

A flock of seagulls may frost you
with dollops of green and white,
a murder of crows may frighten you
with caws in the middle of night.
A gaggle of geese may warn you
of winter's approaching gloom,
but a swarm of bees is unwelcome,
unless you give 'em plenty of room.

A shrewdness of apes may impress you,
their brains like ours on a par,
a pace of asses might strike you,
with just how like us they are!
A quiver of cobras might evict you,
unless a kettle of hawks is about,
but an intrusion of (*shudder*) cockroaches
is very difficult to rout out.

A bed of oysters may lull you
with the temptation to take a nap,
a rhumba of rattlesnakes is definitely not
something you'd want in your lap.
A clamour of rooks may clamor,
a host of sparrows may host,
but if you're having a party, you wouldn't invite
a flink (twelve cows at the most).

A clutch of chicks may grip you,
a clowder of cats detain,
a trip of goats impede you from
your composure to maintain.
A cete of badgers may unnerve you,
a culture of bacteria invade,
but a band of gorillas won't hurt you,
though they're liable to upset your maid.

A yoke of oxen may tow you,
should you suffer a breakdown,
an unkindness of ravens won't help you
catch a lift to the nearest town.
A string of ponies might squire you
along a country road,
and an army of frogs will strike you as
not as quiet as a dead toad.

A smack of jellyfish may accost you,
a mob of kangaroos might, too,
a gang of elk could alarm you,
a horde of gnats you might rue.
A stud of mares might confuse you,
a bouquet of pheasants, too,
but a charm of finches won't bother you,
unless they decide to nest in your "do."

A husk of hares could tell you,
where to find delicious corn,
a lamentation of swimming swans,
might sound like blaring horns.
A pod of porpoises can outswim
your best efforts, you must admit,
and a skulk of foxes won't ever tell
where they've hidden their kits.

A wisp of snipe might swipe you,
a dray of squirrels annoy,
a flock of swifts might swat you,
mustering storks bring bundles of joy,
a bevy of quail might warn you
about a swarm of rats,
and there's few things cuter in this world
than a kindle of baby cats.

And as you attempt to memorize,
study hard to learn the groups,
you'll learn a pack from a pod,
and not to call a team a troop.
When you're done you may figure out,
that most don't give a clue,
which is why animals are often smarter
than a Congress of humans, 'tis true!

The love of animals, like the love of our neighbor,
is not a gift to be condescendingly bestowed,
but a profound and humble acceptance of their kinship.
~ ROBERT R. LOGAN

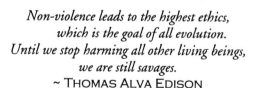

Non-violence leads to the highest ethics,
which is the goal of all evolution.
Until we stop harming all other living beings,
we are still savages.
~ THOMAS ALVA EDISON

PROMISES KEPT

You run in different fields now. *Effortless.*
You jump and play with wild abandon. *Painless.*
Eternally young and carefree. *Timeless.*

There is a shroud over my heart. *Darkness.*
Days are longer and empty without you. *Cheerless.*
I still keep your pillow next to my bed. *Sleepless.*

The years march on. *Ceaseless.*
The memories never wane. *Impervious.*
I feel the moment of my fading, then...*Brightness.*

We run in different fields now. *Effortless.*
We jump and play with wild abandon. *Painless.*
Together for all eternity. *Glorious*

*We who choose to surround ourselves
with lives even more temporary than our own,
live within a fragile circle, easily and often breached.
Unable to accept its awful gaps, we still would live no other way.
We cherish memory as the only certain immortality,
never fully understanding the necessary plan.*
~ IRVING TOWNSEND

THE IMPORTANCE OF BEING ERNEST —
The Life and Loss of a Beagle

Ernest lost the use of his hindlegs yesterday evening and this morning he yelped once in pain. It was time to say goodbye. His two-week fight against kidney failure was over. I thought if I cried all the way to the veterinary clinic, I might not cry in front of the vet. I was wrong. I had remembered to bring a bath towel with me. Ernest doesn't like cold stainless steel tables.

Twenty dollars to end discomfort and prevent suffering – I've spent much more on gifts for my friends which weren't nearly as appropriate.

When you lean over them sobbing as they draw their last breath, does their soul pass upward through yours on its way to Higher Ground? Does it blaze a trail we can follow later? Will we recognize them at our reunion without their earthly appearance, when we can judge them only by their spirit and not their species? I hope so.

I drove home in a torrent of rain and tears, and now know what it feels like to pilot a submarine. I halted at an intersection and watched cars and people bustle about their everyday life. *"Why don't they ring church bells?"* I wondered, *"or stop traffic, or observe a moment of silence? Don't they know that I am chauffeuring one of the kindest, most gentle and loving spirits who has ever walked the planet?"*

I thought about the little things, like how he wiggled his butt when he walked. I thought about the enormous, like why is it that the world's only imperfect species, the only one which sins and suffers guilt, should have been granted dominion over the Earth? And how we should take that stewardship more seriously.

I dug his grave in the rain and obsessed about keeping it dry. Ernest always avoided mud puddles. I looked around at the other graves, each marked by a plant or tree: Amber, Khufu, Sir Edmund, Katerina, Ebony, Viva...too many. Over decades and on two continents, I've done this all before – why does it always seem that it rains, or do they weep with me?

I remembered what a roly-poly riot he and his brother Julio were, the Laurel & Hardy of Beagles. How he'd lose his temper and chase off a wolf when she got to be too obnoxious. How he counted the minutes until dinner and then sang for his supper. I am so grateful to their former hunter owner who abandoned them on my road a couple of years ago, and our neighbors on this road who did as they always do, ignore any stray animal until it becomes our responsibility. They gave me one of the best friends I've ever had of any species.

I remembered how, when he was too weak to eat or drink on his own, he always managed to wag his tail for me. Even when I had to stick needles into him to administer fluids that look of absolute trust and undying devotion never flickered in those beautiful brown eyes.

I closed his eyes and gave him one last kiss.

I have to tell Julio now that Ernest is gone and that he'll have to sing more often and more loudly now to make up for the silence – which he'll gladly do – and explain that, no, he cannot have Ernest's dinner from now on. Then I'll hug him and probably cry some more, and we'll remember that there was something so wonderfully important about the being, Ernest.

Not the least hard thing to bear when they go from us,
these quiet friends, is that they carry away with them
so many years of our lives. Yet, if they find warmth therein,
who would begrudge them those years that they have so guarded?
And whatever they take, be sure they have deserved.
~ JOHN GALSWORTHY
❖

THE SEASONS OF YOUR LIFE

It is the Spring of your life,
the beginning of our love.
I laugh at your foolishness,
show you what you need to know,
protect you from dangers you know nothing about,
and make sure you grow and glow with health.
We will play and practice until...

It is the Summer of your life.
My, what a beauty you've become!
You've grown into yourself and you live at full tilt.
Like the sun, you burn with a passion for life.
You have learned and experienced much,
but you may not appreciate everything until...

It is the Autumn of your life.
You've grown more sedate.
It's been so long since you were the source
of any difficulty that I've nearly
forgotten the Spring of your life.
Your colors are still vibrant,
but I notice the tinge of frost on your muzzle –
foretelling that one season remains...

It is the Winter of your life,
and your eyes have grown as clouded as
the December sky.
I will care for you as I did during the Spring of your life,
and promise that you will pass as gently
as snow falling on frozen fields.
I will sit by your grave and weep,
and remember all the seasons of your life,
for all the seasons of my own.

❖

I LOVED YOU BEST

So this is where we part, My Friend,
and you'll run on, around the bend,
gone from sight, but not from mind,
new pleasures there you'll surely find.

I will go on, I'll find the strength,
life measures quality, not its length.
One long embrace before you leave,
share one last look, before I grieve.

There are others, that much is true,
but they be they, and they aren't you.
And I, fair, impartial, or so I thought,
will remember well all you've taught.

Your place I'll hold, you will be missed,
the fur I stroked, the nose I kissed.
And as you journey to your final rest,
take with you this...I loved you best.

Our animals shepherd us through certain eras of our lives.
When we are ready to turn the corner and make it on our own...
they let us go.
~ ANONYMOUS

HALF AGAIN AS MUCH

The boy sat on the bottom porch step and aimlessly drew patterns in the red clay with a stick. The sound of children splashing in a pool, whooping and squealing, floated over from the next street and he looked up occasionally in that direction. He concentrated on encouraging some fire ants to climb the stick, pretending they were flesh-devouring army ants, and then he gave up and threw the stick into the yard. He stretched his legs out and kicked the built-up sole of his left shoe with his "good foot" in disgust.

Mae watched her grandson from behind the curtains of the living room window and she wore a look of consternation. Something had to be done about the boy, that much was clear, but she didn't know what. She turned quietly and walked into the kitchen with a sigh.

"What's eatin' you, Mama?" Carrie said as she looked up from shaking chicken in a bag.

"Joey," Mae said firmly. "It ain't right, it just ain't right. All the other kids are out enjoying this weather and he sits there the live-long day doing nothin', or he's up in his room playing on that computer."

"Mama, don't start in on me about Joey. I'm doing the best I can by him. I work long hours to keep a roof over our heads and I've tried – tried hard – to find something that would interest him."

"I know you have child," Mae said. "I'm not criticizing you. Maybe if he had a man in his life...I sure wish your daddy was alive, he'd know what to do. Never knew a man to be able to get right to the heart of the matter the way that man could...not like that lying ex-husband of yours."

"Don't go there, Mama," Carrie said and slapped the tray of chicken down on the counter. "He's out of our lives and that's just fine by me."

"Honey, I don't mean to upset you, I'm just worried. Joey needs exercise, he needs some kids his own age to play with. He needs to stop moping around the house and get out in the world.

Lord knows, it's hard enough for our people to make it and he's handicapped."

"Joey is *not* handicapped!" Carrie said. "I've spent nine years trying to teach that boy that he can be anything he wants to and that he's just as good as anybody else...don't you dare even use that word in this house, Mama!"

"Now, Carrie, I didn't mean it the way it sounded...I just mean we have to face facts. What we want Joey to be, how we see Joey...I'm not sure that's the way Joey sees himself. He's withdrawn, child – like he's hiding and puttin' up a wall around him. I'll bet the other kids make fun of him – you know how cruel children can be."

Carrie put her hands over her face and started to cry. Mae stood there shaking her head before walking over and engulfing her into a hug. Carrie just sobbed deeper.

"Don't you carry on now," Mae said. "Me and my big mouth – I never know when to shut up. Remember all the times your daddy lost his hearing aids? Well, I know he did it on purpose just so he didn't have to listen to me flappin' my gums!"

With that Carrie snorted and they both started laughing.

"Mama, I've tried so hard – you know that. I asked the school guidance counselor to talk to Joey last January, and the boy didn't speak to me for two weeks afterwards. I've asked him if the other kids were pickin' on him and he just changes the subject. What am I supposed to do, Mama?"

"I don't know, girl, but we're going to figure out somethin'," Mae promised. "The Lord don't give us nothin' we can't handle. Now if you want somethin' to go with that chicken, I'd better get to the store."

———

Mae backed the car out of the driveway, intending to ask the boy if he wanted to ride along, but the slap of the front screen door told her he'd gone back inside. She fretted her way down the street, through the subdivision, past groups of kids running around lawn sprinklers, laughing, and others whizzing by on scooters or skates.

"Lord," she said to herself, *"I know you have a plan. I just wish you'd let me in on it every once in awhile."*

She knew she could figure this out if she put her mind to it.

She'd raised six children, worked two jobs, and put all of them through college. She and Fred had scrimped and saved, built a nice house and even saved a little nest egg that would help the grandchildren go to college. She wasn't about to let life hold back any grandson of hers. She slapped her fist on the steering wheel to punctuate that thought and nearly ran into the back end of an animal control truck that was stopped dead in the middle of the street.

The animal control officer looked up from trying to load an uncooperative dog into the back of the truck and shook his finger at her. Mae mouthed an *"I'm sorry!"* and waited patiently for him to continue.

"Poor little dog," she thought. *"Your days of running the streets is over – better to be free than to be dragged off to prison."*

The dog reminded her of the terrier who had shared her childhood, "Josh," named for her Uncle Joshua who had been none too happy about the compliment. She'd been the youngest child and after her older brother had gone off to the Army, and her sister had married and moved to Detroit, if it hadn't been for Josh she'd have been one lonely girl. She and Josh went on "expeditions" as she'd called them. They could entertain themselves the whole day and never tire of one another's company. She was mostly surrounded by old people in those days and she laughed at the memory of some of the pranks she and Josh had got up to. No, there was no replacement for those carefree days of running with Josh.

The blaring horn behind her startled her out of her trip down memory lane and as she looked up she saw the animal control truck was long gone. She stuck her hand out the window and waved the other driver around her. She shook her head and chuckled to herself.

"Lord, you sure do work in mysterious ways. The next time you might pay me the courtesy of not dropping the solution directly in the road in front of me!"

Mae put the car in gear and drove off in the vague direction of the animal shelter. It took her three attempts to find the right road and she drove up the gravel driveway and parked in front of the small brick building. A chorus of howls and wails greeted her arrival. She turned off the ignition and sat there quietly for a moment.

"Okay, Lord, I'm here," Mae sighed. *"You just point out the right one and then you'll have to forgive me when I explain to that daughter of mine that you made me do it!"*

———

"Can I help you?" a tired looking woman asked from behind the front counter as Mae walked in.

"Yes," Mae answered, trying to not let on that the animal shelter smells were making her lightheaded. "I'm looking for a good dog for my grandson. He's nine."

"Dogs aplenty we got," the woman said and pointed in the direction of the kennels. "Any preference for breed or size?"

"Somethin' that won't get too big. I saw your truck picking up some kind of terrier over on Eldersville Avenue just awhile ago...is that dog here?"

"That's Buster," the woman laughed. "Buster's a regular visitor. His owner will be calling in a bit, looking for him. Darn dog can climb a six-foot fence! But we got plenty of others...let's go look."

Mae followed the woman with trepidation. She hadn't expected that there would be so many dogs to choose from and she sure hoped the Lord was paying attention.

"I don't want a little puppy necessarily," Mae explained. "Too much work and the boy's mother has enough on her plate already. Somethin' sweet-natured and playful – a boy's dog, somethin' that will get him out of the house."

She wasn't sure the woman was paying attention, as she'd stopped in front of one pen and was making kissing noises, trying to get the little dog in the corner to turn around. The dog slowly turned its head and looked at the two women apprehensively. Mae squinted trying to get a better look at the dog. All she could see in the dim lighting was bits of brown and white and black, and one long ear.

"It's a hound of some sort, isn't it?" she asked the woman.

"A Basset Hound," the woman nodded, "a very unusual one. About nine months old. C'mere girl," she called and bent down, making more kissing noises.

The dog slowly stepped down from her wooden palette and walked calmly to the front of the pen where Mae could get a good look at her. Mae put a hand to her mouth and let out a low whistle.

"My Lord!" she exclaimed. "What happened to her other ear?"

"Born that way," the woman replied. "Her breeder couldn't sell her, couldn't even give her away, so she brought her here. Nothin' wrong with the ear – she's not deaf or anything – it's just shorter than the other one."

Shorter, indeed – a full six inches shorter, Mae figured. She also figured the Lord was in fine form today.

"That'll be the one then," Mae nodded. "I'll take her."

She felt the warmth of the dog as she carried her in her arms and followed the woman back to the office. Her nose told her the pup could do with a bath. She filled out the paperwork and signed a spay agreement, wrote out a check for $25, and toted the dog to her car. She made a pile of bedding on the back seat from a bag of clothes intended for the church rummage sale and gave the dog a reassuring scratch behind the ears.

"You got somethin' important to do now, girl," she said to the pup. "Somethin' real important."

She arranged herself in the driver's seat and composed herself before starting the car. She glanced into the rearview mirror and saw the Basset pup looking at her with complete trust.

"Lord, ain't you somethin'?" she thought. *"For your next miracle, I suggest a good case of laryngitis for that daughter of mine."*

She laughed to herself as she pulled out of the parking lot and onto the road.

––––––

Mae maneuvered into a parking space in front of the shopping center pet supply store. She considered leaving the puppy in the car with the windows down for air and decided against it when she saw other people walking into the store with dogs on leashes.

"Okay, girl, we're goin' shopping!" she said as she hoisted the half-asleep pup out of her comfortable bed of clothes.

Once inside the store she lined the bottom of a shopping cart with a handful of store sales flyers and set the pup on top of the paper. She pushed the cart up one aisle and down the next while marveling at the selection. The shelf of the cart was soon overflowing with toys and supplies, and since Mae had forgotten to bring her glasses with her, she made a formidable obstacle as she pushed the cart with one hand and held bottles out at arm's length with the other hand while attempting to read the labels.

She surprised a stock boy by handing him an armful of products.

"Honey, this ain't what I want. This is cat stuff! Would you mind putting these back for me? Thank you ever so much," she said as she pushed off in the direction of the dog food section.

The pup was wide awake now and accepted her newest mode of transportation gracefully. She took a tentative sniff at some of the items cascading into the cart around her and yawned with approval.

Mae made her way to the checkout line and picked a few pet magazines off the display rack before arriving in front of the cashier. The young woman smiled and asked "A new puppy?"

"Yes. For my grandson," Mae said breathlessly as she attempted to tug a dog bed out from underneath the cart.

"Why, isn't she just the sweetest thing?" the girl commented and then she noticed the pup's two different ears. Mae followed her stare.

"The Lord works in mysterious ways, child," she said. "Indeed he does." And she said it with such conviction that the cashier just smiled weakly and knew better than to ask any more questions.

Mae pushed the cart out the front door of the store with one hand, trying to study the cash register receipt she had clasped in the other. She doubted Josh had cost her family that much money in his whole lifetime. The pup was starting to get restless in the corner of the cart and began investigating the pile of plastic bags surrounding her. Mae loaded her into the backseat first before dumping her paraphernalia into the trunk. She arranged her ample frame in the front seat and glanced at her watch.

"Gracious!" she exclaimed. "Look at the time – and I forgot all about food shopping. Oooo-weee, Carrie is going to have my head!"

She waved and shrugged *"I'm sorry!"* several times to other drivers as she cut diagonally across the parking lot and made her way to the intersection. She drove through several yellow lights before pulling up in front of a fruit and vegetable stand in a spray of gravel and hurriedly bought a dozen ears of sweet corn and some tomatoes. The closer she got to her daughter's neighborhood the more beads of sweat accumulated on her forehead.

"I'm in for it this time," she muttered as she turned the car into the alley behind Carrie's house and parked next to the back gate. She turned around and looked at the puppy sleeping on the back seat before gathering up her purse and the bags of produce.

"You'd better be on your best behavior, little girl," she cautioned the pup. Then she rolled her eyes heavenward and said earnestly, "Lord, don't you be takin' no dinner break now, 'cause I'm surely goin' need you in a moment!"

———

"A DOG!" Carrie yelled and nearly dropped the steaming hot pan of chicken. "Mama, have you lost your mind?! Here I've been holding dinner and worrying where you'd got to, and you come waltzing in here talking about a dog? Mama, we can't afford no dog!"

"Honey, just calm down and let me explain," Mae said, holding the produce bags out in front of her as a shield or a peace offering, or both.

"You don't worry about the money – this is my gift to Joey and I intend to pay for anything that dog needs 'cause that boy *needs* a dog. I've never been so convinced of anything in my entire life, and the Good Lord laid it on my heart to do it, so I did it and that's that!"

"Mama, you and the Good Lord been double-teaming me since I was a child! What is Joey going to do with a dog? I can hardly get him off the front porch."

"The dog will get him off the porch, I promise you that," Mae said and set the bags down on the kitchen counter with a force not in the best interest of the tomatoes.

"Now you listen to me, girl. I have stood by and watched your trials and tribulations since that boy was born...and I have tried to stay out of it as best I can. I have offered you money so you didn't have to work so hard and you won't take it because of pride – foolish pride.

"Hasn't a day gone by that I haven't prayed that a good man would come into your life and look after you and that boy. I love that boy with all my heart and when the Lord tells me that boy needs a dog, he's going to get a dog come hell or high water. And this ain't just a dog, it's a *special* dog and she's going to teach him what we couldn't. Beside the fact that it would be *blasphemy* to not do the Lord's bidding, and Lord knows, I'm a tolerant woman, but if there's one thing I won't stand for, it's blasphemy!"

Carrie stood there with a helpless expression. There was no arguing with her mama when she'd got her dander up and was enlisting the aid of all the legions of Heaven to back her up.

Mae took her daughter's silence to mean she'd won. She walked out into the foyer and called to Joey from the bottom of the stairs.

"Joey, come down here please. Grammy needs some help unloading the car."

――――

The puppy looked up sleepily as Mae opened the car door. Joey wore a bewildered expression as he opened the back door on the passenger side, expecting to find packages.

"You got a dog, Grammy?!"

"A purebred Basset Hound and she's your dog. You'll find everything she needs in the trunk...food, bed, toys, shampoo and some other stuff."

"But Grammy, what's wrong with her? Her ears don't match!" Joey pointed out.

"She was born that way, honey, and nobody wanted her. She needs somebody to love her, someone who understands that all creatures are perfect in the eyes of the Lord. Think you can do that, Joey?"

Joey just nodded with a blank expression and Mae wished she knew what was running through his head.

"She needs to go potty in the backyard and she needs a drink of water now and something to eat. After we have our dinner we're going to take her for a walk," Mae said.

"Why do we need to walk her if we have a backyard?" Joey asked.

"Because dogs need exercise," Mae explained. "They need to get out and see the world. Now let's get her settled in and get to the table before your mama starts carrying on again. Make sure you wash your hands after you're done with her, or we'll be getting a lecture about that, too."

Mae and Carrie maintained a stony silence through dinner except for overly polite requests to pass this or that. Joey didn't seem to notice as he chattered on about the dog and got up frequently from the table to look out the screen door to see what she was doing. The puppy slept on her back on the porch, snoring and burping occasionally. On one of his trips back to the table Joey announced that the dog's name was "Lucy," and the two women glanced at each other before returning to deep concentration over ears of corn.

Carrie declined Mae's invitation to go for a walk and said she had dishes and laundry to do. She watched from the front window as Mae and the boy, with Lucy in tow, started off down the sidewalk. She couldn't remember the last time she'd seen Joey venture past the front gate since school let out.

"Maybe you're right, Mama," she thought. *"You and the Lord and your mysterious ways."*

———

It took hardly any time at all for the odd-eared Basset puppy to work her charms on Joey. If Mae had one complaint it was that she hardly saw her grandson during daylight hours. He and Lucy were out the door first thing in the morning with a packed lunch for the two of them and wouldn't return home until half an hour before dinner. To her daughter's credit, Carrie didn't complain about the muddy clothes, torn shirts and lost caps. Mae believed that her own earlier love of "expeditions" had skipped a generation before finding the two who needed it most. She'd even stopped wearing hats around Lucy, because for some reason the puppy was afraid of them. And she stopped complaining about it when Carrie said "Mama, you've been scaring the whole town with your hats for years, I don't know why Lucy should be an exception."

Mae stayed over some evenings and as she and Carrie sat in the living room watching TV, they heard the thumps and bumps, the giggles and barks of the boy and dog wreaking havoc up in Joey's room. Carrie would purse her lips and Mae would give her an *"I told you so"* look before smiling sweetly.

True to her word, Mae had paid all the costs associated with Lucy and then some. Carrie finally had to tell her she did not think that any puppy needed three beds in three different locations throughout the house. Carrie didn't complain when dinner had to be ready extra early on Tuesday evenings, when Mae came to take Joey and Lucy to puppy obedience class. Carrie had even volunteered to drive Lucy to the veterinarian for puppy vaccinations and then the spay surgery, because Mae claimed she fainted at the sight of needles.

Most nights the three of them took an after-dinner walk with Lucy and usually ended up at the Dairy Delight for dessert, where Mae held court in the parking lot and manipulated the crowd for her own purposes – usually to rope in volunteers to work church socials and fundraisers. She'd even become an apostle for pet ownership and had convinced several neighborhood parents about animals being an indispensable part of a child's life and she'd sent several of them to the local shelter to adopt dogs and cats.

Mae learned that the tired looking woman at the animal shelter was Beth, and Beth learned to count on the times Mae would show up with a boxed lunch for her and a carload of secondhand towels, sheets and blankets for the animals.

"We just buy each other's things at the church sales anyway," Mae explained, "and then we take them back to the church and resell them to one another. Lord knows these poor unfortunate creatures need them more than we do."

Joey had picked out a first "birthday" for Lucy and Mae had proposed a birthday party and then turned it into the children's social event of the season. Some had brought their dogs with them, and childless, dogless neighbors showed up just to see what all the commotion was about.

Carrie sat at the kitchen table and sipped a glass of sweet tea thoughtfully. That Lucy had changed Joey's life and outlook was undeniable. She was sure all the walking and exercise was good for him and thought the boy's limp was slightly less noticeable. Not only had she not once heard a neighborhood child say something mean about Lucy's mismatched ears, they all seemed to treat Joey as one of them. Gone were the days when Joey sat on the front stoop alone and now she usually had to shoo a collection of kids and dogs off the front porch when their mothers started calling for them.

Someday she'd find the right words to thank Mae, but first she'd give it time for some of her mama's gloating to subside. At least Mae had the graciousness to grant that the idea had been the Lord's.

Mae came in the back door huffing and puffing, her arms loaded with bags.

"You're home from work early," she said to Carrie, "you're not sick are you?"

"No, Mama, I'm not sick. I took off a bit early. I've got soupbeans in the crockpot, cornbread just out of the oven – would you give Joey his dinner and stay this evening? I'm going out...I've got a date," she said with a shy smile.

"A date!" Mae exclaimed, setting the bags down and putting a hand to her heart.

"Now, Mama, don't be keepin' me with your questions. I'll tell you about it later – he'll be here in half an hour and I've got to get ready."

She stood up and gave Mae a hug before dashing out of the room.

Mae put away the groceries and set the table for two, all the while wondering and talking to herself. It was high time the girl had showed interest in a man. Her musings were interrupted by the toot of a car horn out front and Carrie flying down the stairs in a cloud of floral pink dress, high heels and expensive perfume.

"Mama, I've got to run. He's here. Please make sure Joey is in bed by 9:30 – don't be keeping him up all night with your stories. And make sure you wipe Lucy's paws before she gets into bed with him. I'll be back by eleven."

Mae just stood there like a stone. She was accustomed to seeing Carrie dressed up and pretty for church, but the girl was beyond pretty now, she positively glowed. She started to open her mouth, but Carrie rushed forward and kissed her, picked up her purse from the kitchen counter and turned on a high heel.

She stopped at the kitchen doorway and faced Mae one more time.

"By the way, Mama – he's a *doctor!* In fact, he's Lucy's veterinarian."

With that she turned and rushed down the hallway and out the front door. She stood on the porch a moment and waved in the direction of the car in the driveway. Then she took the porch steps two at a time and went down the walkway twirling her purse and with a swing in her step. Before she got into his car Carrie looked up toward the living room window, where she knew Mae would be standing behind the curtains, and she grinned from ear to ear. There had been few times in her thirty-four years that she had been able to make her mama speechless. She figured that by the time

Mae lost that slack-jawed look she'd utter one long *"Lord, you sure do work in mysterious ways,"* and then she'd be burning up the phone lines of the Deep South with the news.

Until one has loved an animal,
a part of one's soul remains unawakened.
~ ANATOLE FRANCE
❖

Dogs are our link to paradise...
To sit with a dog on a hillside on a glorious
afternoon is to be back in Eden, where doing
nothing was not boring – it was peace.
~ MILAN KUNDERA
❖

FOR THE UNSUNG

You are the quiet one,
the one whose patience and support I count on.
The one who is used to dinner being late,
or expects that I'll spend more than I should on what matters most,
what matters to me.

This wasn't the life we envisioned,
but you don't complain...much.
You might issue a gentle reminder from time to time,
which I'll probably ignore
and then rush headlong into the next emergency,
or do that thing that must be done that can't wait.
I have to go here, I have to go there, all for a purpose –
all for the good.
But the truth is, I couldn't do any of this without you.

You are the one I turn to when everything is falling apart,
or when I need a hug or a shoulder to cry on.
You are the one who bails me out spiritually and emotionally.
You are the one who stands by me, often behind me –
guarding my back.
I'm the one who flails and fails, who jousts with windmills,
who succumbs to stress.
You're the steadfast one, the rock, ever present and reliable.
The one who dries my tears.

I'm volatile. You're water.
I suffer praise or damnation with grace or guts.
You chide me for my ways and claim they make me endearing.
You are the one who takes me away when I need it most,
from the world I'm trying to change.
You are the one who accepts me as I am
and tells me that what I am doing is right,
even if sometimes it doesn't feel like it.

You are the one who reminds me of what is important,
who leads by serene example.
You are the enabler and as important to my efforts as I am.

And you are the one I don't remember to thank enough –
for all you have done, for just being you, for standing by me.
I can't imagine a life without you.
Thank you.

❖

*The obvious is that which is never seen
until someone expresses it simply.*
~ KHALIL GIBRAN
❖

I HAVE DECIDED

I have decided that I will stop loving anything
or anybody on Thursday noon.
I have realized that the continued cost for me to do so
is five hundred tears per hour.
I have determined that the number of people in this world
whose opinions I can change and whose actions I can be held
accountable for is one.
I have deduced that the number of people who care about
changing the status quo is too few,
and the number of problems is too many.

I have decided to keep my own counsel and company.
There are not enough who understand me, accept me for who I am,
and appreciate what I am trying to do.
If I must pilot this boat alone, better to pray to God
and row for shore.

I have grown tired.
Self-reflection has discovered weaknesses
I did not know about when I began.
That discovery changed everything and I no longer feel prepared.
I have learned a lesson from public apathy:
better to do nothing at all.

I will be taking a leave of absence.
I can be reached at the same locale where people in positions of
authority, who control public coffers, who have influence
and do little can be found.

I will be giving up individuality,
and I will be joining the throngs of the confused, the deluded,
the taken advantage of, the hopeless.
I will be erasing my conscience, ignoring my heart,
forgetting most of what I know to be true and placing the cowl of
selfishness on my head.
I was not cut out to be a king, a bishop, a knight...I will be a pawn.

Yes, I have decided.

On Friday morning, should I be confronted by a person in need
or a creature in discomfort...
if I should be faced with an issue or a problem that I believe
requires my voice,
I might be persuaded to delay my decision.
But only for a decade or two.
After which time it will be impossible to change my mind,
because I will have decided.

For those, O Lord, the humble beasts,
that bear with us the burden and heat of the day,
and offer their guileless lives for the well-being of humankind;
and for the wild creatures, whom You have made wise, strong
and beautiful, we supplicate for them
Your great tenderness of heart,
for You have promised to save both human and beast,
and great is Your loving kindness,
O Master, Savior of the world.
~ SAINT BASIL THE GREAT, BISHOP OF CAESAREA

THE BASSET CHRONICLES:
The Tale of the Telltale Tattletale

I was working furiously on deadline to edit a book manuscript and hoping that the biggest immediate threat to my sanity, Alexis, would stay otherwise occupied. Not likely – I heard the dog door swish and her royal sableness paraded into the living room, weaving her way around half a pack of sleeping dogs.

"You'd better go out and rescue Daphne," she said.

"Alexis, I have to have this manuscript to an express courier by five p.m. – what's the problem?"

"Well, she doesn't do reverse, so when she gets stuck in a corner of the yard she bounces back and forth between the two sides of the fence until she starts making *that* noise."

"Which noise?" I asked.

"You know – the one that sounds like Luciano Pavarotti got his pee-pee caught in his zipper."

"Fine, I'll take care of it and then you must leave me alone for the rest of the day."

"While you are out there, how about giving her a new mantra?" Alexis suggested.

"Mantra? Daphne is Buddhist?"

"Might as well be," Alexis said. "She walks around all day long mumbling '*lovedaddy, lovedaddy, lovedaddy.*'"

I went out and pointed Daphne in the opposite direction and she waddled off happily, chanting as she went. Once again, I took up my red pen and cursed an author.

"This is not English. It's some alien language!" I groaned in frustration.

I heard Alexis shuffling along the hallway making a siren noise.

"Wooo-wooo-wooo – double cat calamity in the bedroom," she warned, looking pleased with herself.

"What happened now?" I asked curtly.

"First, Jasper coughed up a hairball the size of a hamster – we're not missing a hamster are we? Then, Fleck must have eaten something baaad. He did one of his projectile numbers. Colorful, I must say – looks like a Disney film back there."

"THANK YOU ALEXIS, I'll take care of it."

Ten minutes later, smelling of pine cleaner, I returned to the impossible task at hand.

"If I could track down this author's high school English teacher, I would slap her," I muttered to myself. "I'd like to dangle him and his participles over the edge of a cliff."

Alexis sat near me, pretending to focus her attention out the window, but occasionally glancing at me out of the corner of her eye. She cleared her throat.

"Were you partial to that soap-on-a-rope you had in the bathroom?" she asked innocently.

"NO. Why?"

"Amadeus ate it," she announced, looking impressed.

"It doesn't matter, it was organic and Amadeus has been eating things larger than his head ever since he was a puppy without ill effects."

"I think you should come have a look out the window," she suggested. "It gave him gas and now it looks like the Lawrence Welk orchestra is out in the yard. Ooooo – look at the size of that bubble!"

"Please, Alexis, go away – go visit the dogs in the back yard and let me work on this book!"

Alexis flounced off, trying to look deeply offended. I continued forcing tenses to agree, sweeping up commas and scattering them elsewhere, and sweating bullets as I watched the wall clock.

Alexis returned a few minutes later and sat down to stare at the back of my head. I ignored her as long as possible. Then, my concentration broken, I swung around in my chair.

"What is it *this* time?!"

"Apollo and Frasier have dug a HUGE hole in the back yard and now they are filling it in again," she reported.

"It doesn't matter!" I croaked in exasperation. "The back yard already resembles an exploded minefield – now for the last time, will you please go away?!"

"Hmmph!" she sulked and sashayed through the front dog door.

I made a few more corrections before I heard the door flap creak open and saw her brown snout poking through the opening.

"YES ALEXIS?"

"...did I happen to mention that the Beagle Boys are at the bottom of the hole?" she asked demurely.

"WHAT?!"

I ran out to the yard, extricated a livid Ernest and Julio, dusted them off and placated them with a handful of dog biscuits. I returned to my desk and glanced at the clock before giving Alexis a warning look. She stared at the ceiling unconcerned, backed up slowly and sat down on a sleeping cat.

"Rrrowww!" a startled Sergei sprang up and landed on what he thought was an ottoman, with ears. "Woof!" a furious Flash jumped to his feet, knocking over the end table. The table lamp hung in mid-air for a split second before crashing into an easy chair where Danny the Dachshund was snoring under an afghan (crocheted variety). I watched in horror as dogs and cats erupted into the Flying Walendas.

"QUIET!" Alexis shrieked. Involuntarily, my red pen snapped in half in my hand.

"Have you no decency?" she addressed the bewildered bunch. "DADDY IS TRYING TO WORK!"

She looked at me, my face buried in my arms on the desktop.

"And *now* look at what you've done," she continued. "You've made him cry!"

A door is what a dog is perpetually on the wrong side of.
~ OGDEN NASH
❖

THE BASSET CHRONICLES:
Deck the Halls and Alexis, Too!

I put the finishing touches on the Christmas tree and stood back with the animals to admire it. We all instinctively tilted our heads slightly to the right in order to "straighten" it.

"What do you think guys?" I asked.

"It's beeyoootiful!" they concluded.

"Are you sure Martha Stewart recommends attaching ornaments with duct tape?" Alexis asked.

"Martha Stewart does not have badly behaved cats and kittens," I replied.

"Let's follow her example," Alexis said.

"Let's not. Now, Alexis, why don't you entertain the troops with a Christmas story while I make us some refreshments?"

I walked into the kitchen from where I watched as a potpourri of cats and dogs gathered around Alexis and the tree. It wasn't exactly a Kodak moment, but it would do.

"Please, Alexis," they chorused, "tell us about Christmas!"

"Well," Alexis began, pleased with the opportunity to share her encyclopedic knowledge, "Christmas is the birthday of Baby Jesus. Shortly before he was born a bright star appeared in the night sky and..."

"What's a star?" Sassy the Maltese terrorist interrupted.

"I'm a star," said Alexis.

"Ohhh," the group nodded and pictured a glowing Basset in the sky.

"Anyway, these Three Wise Guys saw the star and decided to follow it so they could bring gifts to the Baby Jesus..."

"What kind of gifts?" Danny the Dachshund inquired.

"Errr, well a package of bacon, a side of beef and a couple of roadkills," Alexis answered.

Winnie swooned at the thought of strangers bearing food.

"So," Alexis began again, "the Three Wise Guys rode their camels day and night and..."

"What's a camel?" Tina the Dalmatian asked.

"It's like a llama with humps," Alexis answered, beginning to look peeved. Of course nobody had a clue what a llama is.

"Winnie and Daphne had surgery for bumps," someone else remembered.

"*Not* bumps – humps," Alexis sputtered.

"Isn't that what Daddy says the Beagle Boys do to visitors' legs?" Sadie the Sheltie asked.

"NO!" Alexis fumed.

"*Lovedaddy, lovedaddy, lovedaddy,*" Daphne announced.

"Dearie, someone will be along with your medication in a moment," Alexis patted Daphne's head. "Try to hold on. Now, if I may continue...it was a really long journey, because the Three Wise Guys got lost..."

"Because they wouldn't ask anybody for directions, like Daddy?" Blaze the Labrador wondered.

"*LOVEDADDY, LOVEDADDY, LOVEDADDY!*" Daphne said emphatically and then had to lie down from the effort.

Alexis gave her a very unChristmassy look and took a deep breath.

"Possibly. Finally, they got to the town where Baby Jesus and his mother the Virgin Mary..."

"What's a virgin?" the kittens asked in tandem.

"It's a lady who makes olive oil," Alexis explained.

I glanced at the bottle of "extra virgin olive oil" on the kitchen counter and stuffed a dishtowel in my mouth.

"What's olive oil?" the kittens demanded.

"It keeps olives from squeaking," Alexis replied, "now pay attention! So, the baby's mother and his father, Joseph – uh, well, Joseph wasn't really the baby's father."

"Ahhh," the group exchanged knowing looks.

"Did AKC revoke their breeder's license?" Amadeus the Schnauzer asked logically.

"No!" Alexis roared. "Now listen up. They had the baby in a barn and he was wrapped in swaddling clothes."

"What?" the group asked.

"It's some kind of flea protection," Alexis grumped. "IT'S NOT IMPORTANT!"

"It's hard to waddle when you're swaddled," the Beagle Boys began to sing and do the 'Bump' with each other.

"Teeheehee," the kittens chortled.

"Stifle it!" Alexis yelled. "So, the Three Wise Guys got to town and went straight to the mall, where they bought a Christmas tree with decorations and..."

"Das ist nicht za vay vee do it in Deutschland," Winnie commented.

"Ja," Flash agreed. "Vee offen haf real candles on our Tannenbaum und..."

"Yeah, well you also drive without speed limits – an entire country with a deathwish," Alexis pronounced. "NOW, IF I MAY GO ON...Everyone arrived at the barn and began decorating..."

"Like Daddy!" Sergei the cat said, surveying the plastic splendor everywhere. Meanwhile the kittens argued over who could bring the treetop angel down with one leap, Danny the Dachshund wondered if he'd be allowed to pee on the tree, and Amadeus, who had secretly eaten some of the strung popcorn, was contemplating a bowel movement that our vet would talk about for years.

"...*lovedaddy...lovedaddy...*" Daphne sighed in her sleep.

"Whatever," Alexis snapped. "And when it was all decorated, they had a party and this made the Baby Jesus very happy. It was then that he did something amazing..."

"What?!" the group gasped in unison.

Alexis drew herself up to her full height for the announcement:

"HE DROOLED."

"Ahhhhh," the crowd, especially the Bassets, murmured in appreciation.

It was then I realized how grateful the entire Semetic community must be that Alexis is not Jewish.

Great men have great dogs.
~ OTTO VON BISMARK
❖

THE CONFERRING OF SOULS

Frau Ehrlich slapped the buzzing alarm clock with one hand and fumbled for her eyeglasses on the nightstand with the other. She was accustomed to rising early, but only the two dozen apple cakes she had promised to bake for the village wine festival were justification for getting out of a warm feather bed at five a.m. She flexed her fingers and rubbed her hands, which were still sore from peeling, coring and slicing a bushel of apples the night before.

She dressed quickly and tiptoed past her grandson's room. The smell of apple cakes baking would wake him soon enough. She was glad to have him home and knew that he disliked boarding school even if he avoided the topic. She paused at the window on the stairwell and watched the taillights of her daughter Katja's car disappearing down the driveway and out into the fog. She shook her head. Frau Ehrlich had given up trying to convince her daughter that life in the corporate world was not worth commuting three hours a day on crowded autobahns. Katja had a mind of her own, which was one reason she chose to live in the former guest cottage. She used her background in finance to help keep the family vineyard's books in order, but otherwise showed little interest in wine culture or village life.

Frau Ehrlich continued down the stairs and switched on the kitchen light. She stretched and yawned broadly, grateful that embers still glowed in the hearth. "Schatzi" the wirehaired Dachshund was stretched out on the hearth rug in her usual spot and she did not stir. She walked carefully past as the old dog was easily surprised due to her worsening deafness. Frau Ehrlich put coffee beans into the electric grinder and snapped the lid shut – that would wake the old girl, Schatzi hated the grinder almost as much as she despised the vacuum cleaner. As the beans ground, the dog still did not move and Frau Ehrlich stared at her more intently and with growing concern.

She walked over to the dog and watched for a sign of breathing or a twitch. Nothing. She bent down stiffly and laid her hand on Schatzi's chest. It was cold and hard. As the dog's name meant, she had been a treasure for sixteen years, and tears welled up in Frau Ehrlich's eyes.

Schatzi had never been "her" dog, but she was part of her late husband Heinrich's legacy and family lore. Heinrich, who died six months before her grandson Christian's birth, had won the Dachshund puppy in a shooting contest. The dog had made it clear that she was a man's dog and from the time Christian was old enough to toddle, Schatzi had laid claim to him as her new "Herrchen." Frau Ehrlich had been ready to banish both husband and puppy to the barn after Shatzi chewed the fringe off one end of the Persian rug in the dining room – in fact, the ruined end was still cleverly hidden under the china cabinet.

"Oh, Schatzi," Frau Ehrlich said softly, "and of all days, too."

The annual three-day village wine festival was a time of celebration and reunion as relatives and prodigal children returned to their homesteads. It had brought her grandson Christian home from boarding school and as expected as it was, he was not going to accept Schatzi's death easily. He spent most of his time at home in the company of the dog and when she'd grown too old and arthritic to walk far, he carried her. He had not known his grandfather, although he was the spitting image of him as a boy, and other than his own father leaving after his parents' careers and personalities clashed, he had not experienced the loss of a loved one in his twelve years. Frau Ehrlich had lived through the war years, one learned to get on with life and regard successfully doing so as a tribute to those who had passed on.

"I suppose she's up there with you now, Heinrich," she addressed the ceiling, "ruining expensive carpets."

"Who are you talking to, Oma?" Christian asked from the kitchen doorway and Frau Ehrlich turned around, brushing the tears from her eyes.

"Christian...Guten Morgen. Ach, nobody in particular. I have some sad news to tell you...Schatzi passed on in her sleep last night."

Christian showed no emotion as he walked around the table and stared down at the little dog. He bent down with his back turned toward his grandmother. She saw his shoulders heave slowly with silent sobs.

"Christian...," she said as she started to get up from the chair, but he put his hand up and waved her away. He stroked the dog and made a small whimpering sound. He turned to look at his grandmother with tears streaming down his cheeks, then stood and ran through the kitchen door to the courtyard and kept running. By the time Frau Ehrlich made it to the kitchen window she saw the front gate swing shut and the boy running a race along the field road as the sun burned off the fog.

"Mein Gott," she muttered, "and with no breakfast, too."

She picked up the telephone receiver and dialed her daughter's office number.

———

The boy ran as if Death itself was chasing him. The chilly morning air stung his tear-filled eyes as he churned past fields of harvested tobacco, their pink blossoms frosted remnants of summer. He avoided the rows of wine grapes where workers could already be heard singing and laughing as they picked the last of the grapes and pruned vines. He tore off his flannel shirt and used it to wipe the sweat from his face as he ran past a patchwork quilt of vineyards climbing the steep hillsides high above the Rhine River.

He came to the end of the unpaved field road and leaned over, his hands on his knees as he gasped for breath. He climbed the few ancient stone steps to the old family Friedhof, spread his shirt out on the dew covered grass, and collapsed face down on the ground among the grave stones. The cold ground numbed his underside as the morning sun laid a blanket of warmth on his back, and he sobbed.

"Are you crying because you lost a race, or because you lost someone important?" a man's voice spoke from somewhere above him and Christian rolled over in surprise, his arm shielding his eyes from the sun. An old man wearing a floppy broad-brimmed hat and tattered cardigan sweater, and leaning on a walking stick looked down at him with a kind smile centered in a steel gray beard.

Christian was silent as the old man lowered himself onto a stone bench that had sunk precariously over the centuries. The old man's face was shadowed by the brim of the hat, but there was something familiar about him. He was probably one of the old villagers who lived a hermit-like existence, Christian thought.

"My dog died," Christian said. He was about to continue when a young wirehaired Dachshund jumped up on the bench from behind the man and began pawing his knee for attention.

"You have one, too!" Christian said. "Mine was also a wirehair Dachshund. What's his name?"

"She – her name is 'Schatzi.'"

"Really?!," Christian exclaimed. "My dog's name was Schatzi, too."

The old man chuckled.

"It's a common name...Dachshund people are long on love and short on imagination."

"Yes, I guess," Christian said. "My grandfather named her – she was his dog and then she became mine after he died."

"I see," the old man replied. The little dog tired of her bid for attention and began investigating under the bench. A few clods of dirt were expelled as she dug briefly after an imaginary badger and then she began inspecting the few upright gravestones for other interesting smells.

"Do you think dogs go to Heaven?" Christian asked as he leaned on one elbow and watched the young Dachshund disappear behind a hedgerow.

"They do indeed," the old man answered with certainty. "That's the whole point of giving them souls."

"Animals have souls?" Christian asked hopefully.

"Well, animals who aren't owned, such as wildlife, they have what might be called a 'collective soul' that the Good Lord gives them. But the animals we love – like your Schatzi and mine – those animals are granted an individual soul. God allows us to confer a soul upon them so that we can recognize each other later up there," the old man said and pointed toward the sky. "By our love we instill in them a full and complete soul."

"I'm not sure I understand," Christian said thoughtfully.

"It's not always easy to explain other-worldly concepts in the terms of this world," the old man answered. "It's like...well, take the festival down there," the old man pointed in the direction of the village below where ant-like people were busy erecting booths, tables and chairs, and dressing the red-roofed buildings with garlands and streamers.

"From a distance, we see their group soul – we know they are people like us who we like, even love. We appreciate them...

couldn't imagine life without them. It's a comfort knowing they are there. But that's not the same as looking into the eyes of someone you love, a being like your little Schatzi, is it?"

"No, I guess it isn't," Christian answered. "I see...by loving an animal we give them their own soul and since we are the ones who gave it to them, then we know all about them and can pick them out of a crowd. Is that right?"

"I'd say that's a fairly accurate interpretation," the man said as he used his walking stick to help himself up off the bench. "Speaking of souls, lost and otherwise, I'd better see what that little Dackel of mine is up to."

Christian was about to offer help when he heard his name being called by someone walking quickly up the field road. He turned and saw it was Jens the vineyard manager.

"Christian! There you are...your grandmother is beside herself with worry and she sent me looking for you."

"I'm sorry, Jens. I needed to be by myself – Schatzi died in the night – and then I was talking to Herr...," but as the boy turned around he saw that the old man and dog were gone. He could imagine what his grandmother would have to say about his lack of manners when he told her he hadn't thought to ask the man for his name.

"I know," Jens said. "Your grandmother had me bury Schatzi in the garden and she's going to let you pick a tree to plant there in her memory. Now come along before she sends the Polizei out looking for both of us."

Christian walked silently alongside Jens as far as the vineyard and nodded goodbye as Jens turned into the rows of grapes. The boy continued walking toward the house and outbuildings, and the smell of apple cake greeted him at the front gate.

———

Frau Ehrlich sat at the flour-covered kitchen table with the windows open and the curtains flapping in the breeze. She attempted to ignore a tray of burned apple cakes and instead tried to sort through the cavalcade of emotions that had descended on her in the past several hours. She had already had more phone conversations with Katja in one day than they had had in the past several months, and she was more convinced than ever that her daughter had inherited Heinrich's ability to surprise her.

The first conversation had been full of condolence over Schatzi's passing and concern about Christian handling the grief. The second conversation was the news that Katja had taken Christian's unhappiness over boarding school to heart and he would not be returning there and would be enrolled in the regional school instead. The third phone call was the announcement that Katja had called the Dachshund Society and was waiting for a woman to call her back about dogs in need of a new home, and the fourth call was to confirm that a young Dachshund girl was in a Tierheim not far from Katja's office and she was leaving work early to adopt the dog from the shelter for Christian. Frau Ehrlich doubted anything more surprising could occur all festival weekend, even if Frau Wefelmeyer drank too much new wine again this year and repeated her tabletop rendition of Marlene Dietrich torch songs.

She looked up as Christian came in the kitchen door looking a bit embarrassed, but not grief-stricken as he had earlier.

"Ah, Christian. How are you dear?"

"I'm okay, Oma. I know it was her time. Jens told me he buried her."

"I thought it was best to do it right away," his grandmother said. "I hope you don't mind."

Christian shook his head no.

"She's in Heaven now with Opa," he said confidently. "An old man up on the hill explained it to me."

Frau Ehrlich listened as Christian repeated what the old man had said about collective and individual souls, and try as she did to pry more details out of him about the old man and where he lived, it wasn't until he described the old man's attire that she began to smile with recognition and nodded.

"All well and good, and I'm proud of you for accepting this as you have," she said. "Now you are going to sit down and have a piece of one of the few cakes I didn't ruin, and I need to get some things done. Your mother is coming home early and she's bringing a friend with her."

Christian raised his eyebrows slightly at that news, but didn't ask for more information. Frau Ehrlich was glad he did not press her for details, because she was under strict orders to not betray the secret. She served Christian his cake and a glass of milk, and then excused herself.

She walked into the dining room and slid the heavy drapes back, inspecting the furniture for dust. There weren't enough hours in a day during harvest and festival time and guests would have to overlook dust or gossip about it in the village later. She walked over to the ornate serving board and slid the heavy family Bible toward her, turning open the front cover. A collection of family photographs yellowed and crisp with age slid out. She flipped through them and took one over to the window. It showed Christian's grandfather seated on a log, holding his favorite shooting rifle in one hand, his other hand balancing a wirehaired Dachshund puppy with an impish expression on his knee. He was wearing the worn cardigan sweater she'd darned a hundred times, and beaming below the brim of his floppy hat were gentle eyes and a kind smile centered in a steel gray beard. She kissed the photograph before replacing it in the Bible.

The strains of "Die Loreley" filtered up the hillside from the village below. The Lorelei, the mythical siren who had bewitched sailors on the Rhine – she thought that might be an appropriate name for a little Dachshund girl provided the dog didn't arrive with a name. Frau Ehrlich considered it just as likely they would end up with another "Schatzi." What was it Heinrich used to say? Ah yes, "Dachshund people are long on love and short on imagination."

"Christian," she called as she walked across the room. "When you are done with your cake come in here please and help me roll up this rug."

———

Katja slowed the car as she turned into the roundabout at the edge of the village. She waited patiently as a tractor towing a wagon loaded with hay and festival volunteers pulled onto the road ahead of her. She couldn't remember the last time she had left the office this early in the day, and she felt anticipation for the wine festival that she hadn't felt in years. She looked down at the pair of Dachshunds curled up on the passenger seat. The woman from the Dachshund Society had neglected to mention that the girl, Schatzi, had a brother, August, and after the Tierheim director had informed her that the two dogs were inseparable and had comforted each other after their owner had died, she couldn't very well leave the boy dog behind. The director had assured her that they were perfectly behaved and housetrained. Katja decided that even if that was not accurate it would give her an excuse to buy her mother a new Persian carpet for Christmas.

You think dogs will not be in heaven?
I tell you, they will be there long before any of us.
~ ROBERT LOUIS STEVENSON
❖

If having a soul means being able to feel love and loyalty and gratitude,
then animals are better off than a lot of humans.
~ JAMES HERRIOT
❖

If I have any beliefs about immortality,
it is that certain dogs I have known will go to heaven,
and very few persons.
~ JAMES THURBER
❖

THE EVE OF SAINT AGNES

They told her how, upon St. Agnes' Eve,
Young virgins might have visions of delight,
And soft adorings from their loves receive
Upon the honey'd middle of the night,
If ceremonies due they did aright;
As, supperless to bed they must retire,
And couch supine their beauties, lily white;
Nor look behind, nor sideways, but require
Of Heaven with upward eyes for all that they desire.

– from "The Eve of Saint Agnes, " John Keats (1795 – 1821)

———

Gillian dusted the ice crystals off the park bench with her crossword puzzle magazine and then proceeded to sit on the magazine. It was too cold to remove her mittens in order to hold a pen and work crosswords anyway, and she was otherwise occupied in trying to keep Willow's leash from entangling her legs and preventing the Dalmatian from upending her tote bag and thermos of coffee.

It had seemed like a good idea to spend some hours in Central Park with Willow as part of the dog's birthday celebration, but the brisk cold and rising wind would send them home earlier than expected. The dog wore her new sweater that Gillian had knitted for the occasion, but she worried if Willow's ears were warm enough. She sometimes had to remind herself that most dogs are hardier than thin-skinned humans. She'd even brought along a stadium blanket for Willow to lie on if she chose, but the dog was too busy keeping a look out for other dogs, especially since their humans often carried treats. Willow looked up at Gillian with an expression of impatience as if to say "aren't we going to do any more exploring?"

"In a minute, birthday girl," Gillian said, stamping her feet on the paved path in front of her to stimulate the circulation in her frozen toes. "Just let me get some coffee in me." She wondered if that was such a good idea, since Willow could pee where she wanted, but humans are at the mercy of their bladders and decorum.

She undid the lid of the thermos bottle and cupped her hands around the steam rising from the opening. She inhaled the aroma of the strong brew, hoping it would send a jolt of energy to her brain. She had worked into the wee hours of the morning in order to meet a deadline and then finish Willow's sweater, and as her stomach growled Gillian realized she hadn't eaten since lunch the day before. She needed to take better care of herself, but the life of a freelance children's book illustrator wasn't nearly as much of a fairytale as the scenes she brought to life. Willow had the best of everything, most importantly, unshared attention.

It was the unshared part that sometimes bothered Gillian. She wished she could be as open and gregarious as the dog, who clearly loved the company of other dogs and humans. After her one long-term relationship had ended badly, she'd retreated, gun-shy, to her private world of art, books, strong coffee and whatever Willow wanted. The animal shelter staff had not been able to tell her very much about Willow's former life except that her breeder probably had not been able to sell her because of her handicap. No matter, the dog had the life she deserved now.

Gillian had accepted that being alone was her lot in life and if she had one thing to be grateful for, it was the unconditional love from Willow. Only her mother had accepted her for who she was, and now that she was gone, Gillian felt more alone than ever. She loved her father, but he was reserved and uncommunicative, and even more so now that he was alone. In New York City she didn't feel condemned for her lifestyle, but she also didn't feel that anyone really knew or appreciated her for who she was.

Willow suddenly stood at attention, tail wagging wildly. Gillian looked up from her brooding and saw an English Setter bounding across a grassy area, with a red ball in his mouth and a woman wearing a jogging outfit in pursuit. The dog turned toward the woman, spit out the ball and crouched with haunches in the air, inviting his owner to throw the ball again.

The Dalmatian jerked forward and pulled free the end of her leash that Gillian had been sitting on, and she ran toward the Setter.

"Willow!" Gillian yelled from force of habit and jumped up,

dropping her coffee cup and knocking the thermos over. It landed with the sound of breaking glass on the pavement.

"Grab her leash please – she's deaf!" she screamed as she ran up the path.

The other woman deftly grabbed Willow's leash as Dalmatian and Setter conducted a sniffing introduction. Willow promptly appropriated the ball.

"I...sorry...thank you," Gillian wheezed as she slowed to a walk, still carrying the coffee-soaked crossword puzzle book.

"She'll only go as far as the nearest dog...but I should have been paying more attention."

"Another obedience school drop-out like my boy, only one that lip reads?" the other woman asked. She reached into the pocket of her jogging suit and pulled out a pack of tissues and offered Gillian one.

"You have coffee on your chin and neck."

"I was trying to warm myself...now I'm sweating coffee," Gillian said as she took a tissue and began dabbing at her face, neck and the numerous wet spots on her berber jacket. She glanced at the tall blonde woman and was sure she'd seen the jogging suit she was wearing in a catalog and at a price that would have bought three of them where Gillian shopped.

"You're a bad girl!" she said to Willow. "But it's your birthday, so I'll forgive you."

"Well, happy birthday, Willow," the other woman addressed the Dalmatian.

"I'm Margaret and this is Chauncey. Chauncey is only selectively deaf. Which doesn't present much of a challenge for me, since I'm the medical director for a school for deaf children."

"Really? That must be rewarding," Gillian said. "Maybe you can give me a few pointers."

"On dealing with deafness, yes," Margaret said. "If you are looking for dog-behavior counseling, you're barking up the wrong tree. What are you doing in the park during business hours?"

"I work for myself," Gillian said. "Which means I work twenty-four hours a day. I'm an artist...usually children's book illustrations."

"That sounds like fun," Margaret said. "I'm taking a personal day. I've been covering for a sick colleague beside my normal workload and Chauncey has been behaving badly at doggie daycare. I thought we deserved a play day."

"Other than knitting a new sweater for her royal highness in my free time, I didn't have much time to plan a birthday celebration for Willow, so I thought we could at least manage a park outing without a disaster," Gillian said, trying to self-consciously comb her hair back into place with her fingers.

Margaret looked her directly in the eyes and smiled, and Gillian felt butterflies in her stomach. She pretended to concentrate on trying to get Willow to give up Chauncey's ball. Her stomach growled again loudly and Chauncey gave her a sympathetic look. She began to blush.

"Listen...I have an idea," Margaret said. "You have obviously not had breakfast – I haven't either – and Willow should have a birthday party. I know a cafe that allows dogs a few blocks from here. Let's go have some coffee and muffins. My treat. They even have one of those incinerator things in the bathroom that passes as a hand dryer...maybe you can hold your wet clothes under it."

Gillian sniggered shyly. She was sure she appeared mousy and bookish in comparison to Margaret's natural grace and self-assuredness, but it was also the first invitation by a stranger to any sort of date that she'd had in years.

"That does sound wonderful and I am starving. Anything that has to do with food and dog company is fine with Willow. Sure – why not?" she said and tried to hide her nervousness.

The two dogs propelled them forward and Margaret was such a witty conversationalist that Gillian no longer felt the cold and forgot to notice where they were going so that she could find the place later. They were nearly there when Margaret lit a cigarette and Gillian was almost relieved to see the woman had one flaw. It wasn't until they were installed at a corner table in the cafe with both dogs laying at their feet, laughing and comparing notes about being dog moms that Gillian remembered her tote bag, blanket and broken thermos in the park. They were a small price to pay for such good company.

———

It had been a whirlwind year that had flown by in a flood of long talks, laughter and teasing, outings with the dogs, and changing priorities. It had worked, it was easy, and Gillian finally felt like she could breathe at a normal rate.

In September, Margaret had taken a staff position in Philadelphia, where her new job offered more interaction with the deaf and less administrative responsibilities. They'd found and bought a house an hour from the city, in the foothills of the Poconos. It had a large enclosed sun porch that made the perfect studio for Gillian and more than enough property to exercise her newest passion, gardening. She did the interior of the house in muted tones with English floral fabrics and they spent weekends at auctions and scouring the classifieds for bargain antiques. Margaret allowed her complete range for artistic expression and even complimented her on her frugality. Her only suggestion, after reviewing Gillian's sketches and plans for a rose garden, had been "you had better put a fence around the flowers if you don't want Chauncey drowning everything in urine."

Willow and Chauncey were inseparable. They played in the fenced yard until their tongues were hanging and then flopped down together on the large porch. As a foursome, they went for long walks. Chauncey had acquired manners and was a perfect gentleman, always deferring to his older sister. Willow was now well-muscled and more fit than she'd ever been. She also was now a certified therapy dog and Gillian often took her to visit classes of deaf children. Gillian had lost twenty pounds although she was eating more regularly than she had in her adult life and she attributed it mostly to the lugging around of furniture and turning over and mulching what had seemed like tons of garden soil. She'd even convinced Margaret to quit smoking and with her new job Margaret was losing the harried, overworked look she'd worn earlier last year. Life was good.

Gillian also felt closer to her dad than she had since her mother had died. He lived just two hours away and the first time she and Margaret had visited him, he later whispered to Gillian "that one's a keeper." Gillian had nodded in agreement. Margaret had trounced them both at cribbage and then drank them under the table, and her dad now called them both "his girls."

"I don't know how I'll ever thank you, Willow," Gillian said to the Dalmatian, giving the dog a bear hug and kissing her on the cheek. Chauncey flopped over on his back at her feet with his "I need a bellyrub" pleading look.

"And you...you big baby," she said to the Setter. "You've managed to wear out two moms!"

———

Gillian picked up the skein of wool that had rolled off the loveseat, before one of the dogs decided it was a new game, and she carefully folded the sweater she was knitting for Margaret. She stuck the knitting needles into the skein and set them on the coffee table, and then picked up the day planner book Margaret had given her for Christmas. It was filled with classic art and interesting notes about women in history. She repositioned herself on the loveseat and adjusted the pillows. She was concentrating on making notes in the book about ideas and deadlines when Margaret walked into the room, talking into her cell phone.

"Ummm-mmm, ummm-mmm," she said into the phone as she settled into the easy chair. She pointed to the phone and made a gagging motion that told Gillian it was a colleague she didn't approve of. She reached over with a slippered foot and playfully nudged Gillian's knee. Gillian looked up and smiled and went back to her notes.

Gillian turned a page and admired a painting of a young girl wearing a halo and carrying a lamb in one arm, with some sprigs of what looked like rosemary and thyme in the other hand. At her feet lay a bloody sword. Then she noticed a notation for today's date, January 21, "The Feast of Saint Agnes," and began reading the corresponding margin note. As she read, she had an eerie feeling and shook her head back and forth in disbelief.

"No, doctor, I do not think the boy needs medication for behavioral problems," Margaret said forcefully into the phone. "I think what he needs is a lot of activity out in the fresh air and two parents who had better put career goals on hold until they help the boy develop some coping skills and deal with his deafness as a family! ...ummm-mmm. Fine. We'll discuss it at the staff meeting Monday. You, too."

Margaret ended the conversation by loudly snapping the cell phone shut.

"I could do the world a large favor by hiding that man's prescription pads," she said. She readjusted Chauncey's head on her lap and looked over at Gillian. "And why do you look like you've swallowed a bug?"

"I've just been reading...the oddest thing," Gillian said. "You went to Catholic school – what do you remember about Saint

Agnes?"

"Saint Agnes?" Margaret asked thoughtfully. "I think she was my fourth grade social studies teacher. No, wait a minute, that was Sister Agnes. Saint Agnes...give me a clue...which body part did she lose?"

"Her head," Gillian said. "It says here that she refused to marry or renounce her faith and she was beheaded in Rome. Later on, especially in the British Isles, they believed that on Saint Agnes's Eve, if a young virgin goes without supper that evening, she will dream of her future love. The young people in Northern Scotland scatter grain in a corn field and recite a verse, 'Agnes sweet, and Agnes fair, Hither, hither, now repair; Bonny Agnes, let me see, The lad, or lass, who is to marry me.' And they still celebrate her feast in Rome, and one of the special observances involves shearing two lambs and weaving a religious article from the wool called 'palia' that is only worn by the Pope and archbishops."

"Fascinating," Margaret said.

"I'm not finished...do you know what today is?" Gillian asked.

"Considering that I tripped and fell over a large new dog bed this morning, I'd say it is probably Willow's birthday," Margaret replied.

"And what else?" Gillian continued.

"And that would make it the anniversary of the day Willow threw us together," Margaret said. "How many points have I accumulated so far?"

"Not enough," Gillian said. "Today is also the Feast of Saint Agnes. The evening of the twentieth is the Eve of Saint Agnes."

"That much I got," Margaret said. "If there is going to be a test later, I hope it's multiple choice."

"Silly...don't you remember, the day I met you I was nearly faint with hunger?"

"And all along I thought you were swooning in my presence," Margaret said snidely.

"Grrrr," Gillian shot back. "I hadn't eaten anything since the day before. I'd been up late that night finishing Willow's wool sweater. Isn't that uncanny...the fasting and the wool, deafness and everything? Saint Agnes is even the patron saint of gardeners! Don't you think it's too coincidental?"

"Maybe, with the exception of the virgin part," Margaret said. "I don't know. However it came to be, I'm just glad it did. Personally, I think Saint Willow had a lot more to do with it than Saint Agnes."

"Yes, she did," Gillian said and threw a throw pillow at Margaret, then shut the book and set it back on the coffee table.

"Now I'm going to the kitchen to fix us some brunch and bake the birthday girl and her brother some dog biscuits. What are you doing?"

"I'm going to take the kids out to the yard and help them dig up some of your spring flower bulbs, and then I'm going to get cleaned up and presentable for the Feast of Saint Willow."

Willow and Chauncey raced her to the porch door and Margaret blew Gillian a kiss before pulling the door shut behind her.

"You should be wearing a jacket!" Gillian said to the empty room.

———————

Wisdom of serpent be yours,
Wisdom of raven be yours,
Wisdom of valiant eagle.
Voice of swan be yours,
Voice of honey be yours,
Voice of the son of the stars.
Bounty of sea be yours,
Bounty of land be yours,
Bounty of the Father of Heaven.
~ TRADITIONAL CELTIC BLESSING
❖

ON BEING AT HOME

I had noticed the bearded man of about my age and his dog sitting on a blanket in a corner of the restaurant and pub district adjacent to Halifax Harbor, as I hurried into one of the seafood restaurants. It was late October, after the tourist season, and I didn't have to wait long for a table with a view of the harbor and the darkening skies. Severe thunderstorms were predicted for later in the evening so I rushed through a good dinner and a glass of wine, hoping I wouldn't have to drive back to my hotel on unfamiliar roads in a gale.

As I exited the restaurant and zipped my jacket against the rising wind, I saw that the man and dog were still there, and I walked over. Dogs are magnets for me and I can't pass one without stopping.

My impression of Nova Scotia is that everything is clean and picturesque, so it was no surprise that a homeless man and his dog and their blanket should appear well-groomed and laundered. He, John, had a plastic bag of dog biscuits and a hat with a few coins in it displayed on the blanket. The deal was that you made a contribution and then you could feed the dog, Annie, a few biscuits. There aren't too many enterprises where all parties leave satisfied and it seemed like an excellent idea to me. After I struck up a conversation with him, he told me he was from Newfoundland. I imagine a Newfie might think of Nova Scotia as a southern climate and well worth migrating to.

Annie is a bright-eyed, black and white shorthair of mixed parentage that perhaps included an Australian cattle dog. She looked to be three or four years old and the picture of health. John is articulate, intelligent and friendly. I asked him if Annie was spayed and vaccinated. She was due for her shots, he said, but he didn't think he could afford them and, no, she wasn't spayed. I gave him ten Canadian dollars and extracted the promise that he would contact one of the local animal welfare agencies and see about having that done. I also gave him my business card, for what little good it would do him. I asked him if he had some place to sleep out of the weather and he said he did. He and Annie are obviously best friends and I walked away content, perhaps a bit jealous of their vagabond life, and it made me miss my dogs. They had also been the first homeless beings I had ever met who I didn't feel sorry for, or feel that as a society we had failed.

Something about that pair intrigued me. Was it the look of complete peace and contentment they both wore? Was it the fact that they didn't regard themselves as homeless, but believed that wherever they were, together, was home? Was it that they both behaved as if they had self-esteem, that their "plight" wasn't a plight at all, that it was a blessing, blessed freedom, or that they could accept help graciously without any evidence of foolish pride? That, of course, is a quality we admire in dogs, but it is unusual to find it in a human.

Meeting John and Annie was not accidental, nothing in life is. Every experience in life has meaning, even the seemingly innocuous occurrences, but it took me awhile to delve deeper for the meaning. I had gone from the wanderlust of youth to struggling with the concept of "home." Where is "home?" Now that my parents and many loved ones have passed on, taking with them much of my affinity for my hometown, will I ever feel "at home" anywhere?

A wise and well-traveled woman once told me that wherever you move to, it will take about one and a half years before you feel at home. In a practical sense, I have found that to be true, and with any move it has taken me that long to find my way around, to know what an area has to offer, to be on a first-name basis with some people and to feel that I have made some new friends. But I wasn't sure I had felt "at home" anywhere. Oh, there were places I had lived that I liked and some I didn't, but I spent my childhood wishing to grow up and live in foreign places, and as an adult I lived in foreign places wishing that I could go home.

What did John and Annie know that I didn't? After some heart-wrenching human and animal losses in my life, and having to sell the only house I'd owned and truly loved so that my wife and I could be available to care for sick and dying parents on two continents and still support a large family of rescued animals, after selling my childhood home...and after accumulating enough life experiences, I could be more introspective than I'd ever been and I think I now know.

Home *is* where the heart is and because we carry our hearts around, beating in our chests, wherever we are is home. The heart has many more than its anatomical chambers and we furnish it with favorite memories, our present loves, and our aspirations. Those we love, human and animal, are installed there with honor, and their physical presence or whether or not they are still with us in this world have nothing to do with their reality for us, their accessibility, or their ability to make us feel comfortable and at home. We will always appreciate the familiarity of favorite places, but we have also distilled their essences and we carry them with us in our hearts. They are all in there, like a well-packed suitcase we'd travel with...reach in and pull them out as you need them. Otherwise, look to your new surroundings for the fresh and rewarding, the old and the similar. As we move through the journey called life, we learn to pack the necessities and to leave the burdensome and the fluff behind. Yes, we might look at the heart as an amazing muscle that beats of its own accord, but it is also a microcosm, the seat of our universe, of our being, and the repository of our home.

Life and responsibilities have required my wife and I to have long separations over the past few years. That has done nothing to lessen the bond and commitment between us, if anything, it has strengthened them. No matter where we are, we still look up at the same moon at night. Our animals will soon be accompanying us on our second trans-Atlantic move. I learned with the first move that all my worries about how they would handle the travel and adjustment upon arrival were unfounded. It was for me yet another example of what we can learn from animals. After a brief investigation of their new quarters, they were home! We were there, they were there, all was right in their world and they had brought everything they needed with them. They strengthen my resolve to have resiliency, to take whatever life hands me and to make it work for me, wherever I am, and to allow myself to be at home.

My chance meeting with John and Annie that blustery evening didn't change their lives. John left ten Canadian dollars richer and with the assurance that another human being was concerned about Annie's welfare. Annie received a few pats from a stranger and a few more dog biscuits that she would have gotten anyway. I took away a lesson I hope to hold on to for life...pack carefully, travel light, use what you have, and make where you are in life "home."

As we talked of freedom and justice one day for all,
we sat down to steaks. "I am eating misery," I thought,
as I took the first bite. And spit it out.
~ ALICE WALKER
❖

When you believe there is no love in the world,
just gaze into the eyes of the cat in your lap.
~ WELSH SAYING
❖

WIND AND WATER

Wind and water, ocean breeze,
and I alone on bended knee
can while away contented hours,
for while the others sleep at night,
I watch the seagulls' endless flight
across thy surface, to the moon
that bathes in light the golden dunes.
Here thou once did implore
sailors' vessels to explore,
with fluid motion thou did reach
and dashed their boats on rocky beach.
And even yet thou plays this game
to roll and billow, kill and maim.
But thou are a puppet on a string,
thou heeds the Moon for when she sings
thy tides must course along the path she chooses,
to escape her wrath –
But who controls the Moon, you say?
What ethereal force at end of day
makes her orb in stillness stand?
I do! For by my hand her crystal globe
ebbs and sways across the night 'til break of day.

PRAYER TO THE PILLARS OF THE DAY

Morning star that heralds the dawn,
make this a good day.
Make it sweet and gentle and memorable.
Let every minute have meaning, conscious, pure.

Sun, giver of life, dazzle us!
Illuminate colors and add sparkle to our hours.
Shine on our lives and gild our actions with rays of blessing.

Evening star, give us direction.
A point of reckoning,
a reason to reflect upon the day past,
and that which will dawn tomorrow.
May we be found worthy.

Moon, precious orb of hope!
Deliver us from the cares of the day.
Assure us that tomorrow will be better.
Paint our love in silver,
and guide us safely through the darkness.

AUTUMN'S DEATH

A quilt is laid upon the world
of colors red and gold,
a sheet is placed of frosty white
peace tucked in every fold.
The air is ripe with cinnamon,
wood smoke and apples tart,
the harvest fields of golden grain,
their richness do impart.
A hunter stands, a shot rings out,
a fallen stag lies still,
Autumn's splendor melts away,
replaced by winter's kill.

We can not have peace among men whose hearts find delight
in killing any living creature.
~ RACHEL CARSON

SONG OF ORCA

Sleek profile that cuts through gray water cold as steel,
terns and gulls circle overhead,
squeals and clicks echo off the rock sentries.

A dorsal fin traces patterns in the sea foam as
schools of fish race on ahead in a ballet of flashing silver.

The sun breaks through clouds
and strews a diamond glint on the sea.
A tail slap sends up shards of glass and Orca breaks the water's
surface into concentric circles.
His mate, heavy with calf, undulates through a curtain of jewels.
They glide together, touching and rolling,
their calls of joy reverberate to the abyss below.

Sleek profile that cuts through turquoise water,
a dorsal fin traces patterns in a pool.
A silver fish flashes above and Orca breaks the water's surface
as the crowd applauds.
He dives in a crystal fountain of sadness.
His mate calls from the gray water cold as steel.

❖

ON ANIMAL RIGHTS FROM THE ANIMAL PERSPECTIVE

We are the animals. We have neither more nor less worth than the human animal. We were not placed on this Earth for your use, benefit, or entertainment. Most of us preceded you by millions of years. We are all, including the human animal, part of the fabric of Life and we each serve our purpose. For centuries, you have made subjective assessments of our "value" and "intelligence," and the intelligent among you have recognized that we are as "valuable" and "intelligent" as we need to be to fulfill our purposes.

While your championing of our "rights" is often noble, it is also an artificial human concept. In most instances you are simply seeking to restore to us what you have taken away – our freedom, our habitats, our inherent right to live without confinement, fear, pain, abuse, exploitation, manipulation and destruction.

We are not a replacement for human companionship. We are not your children. We are not a commodity. We are to be respected for who we are and our animal natures and our specific needs must be taken into consideration. Every attempt to make us what we are not, human – or worse, possessions – is an insult to the sum and substance of what we are: Animals. Whenever you acquire us it is your responsibility to ensure that it is a mutually beneficial relationship for all of our natural lives. You may earn our trust, respect, and even love, but you "own" us by your definitions, not by ours.

It defies logic that despite thousands of years of interaction between our species and yours, humans still do not comprehend some of the basic truths – that all dogs have the capacity to bite, that all cats may scratch, that all horses must run, that cows need pasture, that wildlife belongs in the wild, that most animals need the companionship of their own kind, that if you upset the natural order the result may be extinction or population explosion, and that we all feel pain and discomfort to the same degree as you.

While we appreciate your efforts on our behalf, we urge you to look to your own history that shows lasting change is accomplished by reasonable people, by intelligent debate, by carefully considered legislation, and by compassion. Anything less may make a mockery of the goals and jeopardize that which you strive to accomplish for us.

Every use of an animal, for research, for meat, for fur and hide, for profit, for education, needs to be considered individually. Your ethics committees may debate those uses, but they frequently do so on the basis of a perceived "need" and the human assumption that humans were endowed with the right to make decisions for animals. You have usually demonstrated by your ignorance that you are not qualified to do so.

There is one basic premise from which taking a life must be considered: *All Life is Sacred.* Your academics may debate that, your religious scholars may argue the point, and your nonbelievers may scoff at it...however, we believe you know it in your hearts to be true, as we know it in ours. Our blood runs as red as your own. We kill for sustenance, in self-defense, from instinct and without malice. Should your reasons be any less honorable? Imagine yourself in our place, where the sanctity of life is not ideology but the very instinct of survival. It is not in our power to hold you accountable for your actions, but most of you believe you will answer to a higher authority. Your actions toward animals will not be exempt and turning away from the problems will be judged as complicity.

We are the animals. Appreciate us for who we are. Protect our habitats. Spare us pain and suffering. Stop exploiting us for financial and other gain. Pay attention to our needs and our natures. Fulfill your obligations as stewards and regard our lives as sacred as your own. In so doing, you will achieve a harmony that has been lacking in your lives and which is abundantly apparent in ours.

---

*A thinking man feels compelled to approach all life
with the same reverence he has for his own.*
~ ALBERT SCHWEITZER
❖

RAIN

The tears of God,
baptism of the spirit, life giver,
trickles down the window glass,
adding an impressionist painter's brush
to the view.

Rain...
that patters with staccato in tempo to the heart,
a tympanic accompaniment to creation,
a promise of renewal.

Rain that runs unceasingly,
threads of liquid silver,
prisms of light carried away in torrents,
bathes all with freshness.
Mist that rises from surging streams,
herding the debris of life,
sweeping clean the slate.

Rain that lulls, mesmerizes,
comforts like a cool splash on the brow.
Rain that soaks,
washing away the grime of toil,
and troubles.
Rain that glosses all with sheen,
fades,
spent,
and as gray skies part and bow before the sun,
gives birth to a rainbow.

SACRIFICIAL OFFERING

This is my body broken for you. Use it.
This is my life's blood. Spill it
...when you hunger.

If you must shield your nakedness from the cold,
take my skin.
When your children cry for the ache in their bellies,
feed them,
though my children may starve for the loss.

Do it!
Make the knife flash swift and clean.
If I cry out as my spirit is released,
Cry, too...
in a communion of our spirits,
in praise to the Creator for His goodness,
in thanks to the Spirit of the Earth for Her bounty,
in apology to my kind for my sacrifice
...for your hunger.

Consecrate the ground unto which my blood spills.
It is holy.
Say a benediction for the survival of my kind
...when you hunger.
As your knife cuts into the mystery of life,
rejoice in it.
Waste nothing.
Make a burnt offering in thanks
...for sated hunger.

This is my body broken for you. Use it.
This is my life's blood. Spill it.
When you hunger.

And if there is another way,
find it!
Was it hunger?

AN OPEN LETTER TO THE HUMAN RACE

From: The All Creation Society

To: The Human Race

Dear Monsieur & Madame *Homo sapiens*:

We regret that you were unable to attend our recent General Meeting. However, it is my sad duty to inform you that your continuing membership in our Society is currently under review as a result of allegations made against you at said meeting. (Some of which were rather shocking!)

To begin with, *Canis lupus* complained that your species has been the reason for extinction of several of his cousins and that recently you have even been shooting at him from your airplanes. *Alligator mississippiensis* alleged that some of your kind have been wrestling him for sport and *Crocodylus niloticus* said he could top that and claimed you had made belts and purses out of his family members!

Ursus maritimus reported that you have recently been drilling for oil in his habitat and upsetting the order of things, and *Nyctea scandiaca* confirmed the charge and said she was so upset she could barely sit her eggs for the intrusion.

Odocoileus virginianus and *Oryctolagus cuniculus* explained how they had hoped for better days after your "Disney" made movies featuring them, but that many of your kind make a habit of storming their woodlands and shooting at them, often with lethal consequences.

Rattus norvegicus and *Mus musculus* said they were first enticed into your homes and barns with offers of food, and then had been beheaded by some cruel mechanical device – while several of their cousins opined that that was a relatively painless death compared to what they had endured in your laboratories.

Orcinus orca claimed that he had been sold into slavery by you and forced to jump through hoops. *Lynx rufus* told how his kin had finally reclaimed some of their former habitat, at which point you opened a hunting season. *Panthera tigris sumatrae* said that in his part of the world he can barely find a plot of ground large enough to raise his family.

Gorilla gorilla beringei wept when he told how your wars threatened both his habitat and his offspring. *Eubalaena glacialis* said he had swum the world's oceans in an attempt to get away from you and had been harpooned for his troubles.

Equus caballas, that most noble of creatures, explained how his kind is wagered on by you, then sold by you at auction and transported without food and water to slaughter (surely he exaggerates?). One of the worst stories we heard that evening was from *Selenarctos Thibetanus*, of how his kind is cruelly imprisoned by you in cramped cages for their bile. His cousin *Ailuropoda melanoleuca* said she could hardly believe it – that you had chosen her as the symbol of one of your largest wildlife protection organizations!

We realize that you are relatively new to our membership (speaking in evolutionary terms). In the past, we have enjoyed a most pleasant relationship with some members of your species. We are eternally grateful to your Noah for rendering transportation assistance during that unfortunate incident. One of your members, Dr. Albert Schweitzer, is legendary for his kindness. We hold your Miss Rachel Carson in the highest esteem for trying to warn you about environmental concerns that threaten us all, and of course we are all aware of the efforts of Dr. Jane Goodall on behalf of *Pan troglodytes*.

However, we simply can no longer tolerate some of your behaviors and ignorance. In fact, our chairman, *Panthera leo*, called on two of your closest allies, *Canis lupus familiaris* and *Felis domesticus* to speak on your behalf during the meeting. Well, it was nearly impossible to restore order. They told how they had been abandoned and killed by the millions, allowed to breed out of control, acquired as companions and then ignored, passed around like pieces of old furniture, and had been targeted for such abuses that *Struthius camelus* could not hear any more and buried her head in the sand.

Many species said they felt so defenseless in your presence that they may was well be a sitting *Aix sponsa*. *Alces alces* concurred and said not only had they every reason to worry, but his kind was frequently shot by your species and then suffered the added indignity of having their heads hung on your walls! *Elephas maximus* said she has so many unpleasant memories of her relationship with your kind that she does not think she will ever forget them.

Please do not think us intolerant, or that we do not have a sense of humor (if I might offer *Platypus compertus* as proof of the latter), but this unseemly behavior simply must stop for the good of our entire membership. We respectfully request that you review our rules for peaceful coexistence on this planet and rethink some of your practices and behaviors. We are not insensitive to the dilemmas you face, particularly with some of your kind being herbivorous and some carnivorous. However, if there is not an immediate improvement in the current situation, we will have no choice but to take this matter up with *The Creator*.

Thank you in advance for your prompt attention to these matters.

Warm regards,
Sagittarius serpentarius, General Secretary bird

The animals, you say, were "sent" for man's free use and nutriment.
Pray, then, inform me, and be candid, why came they eons before man
did, to spend long centuries on earth awaiting their devourer's birth?
Those ill-timed chattels, sent from heaven, were, sure, the maddest gift
ever given "sent" for man's use (can man believe it?)
when there was no man to receive it!
~ HENRY SALT
❖

THE BASSET CHRONICLES:
Surviving Alexis

The sound of someone beating on our metal trashcan was interfering with my concentration and I went outside to have a look. Alexis had a large stick in her mouth and was rhythmically pounding dents in the can.

"ALEXIS! What do you think you are doing?!" I sputtered.

"I am calling everyone to a tribal council meeting," she replied innocently. "We're playing 'Survivor'."

"Oh really. And which tribe are you a member of?" I inquired.

"I am the leader of 'Bassetonia,' and Shania is the leader of the 'Dingdong Tribe'."

"But there are only seven Bassets and..." I was interrupted by the sight of a large pack of dogs, all colors, breeds and sizes, rounding the corner and wearing headdresses of long "ears" made from shredded pet blankets.

"A-ha – and you think it's fair that there are twenty-three of you versus Shania, Apollo, Frasier and Julio?"

"Yes," Alexis replied. "I make the rules and there is no point in playing if I don't win. Considering that you spent your boyhood being beaten to a pulp at backgammon, I do not expect you to understand."

I looked past the decorated pack, some brandishing kitchen utensils, and poor little Harry Potter, the newest foster dog, wearing a confused expression and a colander on his head – and my eyes narrowed.

"May I ask WHY my garden tiller is sitting in the middle of the dog pool?!"

"Wave action," said Alexis. "How do you expect our rafts to get around – doggie paddling?"

"Get it out immediately! By the way, where is Shania and her tribe?"

"We sent them out back on an 'immunity challenge mission.' They are to bring back a herd of bloodthirsty deer. We fear they may have been eaten."

"Deer don't eat meat, they're herbivores."

"You humans just think that because they also eat the bones – no evidence."

"I don't know what you are up to, but you'd better not be endangering anyone with your antics."

"Just because we're rabidly hungry from eating nothing but rice for the past thirty-nine days, when our diet usually consists of yuppies, doesn't mean we are going to hurt anyone," promised Alexis.

"Rice? Yuppies? Whatever are you talking about?! You guys eat a homemade diet with human quality meat."

"Oh," said Alexis, "a misunderstanding – we thought it was 'quality human meat'."

"Don't be ridiculous. Now then, do you think you could play at something that doesn't require banging on metal, so that I can get some work done?"

"Sure. OUTWIT! OUTPLAY! OUTLAST!" she bellowed until even Harry's colander slipped down over his muzzle.

"You there!" she barked like a drill sergeant at the nearest group of dogs. "More foxholes! The rest of you, move the retaining wall, that utility pole is in the way, sharpen those sticks, we need more tarps, keep your eyes peeled for pit vipers and cannibals...What time is it?" she asked me.

"Almost two o'clock," I replied, thoroughly confused and gravely worried about some of the new activities. "Why?"

"CARRY ON TRIBE!" Alexis ordered. "I have to go," she said to me. "My 'soaps' are on."

The soul is the same in all living creatures,
although the body of each is different.
~ HIPPOCRATES
❖

SOPHIA AND THE WOLF WITHIN

The wolf peered out from her vantage point behind the shrubbery. The house and yard were clearly in view and she could see the dogs slumbering on the lawn and under a shade tree. She inched forward, staying in the shadows and following the treeline. She stayed upwind of the dogs, knowing that their sense of smell was nearly as keen as her own.

As she crossed under a tree a bird sentry began chattering an alarm and she froze – but some of the dogs only stirred and returned to their deep sleep. She placed a forepaw ahead of her and continued her pace as silent as a shadow.

She rounded the corner of the house and could see that the backdoor stood ajar. It was as she'd hoped. She sat back on her haunches and surveyed the area. The only sounds were of birds, a rabbit scurrying through the underbrush, and the faint tones of the human's music. Minutes passed as she prepared herself mentally to cross the threshold of human inhabitance. She licked her muzzle with nervousness.

She stealthily approached the back door and froze again at the step. She inhaled deeply and a flood of information invaded her. She knew instantly that in this place resided domestic dogs and cats, and one human male and one female. Not even the humans' chemical perfumes could disguise the number and sex of each. She curled her lip against the assault of scents and waited.

She entered and froze again, waiting for her eyes to adjust to the dim light. Her pupils dilated and attempted to comprehend the human's world of manmade clutter. She moved silently through the first room. Her hackles were raised in anticipation.

The human male, her prey, was asleep directly in front of her on a bedding platform. He moaned softly, rubbed his nose and resumed breathing deeply. Again she waited. A cat regarded her without alarm from the top shelf of a bookcase.

The wolf planned her leap. She slowly wiggled her hindquarters as she coiled the muscles of her haunches and the nub of her tail gyrated. She leapt.

"UHH!" I gasped as sixty-five pounds of brindle Boxer landed on my midsection and I drew my knees up in self-defense. I struggled to a half-sitting position and stared wide-eyed into a beautiful ugly Boxer mug.

"Sophia..." I struggled for breath. "HAVE YOU LOST YOUR MIND?! That hurt!"

Sophia blinked innocently and her pink tongue apologetically licked the tip of my nose. She slunk away to the far end of the couch thoroughly chastised, as I swiveled my feet onto the floor still clutching my stomach.

"Honestly," I said and gave her an exasperated look. "I wonder sometimes what goes through that Boxer brain of yours!"

If you take a dog which is starving and feed him
and make him prosperous, that dog will not bite you.
This is the primary difference between a dog and a man.
~ MARK TWAIN
❖

We have not to gain his confidence or his friendship.
He is born our friend; while his eyes are still closed,
already he believes in us, even before his birth
he has given himself to man.
~ MAURICE MATERLINCK
❖

ARTIQUE AND THE CHILDREN
OF THE NIGHT

Listen to them – the children of the night.
What sweet music they make!
– from "Dracula," Bram Stoker (1897)

———

The pilot of the single-engine plane banks sharply and heads over a rocky outcrop and pine forest.

"Get ready," he instructs the sharpshooter, who is already leaning out of the window with hands poised to bring the gun to firing position. "I'll dip down and see if we can flush any out of the trees."

Both men are employed by the Canadian province to kill wolves from the air. On the ground the trappers are the wolf's principal nemesis with their steel-jawed traps set in ingenious ways to hold the wolf until shock, blood loss, starvation or the trapper can finish her off for her pelt. Against this aerial menace the wolf has no chance and she is killed because she preys on caribou, elk and deer – not to excess, because for the wolf only one in ten hunts is successful. Without the wolf the natural balance of selection is threatened, since wolves cull the weak, the infirm and sick from among their prey, thus ensuring a healthy gene pool. Man, on the other hand, shoots the strongest and finest examples of his prey for such frivolous reasons as to hang their heads on his den walls. In this territory the wolf is only a threat to economics because tourist-hunters can't abide the slight competition from the wolf and want to pay extravagantly for the privilege to hunt the choicest trophies.

It is spring, but the long awaited thaw is late. A wolf stops near the edge of a clearing and raises her muzzle to sniff the chilly air for the scent of prey. No large prey are about, but she will settle for a hare or a field mouse, anything to appease the hunger that has intensified during her confinement with her pups. Her litter of four needs to nurse often and although her mate and pack members bring parts of fresh kills for her or regurgitate partially digested food, nursing the pups has caused her to lose a third of her body weight.

Hunger overrides cautiousness and she moves further from the treeline. In the open she will have a less encumbered chase if she does flush a hare. She paws at some rocks that might disguise a burrow, but they do not. She ambles on, stopping frequently to cock a hindleg and mark her territory with urine, and she scans the flat snow-dusted terrain ahead for any sign of movement. Her gray coloring offers no camouflage against the white backdrop. She hears the drone of the plane before it bursts over the crown of the forest.

"There's one!" the sharpshooter yells, "To your left – turn!"

The pilot maneuvers the aircraft into position as the wolf begins the flight of her life. Her nostrils flare and she lays her ears back. Her eyes dart in fear and she turns and weaves, trying to elude this winged death. The snow is deep in pockets and long-legged as she is, she plunges in up to her chest. Frantically she springs free and sees there is no cover ahead. She turns and races back toward the forest, froth flying from her muzzle. She can bound up to sixteen feet on hard, flat ground, but the snow and low brush impede her. In peak health she could reach a speed of forty miles per hour, but nursing and hunger have weakened her. She whirls one last time toward her attacker, terror and desperation flash in her yellow eyes, and with one growl of rage she races directly toward the approaching plane.

Crack! The shot cleaves the stillness and sends startled birds and hare from their hiding places. The wolf slides in a spray of blood and snow and crumples...not dead, not yet. Searing pain from her shattered shoulder and pierced lung, shock and the fast falling temperature will kill her later, while the shooter and pilot share a celebratory beer in front of the lodge fire.

Her pups will also die within a few days. If they were old enough to eat the solid food their father and other pack members regurgitate for them, they might survive. But they are too young and must have milk. Because their mother, the "alpha" female, has been the only female pack member allowed to breed, no "wet nurse" is available. Their cries of hunger disturb the adult wolves who pace frantically until the den is permanently silent.

———

There is a North American grey wolf, a "timber wolf," asleep under our kitchen table. His name is "Artique" and he's nearly one year old. The Italian-made kitchen table, chairs and floor-to-ceiling cabinets were my gift to my wife, and I had attempted to justify their price by claiming they would last us a lifetime. The furniture at Artique's level looks like it has been blasted by a shotgun...it had been his favorite teething toy as a pup and before he progressed to woven rag throw rugs and rolls of paper towels.

"Come Artique, we're going out in the garden," I say.

Artique explodes from his hiding place, anxious for a romp with our dogs. He bowls over the Dachshund in the courtyard, leaps over the Basset Hound, careens off the Great Pyrenees, who tries to nip him in protest, and races the Weimeraner shoulder to shoulder until with one bound he's lengths ahead of her. They tear and race around the fruit trees until they are exhausted and fall asleep together in a pile of tangled legs.

———

The lead or "alpha" male wolf stands alone on a rocky precipice. He surveys the area and periodically sniffs the air for any useful information. When downwind he can smell large prey one and a half miles away and his high-set ears can detect the slightest rustle within several hundred yards. All is well and he turns his gaze to the young wolves born two springs ago. They race and wrestle, play tag and leap over one another's backs, and make playful lunges at the older wolves. Even the alpha male is not immune from their marauding, but he is tolerant by nature. His second-in-command, the "beta" male, might be less so – he's often the disciplinarian of the pack.

The alpha male descends from his vantage point and walks among the pack. He holds his tail erect as a symbol of his status. One of the young males lowers his head and eyes as the alpha approaches. A direct stare could be taken as a challenge to his authority. He wags his lowered tail nervously and then flops to the ground, exposing his belly to the older male. The alpha nuzzles him and the teenager licks the corners of the alpha's mouth – another sign of submission and a holdover of the "feed me" pleadings of a young pup.

The alpha male cues all the adults and they follow him away from the den, anxious to hunt. One subordinate wolf will stay behind and babysit the weanlings in the den. The alpha female emerges from the den and blinks in the sunlight before trotting off to catch up with the others. They stop and sniff her, and lick her muzzle in greeting, pleased that she has decided to join them.

――――

Our Great Pyrenees female, a breed created to guard sheep and kill wolves, watches as Artique and our Weimeraner female continue their shenanigans. She often participates in the games, but has a short temper and gives him a warning growl when he gets too nippy or rambunctious. They spend a lot of time marking the premises with urine and each marks over another's calling card in a contest of one-upmanship. The Dachshund has an ego far greater than his stature and he strains to mark as high as possible against any vertical object. He's famous for running off Artique when he gets to be too bothersome and the sight of a "weiner dog" chasing a wolf never fails to amuse me. Their other playmate is a wild moorland sheep named "Hannelore," and she doesn't take guff from anyone. I'm even more amused by a sheep, head down in "I'll butt you to kingdom-come" position, threatening a timber wolf.

"Dinnertime!" I announce. "Let's go, guys." The assortment of canines pummels each other as they race through garden and barn. As usual, Artique jostles and leaps his way to first place.

――――

The alpha male tests the breeze with a sense of smell one hundred times greater than a human's. This time his probing is rewarded – caribou. He gives a low growl and the other wolves halt their play and grooming. He switches his tail in excitement and the other wolves also sample the air. They begin to throng around their leader. He moves off toward a trail and the others follow him single file.

They gather near the edge of the treeline, peering through the underbrush and careful to stay downwind of the caribou herd. Gold, brown and yellow eyes flicker in anticipation and as their excitement mounts they raise the mantle of long fur along their backs and shoulders.

The caribou walk placidly over the crest of the hill and only a sunlit expanse of wiry grass separates them from the unseen hunters. Older animals at the perimeter of the herd stop frequently to listen. Mothers with calves are in the center of the herd where they can be surrounded and protected.

The alpha pair and beta wolf crouch low to the ground, tails lashing. The younger wolves begin to pant with excitement and a young male with more enthusiasm than experience takes a step forward, but the beta male turns toward him and issues an admonishing growl. The wind shifts and carries the growl and smell of wolf to the caribou scouts. They trumpet an alarm and begin to close ranks around the cows and calves. The herd turns in unison and begins to stampede. Calves bleat in fear.

The wolves leap from the underbrush in a "V" formation. They yip with excitement as they ride the fringe of the caribou herd. They dodge clods of earth flung up by hooves as the caribou stags grunt, urging the herd to pick up speed. An older cow at the back of the herd stumbles, regains her legs, but the break in rhythm is enough to allow half the wolves to cut between her and the herd. She realizes her mistake and falls in a sit-spin as she attempts to change direction. The wolves reach her in a bound. The alpha male sinks his teeth into her hindquarter and uses his one-hundred-fifty pound weight to knock her off balance. Another wolf locks onto her muzzle, but she tosses her head and throws him off. The beta male springs and takes her throat in a death grip. She spasms, kicking her legs, and dies.

The ten members of the pack gather around their kill. The older wolves begin to feed and then the younger ones join in with only a few skirmishes. They will gorge themselves and then bury part of the remains. Strategically placed food caches might be all that stand between them and starvation if capricious weather or the migration of prey species reduces their opportunities for a successful hunt.

––––––

The twice-a-day feedings at our house are the highlight of our pack's day and are carefully orchestrated events. Some people's dinner parties are less complicated. Meals are adjusted to each individual's needs and then there is the matter of the seating arrangement. The oldest dog, "Dudley," is on a meatless diet and he eats small, easily chewed meals scheduled around his various medications and served in the front hallway. The Dachshund, "Danny," refuses to eat breakfast and is hungry by early afternoon; he eats in the front entrance way. The Basset, "Winnie," lives to eat and her food portion is strictly controlled. Since she shares dining space, the summer kitchen, with the Weimeraner, "Amber," I have to make sure the latter finishes her meal or "Winnie" will. The Pyrenees, "Coco," must eat alone because she is food aggressive and will attack any dog who approaches her bowl. Artique will only eat when his bowl is placed under the kitchen table, his "den," and I stand guard in the middle of the kitchen while Coco eats at the opposite end. She's also our slowest eater.

Artique's meal takes the longest to prepare. It has taken consultations with several wolf biologists and the Royal College of Veterinary Medicine in England to come up with a diet that manages the colitis he's had since puppyhood.

Artique paces back and forth as I prepare his dinner. The Basset howls, trying to convince me she is faint with hunger. The Pyrenees sprawls in the middle of the kitchen, bored with the whole process. Artique stands up with his front paws on the buffet next to where I'm grinding whole peanuts in the shell to add to his dinner and he sniffs a plastic container.

"It's just boiled chicken, Artique. They were all out of caribou-in-a-can at the local market."

He twirls in circles in the middle of the kitchen until I set his bowl down under the table. I then place the Pyrenees's bowl on the other side of the kitchen island counter and take up my guard position. Artique stands over his bowl, ears cocked, waiting for the sound of the Pyrenees to begin lapping. Only then will he begin to eat. She's also our pickiest eater and sometimes refuses dinner, in which case I turn my back to Artique and imitate the sound of a dog eating. I don't know whether I successfully fool him or if he just humors me, but he always begins to eat.

———

Dusk has settled over the mountains like a sheet of gauze. The forest rustles with nocturnal life. Bats fly overhead, owls hoot, and somewhere a twig snaps and scurrying is heard. The colors dim to twilight and the wolves gather. From various directions they abandon their activities or slumber and meet at this common spot.

The alpha male begins softy. A wailing sound rises from his throat and as he arches his neck and raises his muzzle toward the crescent moon the howl waivers and trebles, increasing in volume. Another wolf joins in with a different pitch and tone, then another and another until all the pack members are silhouetted against the darkening sky, chorusing in discordant harmony.

This unearthly music will continue to increase in fever and pitch, and perhaps be answered by another pack in the vicinity. We assume it is part of the wolf's communication repertoire, but we suspect that he may also howl for the sheer enjoyment. It is an eerie, savage sound that has struck terror in the hearts of Man for centuries. It is the cry of the Children of the Night.

———

W e are all asleep in our beds.
 Ahhhaauuwooooo...

"What the...?" I sat up in bed, jolted awake. Again Artique repeated the howl from his bed at the far end of our bedroom. He ended in a snuffling snore. I gazed at him as adoringly as any father whose son had just uttered his first word. I shook my wife awake.

"Honey, did you hear it?"

"Hear what?" she mumbled.

"Artique...he just howled in his sleep!"

"That's nice dear," she said drowsily and drifted off to sleep again.

The Weimeraner raised her head from her bed near Artique and looked at me as if to say *"Well, I heard it!"*

This had been his first howl since he came to us in Germany at the age of fifteen weeks. He had howled in Vermont in the company of his parents and the other captive wolves, we'd been told. After months of complete silence here, he began making other sounds – a small yelp when his playmates nipped too hard, a high-pitched *yip* during a chase, a soft whine when his toy rolled under the kitchen cabinet, and an occasional *woof* when I surprised him during our hide-and-seek games. Maybe he didn't have a reason to howl and since he was always indoors during a wolf's favorite howling time, late evening, maybe our domestic life was handicapping him.

Wolves in the wild will even howl in response to a human's pitiful imitation of the sound. One evening I was alone in the garden with Artique and the dogs, and I decided to experiment. I looked around to see if anyone was walking on the field road behind our property and no neighbors were evident. I let loose a few howls that I thought were quite respectable. Artique cocked his head and looked at me with concern. Had I been injured? Was I in pain? Several hundred yards away an elderly neighbor lady straightened up from behind the roses she'd been pruning and regarded me suspiciously. *"That Herr Willis,"* I imagined her thinking, *"he's an odd one."*

I watched Artique in his bed breathe with deep contentment and decided he probably wouldn't perform an encore. I'd painstakingly crafted the wood bed for him before his arrival, with his name and a howling wolf motif burned into the wood and then gilded with gold leaf. Now the bed was ruined, chewed along every edge.

What do you dream of, Artique? I wondered as I switched off the bedside lamp.

————

Tomorrow the men of the tribe will hunt and tonight they will dance to create a powerful magic to ensure their success. The day has been spent in preparation for both the ceremony and the hunt. The fire has been lit and the elders take their places. The drums begin.

A lone dancer dressed in caribou hide and an antlered headdress begins to move slowly to the drumbeat. Other dancers enter from the dark beyond the firelit circle. Each wears a mantle of wolf fur, their faces streaked with red paint, and the strings of wolf teeth around their necks click as they raise spears and begin to dance. They follow the lead dancer in a large circle that begins to enclose the "caribou." The drums increase their tempo and the dancers stamp their feet to the rhythm. Perspiration glosses their taught bodies as they crouch and rise in mimicry of a wolf pack bounding in chase. The caribou dancer is surrounded. Spears glint and stab in the firelight and the caribou falls in mock death. His body is carried and laid before the elders who nod their approval. The chief elder stands and raises his arms over the "kill."

"May the Great Spirit reward us. May our Brother Wolf lend us his eyes and ears, his silent walk, his stamina and power, and his cunning. May the caribou understand and forgive us."

Their hunt the next morning is successful and they carry their bounty back to the camp, tethered and hanging from wooden poles. The entire tribe will spend many days processing the kill. The meat will be roasted, some will be smoked and dried. Hides will be cured. Teeth, bone and antlers will be worked into musical instruments, implements, amulets and jewelry.

The tribe members perform their tasks solemnly, with gratitude – to the Great Spirit, the caribou, and especially the wolf. One animal has been elevated in their mythology to equal status with themselves and in their language they have one name for both their own people and their Brother Wolf.

The canines and I do our "happy dance," but only when no one is looking. More dogs have been added to our growing family – a young male Giant Schnauzer mix, "Amadeus," who lacks social skills, an older male Basset Hound, "Flash," relinquished to a shelter with even less social skills, a beautiful Sheltie girl, "Sadie," given up because of problem barking, a deaf, epileptic and slightly mentally retarded Dalmatian male, "Pongo," and a Dalmatian female, "Tina," formerly abused and afraid of men. It is a colorful "tribe" and since I work from home, I feel blessed to be in their company most hours of the day.

Artique takes every new addition and change in stride. He is becoming more self-assured. Months ago even the slam of the screen door was enough to make him dive for cover under the kitchen table. I remember when he first arrived and destroyed his first "den," my office. He had been born and raised outdoors and objected strongly to indoor life. I created a den for him in a corner of our barn and he lived there the first three months, venturing out only at night. The other dogs went into the barn to visit with him, but the moment he heard a human approach he hid. One day he followed the Great Pyrenees into the kitchen, walking behind me as silent as a shadow. I nearly dropped my cup of coffee when I turned and saw a wolf sitting under the kitchen table peering at me apprehensively. It was a good illustration of an old saying, "the wolf will see you ten times before you see him once."

I'll never forget the day he first licked my hand, or carrying a full grown wolf up the stairs to bed at night and down again in the morning. Artique tolerated many human conveniences, but not stairs.

How gentle and sensitive he is. I found it incredible that people still believed the mythology of the wolf. No non-rabid, unprovoked wolf with room to flee had ever attacked a human in North America. Even a hungry pack of wolves will run from a human.

I had recently stood in front of the selection at a local video rental shop and shaken my head. The covers of many horror films had depictions of snarling wolves, blood dripping from their fangs. Even in the children's video section "big bad wolves" walked on their hindlegs and threatened to impersonate grandmothers.

American settlers had spread strychnine poison across the whole continent and wiped out one wolf species. Other wolf species were endangered and hanging on by a thread. I wondered if the American Indian had any premonition that he and Brother Wolf would share a similar fate.

Lost in thought, I knocked my notebook off the kitchen table and the slap of it on the ceramic tile sent Artique bolting out the kitchen door.

"Sorry, Artique," I called. "Come here, it's okay."

Artique peeked around the corner to make sure the danger had passed and then came slinking back into the kitchen. He walked to me in his submissive posture and licked my hand.

I hoped the Great Spirit, the Indian and Brother Wolf would all forgive us.

———

A solitary wolf stands several hundred yards away from a wolf pack. They have finished feeding and will move on to a favorite napping place. His eyes follow them, wishfully? They are aware of his presence, but they choose to ignore him. He will wait for them to leave and then pick the remaining scraps from the carcass of their kill. Given the social nature of the wolf, he probably regrets not being in their company, but if he approached them at the least he would be driven away, at worst they would kill him.

He is a lone wolf and there are many like him, perhaps more than twenty percent of the wolf population. Some may be adult wolves who lost their mates and left the pack to search for a new mate. Some lost their position in the hierarchy of the pack and were driven away. Some are young wolves who left when the pack population density became too great and they went off in search of greener pastures.

———

We don't have central heating in our hundred-year-old lovingly restored farmhouse in Germany's Rhine Valley. Each room in this rambling architectural monstrosity has a different oven or fireplace and cutting wood to specific lengths for each is a chore.

The kitchen is heated by an old cookstove that burns wood and coal and Artique and the dogs like to sleep in its warm glow. I made a huge pillow out of polyvinyl stuffed with straw, large enough for the whole pack, and my wife and a friend sewed giant flannel pillow covers for it.

I like to work at the kitchen table rather than in my office upstairs, partly to be near the pack, partly to keep them from mischief. Editing manuscripts is tedious and I yawn. I'm jealous of their snoring and cuddling. Sometimes I can't resist and I lie down with them. After some initial sniffs and licking, and rearranging to get as close to me as possible, they resume their naps. Artique lays his head on my chest and I scratch his ears before I doze off myself, often with tears in my eyes.

———

The lone wolf keeps a watchful eye for the return of the pack as he feeds. His hunger satisfied, he walks deep into the forest. He stops frequently, sniffs, and then rolls around on his back. He's found something odiferous and is covering himself with that unsavory scent in order to disguise his own. His mission accomplished, he walks along a trail blazed by other wildlife.

A strange scent catches his attention and he steps just off the trail to investigate. He paws the ground inquisitively and a bit of steel under the leaves catches the sunlight. He woofs in surprise at this unnatural find and turns to run. There is a loud *chink* as the steel jaws of the trap seize his foreleg to the bone and send leaves and twigs flying. His scream of pain carries and runs through the dozing wolf pack like a jolt of electricity. They spring to their feet with muffled growls and hackles raised and they run.

The setting sun sparkles on the guard hairs of the six wolf carcasses hanging from their hind feet from the porch roof of the ramshackle cabin. The boy struggles to help his father lift and string up the last and heaviest body. It is the lone wolf.

"Whew!" the boy exclaims as he uses his neck and shoulders to help lift the body. "This one stinks!"

―――

Standing in the check-out line at a German grocery store to pay at the *Kasse* can require patience. Customers bring their own bags and bag their own groceries. There aren't any magazines in a rack near the cashier as there are in America, so I people-watch to take up the time.

My eyes fix on the girl in front of me. She's wearing a parka of synthetic material and the hood is trimmed in fur. The fur is luxurious with long black guard hairs and it is various shades of gray mixed with tawny beige, brown, silver, black and white. I am very familiar with this fur, I have one just like it at home – probably at this very moment under the kitchen table chewing on a table leg.

"Stupid girl," I think. *"The fur looks much better on him that it does on you."*

―――

The long winter and spring thaw are over. Wildflowers bloom, migrating prey species have returned and food for the wolves is abundant. The streams and rivers run high and it is another season of new life. Again the whimpers of a new litter of wolf pups issue from the den.

The wolves camp near a stream. Attempts to catch fish are more of a game, but occasionally one of them is successful and he trots his prize away from the pack, refusing to share. Half of last spring's litter did not survive the winter, but the remaining two are strong and engaged in a splashing contest in the shallows of the stream. The alpha male has aged and is near the end of his reign.

He rolls over on his back, exposing his belly to the sun and all is well in his world.

———

Artique takes a tentative taste of the bubbles and lets the warm water wash over his back. He rolls over on his side and lets me shampoo his belly. He would probably stay in the bathtub for hours if we let him. He'd rolled in something foul smelling this morning, maybe not out of any wolf instinct, but as another excuse for a bath.

I can see his anatomy more clearly when he's wet. The angle of his skull running from below his ears to his temples is more severe than a dog's. He has a long muzzle and impressive canine teeth. His legs are long and his toes are longer than a dog's. He has the same number of chromosomes as a dog and close to ninety-nine percent of his genetic matter is identical. Still, he isn't a dog. He knows it and we know it. He is the domestic dog's closest primeval cousin, fifteen thousand years older, and as highly intelligent as the dog is, the wolf is the true genius.

I give his stomach a final tickle and Artique groans with enjoyment. I rinse the suds from his luxurious pelt. When wet his coloring is even more striking. I comb the water from his fur with my fingers and lay my hand against his chest, just to feel his heartbeat.

———

The three-week-old wolf pups toddle unsteadily as their mother leads them to the mouth of the den. They are afraid of the bright light and new world ahead and whimper. She takes turns nuzzling each and gives them a reassuring nudge. The rest of the pack waits outside expectantly. They are respectful and none approach the pups without their mother's permission.

The pups have made it to the lip of the opening and stand there blinking. Their baby eyes of blue gray are beginning to change to various shades of brown or yellow. Their very dark puppy pelts are beginning to lighten to a range of feral shades including one pup who is almost a cream color like his father. Even at this young age he is the heir apparent and dominates his littermates.

Their mother shows by her body language that the other pack members may approach. They are a doting family, they whine with excitement and the pups squeal as they are rolled over by inquisitive noses. They taste and smell each other and will remember the information for their lives.

The pups are allowed a brief adjustment period and then they will be carried to a new den. Their mother has prepared two other dens in the area. It is her instinct to have a contingency plan and for reasons of safety they will be moved to each den in succession until they are old enough to travel with the pack.

The young wolves sleep much of the day, nurse frequently, and begin to eat the food that is regurgitated for them by all members of the pack. Finally, the burden on their mother eases as "aunts," "uncles," and siblings from previous litters share in their nurturing. The pups conduct mock battles and wrestle, and begin to imitate the behavior of the older wolves. Their attentive role models control and direct them and gently discipline them with warning growls and nips.

The pups have cut their first teeth and are intent on trying them out. The largest male pup methodically strips the bark from a stick and directs a raspy growl toward any wolf who approaches him.

———

I attempted to work in my office upstairs, but my concentration was broken by a loud *thump, thump* noise coming from the kitchen downstairs. Since Artique's arrival I had learned to not ignore strange noises.

I tiptoed down the stairs and quietly opened the door from the hallway into the kitchen. Artique's rear end was visible, protruding through the dog doorway in the screendoor leading to the summer kitchen. He was attempting to drag in a long section of two-by-four, but it was hung up in the narrow opening. He sensed me behind him and dropped the wood.

"Artique, what's going on in here?" I asked as he sat on his haunches and gave me an innocent look. He glanced at the wood and tried to wish it away.

"Woof." (My wood.)

"Yes, that's your wood, but it doesn't belong in here. Look at this mess you've made."

Bits of wood littered the kitchen floor, either the remains of another piece or he had tried to whittle down the present piece.

"Woof!" (My wood!)

"I don't want your old piece of wood, but I want you to take it back outside."

Wolves can be much more single-minded than a dog, and twice as destructive, which is another reason they don't make good roommates.

"Woooof." (Want my wood in here.)

"Enough, Artique. Take it back outside and behave yourself."

I looked around the kitchen at Artique's handiwork. It was difficult to open any drawer because Artique had removed the wooden pull knobs. My wife had been surprisingly understanding about all of this. Maybe she was even relieved when I told her it was only a wolf who would be joining our family, because she knows I'm also fascinated by elephants.

"Rrrrr-woof!" (MY wood!)

"OUT!"

Artique snorted with frustration and stepped through the opening.

"Wooffff." (Taking my wood.)

I heard the two-by-four sliding along the summer kitchen floor as the connoisseur of fine woods dragged it out to the courtyard. As I walked back up the stairs to my office I wondered if it was genetically possible for him to be part beaver.

————

The summer heat is oppressive. The wolves do little more than sleep in the mid-day hours and hunt in the early morning or after dusk. The pups are nearly old enough to travel with the pack, after which time the pack may travel twenty-five miles a day. The pups will learn survival skills along the way. Staying on the move conserves prey populations, brings variety to their diet, and helps them escape detection. Their only enemy in the wild is man and it isn't safe to establish a permanent camp where they might be discovered.

They loll about in the shade. Some are still shedding out their thick winter double coat and have a raggedy appearance. The pups yip in their sleep.

A deer bursts through the trees and runs by them, only yards away. The adult wolves are alert now and wear a comical look of surprise. They hardly have time to interpret the deer's unusual behavior when more deer are heard crashing through the underbrush. Then they smell the smoke.

The alpha pair both jump to their feet with short woofs of alarm. The pups are awake now, yawning sleepily. All the members of the pack mill about, nervous, their ears laid back, their eyes searching in all directions as they try to formulate an escape plan. There is none. Fire is the confusion that overrides their senses, their only instinct is to flee, and it's every wolf for himself with the exception of the alpha female who will stay with her pups no matter the cost.

The raging wall of fire rips through the forest, the front wave of heat ignites trees before the creeping river of red flows along the forest floor like lava. The cracking and popping of branches exploding in flame sound like gunfire and the wolves run in every direction in terror. Cross winds whip the flames and choking smoke blinds them. Some of the wolves make the right choices, some do not.

Most of the pack gathers on a hill hours later, exhausted, their eyes red rimmed and inflamed, their paw pads burned and fur singed. They pant and heave and collapse on the rocks. Below, the blackened landscape smolders. They can see the glow of the wildfire in the distance like campfires of the enemy. Missing from their number is the alpha female, the pups and the beta male.

———

It had become chilly in the kitchen, the room we lived in most, and I shivered. A rare Siberian cold front had moved in and had Europe locked in its icy embrace. The fire had died down in the cookstove and I stepped over the canines on their pillow and gently slid the Basset girl's rump away from the door to the firebox. She grumbled in protest. I picked up a pair of tongs and forced as many compressed coal bricks into the tiny opening as I could.

"Don't mind me, guys," I said, "sorry to disturb you."

What a life they have, I thought, and shook my head jealously. An excellent life for a dog, of that I was sure, but for a wolf? Of that I wasn't so sure. If I could give Artique a bed of pine needles in the forest instead of a pillow in front of my fire, I would, but I couldn't. He was captive-born, bred by an uncaring breeder, and could never be returned to the wild.

The issues and problems that surround wolves are enough to give Solomon a headache. Private ownership of them isn't an issue in most countries, but it is in North America, where breeders of wolves and wolf-hybrids (wolves mixed with various dog breeds, also called "wolf-dogs") contribute to the problems under a misguided sense of appreciation for the wolf.

I have no doubt there are people who love and properly care for their wolves and wolf-dogs. However, I'm also part of a rescue network and a member of a sanctuary association whose few members with facilities for wolves are deluged by requests to take the privately owned ones who don't work out, and as "pets" most do not work out. Wolves are escape artists and even those who are loved and properly cared for may eventually heed the call of the wild, usually with lethal consequences.

Many people who own wolves and hybrids abandon them in the woods later, believing they'll be able to survive. They can't and they become a threat to livestock, are shot by farmers, killed on roads, and may hurt humans out of fear, especially the hybrids whose "dogness" means some of the wolf's natural fear of man has been bred out of them. American animal shelters kill them by the hundreds.

Not even reintroducing wolves to some of their former range is an easy endeavor. The amount of public hearings, written opinions, studies, protests, and taxpayer dollars it takes in America to do so verges on the ridiculous. Thankfully, a few wolves have started to take back some of their former habitat without human intervention. The job now is to continue to protect them from humans.

I'm not wise enough to offer answers to the issues that surround wolves. I only know that every decision about the wolf should stem from the truth, that he is the ultimate wild animal, a symbol of freedom, and that we took away his habitat, imprisoned him, killed him, exploited him, wiped out some of his species forever, and were so jealous of what he represents in the scheme of nature that we tried to destroy him. If you look at a map of the wolf's range in the world of a century ago and compare it to a map of his present day range, it's enough to make you cry. What Man didn't accomplish purposefully he succeeded in by his ignorance.

Years after Artique's arrival I was in Nova Scotia and talked with a wolf biologist who ran a university study of a captive wolf pack. Such studies are mostly a thing of the past since the reintroduction of a pack to Yellowstone National Park, where the wolves can be studied in a natural habitat. Her study's wolves were "retired" and will live out their lives in a refuge.

She told me of one wolf her program had rescued. He had been confined for years in a small cage in a roadside zoo, where spectators could view him from all sides. Knowing the wolf's love of privacy and instinct to have a den, that was alarming enough. This animal's quarters were so cramped that his muscle tone was poor and his hindlegs under developed. The wolf biologists weren't sure he would ever walk properly.

After he recovered some strength, he was turned out in a large fenced enclosure with a few other wolves. He ran...he runs for the sheer joy of running, he may never stop running because he still has years of cruel confinement to make up for. By the time she finished her tale I had a lump in my throat and a murderous rage glowed in my eyes. The only thing I could think of is how much I might enjoy calling on the owner of that roadside "zoo" with a baseball bat in my hands.

———

I'm sitting alone at the dilapidated kitchen table after a late dinner, looking out the window into the courtyard and admiring the roses, marveling at how much the grape vines have grown in just two summers. Nicole is upstairs in her never ending quest to keep a house inhabited by animals clean to her German standards. It is the end of summer, time for wine festivals and local delicacies along the Rhine River and its romantic villages. It is time to take in more orphaned hedgehogs after their mothers meet an untimely end, usually on the roadways. There are already eight of them and their nursery is the *Wintergarten*, the glass conservatory I had built next to our bedroom to house my wife's plants. Their nocturnal rustling in their wooden cribs keeps Artique awake, and he in turn keeps me awake.

Artique will grow his winter coat soon and it will be magnificent. I am sometimes hypnotized by watching him, dumbstruck in the presence of such beauty. The gas street lamps flicker on and I decide I should go out to the garden to put Hannelore in her stall for the night and bring in the canines. It's an effort to get up out of my chair – it's been a long day of gardening and renovation projects. The animals are all unusually quiet. Hannelore has likely tired of stalking the wolf, one of her favorite games, the dogs have all eaten and are probably napping in their various favorite spots. The older dogs will have sequestered themselves in corners out of Artique's way, his boundless energy exhausts them.

If they are quiet it means there is nothing going on anywhere behind our barn and property. I know their every bark and even from inside the house I can tell if they see someone in a neighboring garden or on the field road who they know, or if it is a stranger, and if that person has a dog with them. After all these years of living with them I've become fluent in "dog."

My mind wanders with fatigue until a howl comes from the garden, slides over the barn roof and reverberates in the courtyard. *"Aaauuuwooooo."* The dogs are evidently too tired to join in. Is it a howl of loneliness? I wonder. Artique's howls are beyond my canine communication skills. Or a howl of regret? Of longing for that which he can never have, the company of his own kind in a life that is wild and free.

I hoped he was happy. We had certainly given our best effort and sacrificed a lot, including the kitchen furniture, to give him a life he might deem acceptable. Still, his very presence in our lives posed a moral dilemma. With advancing years comes wisdom and the foolish assumption that the older we get, the better we become at sorting out moral dilemmas, when the truth of the matter is that the wiser we get and the more caring we become, the more moral dilemmas there are to decide on.

I don't know if what I did was right by Artique, but given the choice of having him here with us or allowing his breeder to sell him to anyone who'd buy him, I'd do it all over again.

"Aaauuuwooo...oooooo," Artique calls again. This time perhaps the howl instinctively avoids the concrete, brick and red-tiled roofs of our crowded village and soars over vineyards toward the Alsatian mountains visible in the distance. Possibly it reaches other wolves hidden in isolated pockets of wilderness. Maybe they

howl in reply, in a chain of communication that says *"against all odds, we are still here."*

I know in my heart that he howls for the Children of the Night.

———————

On the ragged edge of the world I'll roam,
And the home of the wolf shall be my home,
And a bunch of bones on the boundless snows,
The end of my trail...who knows, who knows!
~ ROBERT SERVICE, FROM "THE NOSTOMANIAC"
❖

THE BASSET CHRONICLES:
Alexis and a Not-So-Grimm Fairytale

It was a long drive home from the airport with the wolf. She was mildly tranquilized and calm. When I arrived home I put her on a lead and took her around back and in through the uppermost gate. She lapped up half a bucket of water and then began to investigate her new surroundings. She was surprisingly unafraid and trusting. I left her there and went inside to face the troops.

As I entered the house the dogs gathered around me excitedly and sniffed my hands and pants legs. Nicole gave me a hug. She knew what a nervous wreck I'd been over this particular rescue and transport. It had involved over two dozen abandoned wolves and hybrids, months of worry, hundreds of e-mail messages, dozens of volunteers and much bureaucracy.

"Whew!" Alexis wrinkled her nose. "What derelict dog have you dragged home this time?"

"Well, guys, this is a very special animal who had a terrible life and she's traveled a very long way."

"Not another Basset Hound?" groaned the Beagle Boys.

I shook my head "no."

"So after a brief pit stop then she's going to be on her way?" Alexis asked.

"No, Alexis, she's here to stay and I want all of you to be kind to her. She's very sensitive. She deserves to live in the wild, but because of her past circumstances she can't. She's going to be an ambassador for her kind and together maybe we can teach people to work toward conservation and protection measures."

"Good luck, Gandhi. You said I am an ambassador for Bassets," Alexis reminded me.

"No," I corrected. "I said you were the poster-child for Bassets."

"Whatever," Alexis said. "How old is this bitch, I mean girl?"

"About your age, between three and four, but speaking in evolutionary terms she is about fifteen thousand years older than you guys."

Alexis pondered that and was about to ask another question when I suggested "Alexis, why don't you go out back and introduce yourself to her?"

Alexis waddled off with a superior air.

The wolf stood at the top of the yard and looked through the fence at the silhouette of the forested hills in the distance. She felt their pull like a magnet. She turned and regarded Alexis as she huffed and puffed up the hill.

"Yo there, howdy do?" Alexis said in a poor imitation of what she thought was country lingo. "My name is Alexis and I am in charge here. If you need anything, just ask and I will say no."

The wolf regarded her with amber eyes that held secrets thousands of years old.

"My! What unusual eyes you have," Alexis commented. She sniffed in the wolf's direction and considered that a bottle of shampoo was in order.

The wolf drank in the night air and one of the greatest senses of smell in Nature told her volumes about her new surroundings.

"And my! What a big nose you have," Alexis noted.

The wolf cocked her ears and listened. She heard the sound of a truck approaching from miles away and heard field mice scurrying in the underbrush hundreds of yards away. She smiled and licked her muzzle as her long incisors glistened in the moonlight.

"My, my, my! What big teeth you have!" Alexis said and laughed nervously.

The wolf looked at the ground shyly. She took a deep breath and slowly raised her muzzle toward the night sky. First a low moan escaped her and then a howl rose in pitch and reached a crescendo that echoed in the valley below. Deer stopped their grazing and huddled in alarm. An owl took flight in celebration. It was a sound not heard here in over a century and if this particular sister was calling, then perhaps Nature had won and all would again be as it once was.

Alexis was dumbstruck and then the realization hit her like a splash of icewater.

"AAUUUGGGHHH!" she shrieked as she plummeted down the hill, tripping on her ears. She shot through the dog door like a cannonball. She made a four-paw slide down the hallway and ended in a wrinkled heap at our feet.

"MAMMAA! DADDEE! Ohmygosh *pant, pant* oh, dear...help! Call the game warden. Call somebody! I...*huff*...she...*puff*...She's a..."

Just then another howl reverberated through the air and Nicole and I stood solemnly as something soared within us. The dogs remained quiet and respectful.

"Uuuhhh," Alexis moaned softly and slumped to the floor.

"Oh Gott! She's fainted," Nicole exclaimed. "Quick! Get me some cool water and a towel."

"What – no chamomile tea?" I teased. "Leave her be. She'll come 'round soon enough and this is the quietest I've ever seen her."

I stepped over Alexis on the way out to go visit our new friend. I sat down on the ground near her. The wolf came toward me and paced back and forth before sitting down near me. I reached out my hand. She sniffed it and moved closer until she was leaning against me. I pressed my face into the ruff around her neck. I slowly moved my arm around her and gave her a hug and I felt the tension in her muscles relax. She knew she was home. She sniffed my ear and gave it a lick before getting up and walking back up the hill. She gave an odd *woo-woo* howl that I took to mean contentment.

I looked up at the stars and gave silent thanks to the Great Spirit for keeping her safe. I remembered a quotation from the book *Ordinary Grace*: "Grace doesn't just live in the blessed sounds emanating from great cathedrals and holy ashrams – the sacred is all around us. Listen. Open your eyes."

I got up and walked back toward the house. As I neared the back door, I heard Nicole trying to placate Alexis. I mostly heard Alexis.

"I have rights! I want an attorney. He's a madman – and YOU...Mrs. Madman! I'm ashamed of you. I could have been killed! We could all be murdered in our beds! He's gone too far this time..."

I smiled and whispered back into the darkness, "Sleep well, beautiful girl."

EARL WILLIS BEING INTREPID.
CYNNAMON, JIM AND HIS SHELTIE SADIE

LEGS – MY FATHER, MY HORSE, AND ME

When a child, my dreams rode on your wishes,
I was your son, high on your horse.
My mind a top whipped by the lashes
Of your rhetoric, windy of course.
– Stephen Spender from "The Public Son of a Public Man"

Someday, someone you love may say something to you that contains such an obvious truth that your cheeks will burn in embarrassment for having overlooked the fact and you will be too moved to speak. Such was the time when my father looked up from the Sunday morning breakfast that we shared weekly in a restaurant, with eyes nearly blind from macular degeneration, and he said of his boyhood horses, "They weren't just horses...they were my legs." His own legs hadn't worked since he was stricken with polio at the age of three years.

My father had grown up near Pittsburgh, and he moved with his family to Arkansas when he was a teenager, where his dad worked construction. He had two mustang mares in those days, Stormy and Star. His mother was an excellent rider. She used to send my dad to town on horseback to buy groceries. He would tie his crutches behind the saddle and since he couldn't use his feet the stirrups were tied under the horse so they wouldn't bounce. Stormy liked to wait until my dad's hands were full with grocery bags and then she'd act up. Once she walked into a pond and dumped him. Sometimes she just threw him along the side of the road and would walk home alone. My grandfather would see her coming riderless and yell, "Jesus Christ, she threw Sam again! I'm going out to look for him." I don't think anyone knew why he called my father Sam, when his son's name was the same as his own, Earl, or perhaps that was the reason.

My grandmother died during a hysterectomy when my father was a young man. She had predicted her own death during the drive to the hospital. My scientifically minded father who didn't believe in "such things" did not deny later in life that he couldn't explain the premonitions his mother had that had come true. She doted on him and had a heart of gold. One day she and my father were riding their horses home from town, carrying groceries, when they came upon a poor family along the road – so poor they were shoeless and their pants were held up by pieces of rope. My grandmother gave all the groceries to the family and sent my dad back into town for more.

In his last years, my father often talked about his boyhood friend in Arkansas, Boyd Hickman. Boyd owned the fastest horse in the county, but he was so poor he had a beat-up saddle held in place by a girth made from an old tire inner tube. When my dad and his family left Arkansas, he had to leave his horses behind, and he gave Boyd his saddle and tack. Those stories came to mind one evening a couple of years ago and I used a people search engine on the internet and came up with a list of Boyd Hickmans. I went down the list and began calling them. "Did you live in Arkansas as a boy and did you have a friend named Earl Willis?" The fifth man on the list, living in Florida, said "Yes! Who is this?" I told him who I was and that my father still talked about him and his fastest horse in the county. He asked for my dad's phone number and as soon as I hung up, I dialed my dad's number. It was already busy and stayed busy for the next hour. My phone rang later and my dad on the line said "How in the hell did you find Boyd Hickman?! He just called me." It was one of the nicest things I ever did for my father, allowing him the chance to talk to a friend he hadn't spoken to in over sixty years.

————

To create the Arab horse, God spoke to the south wind: "I will create from you a being which will be a happiness to the good and a misfortune to the bad. Happiness shall be on its forehead, bounty on its back and joy in the possessor."
– Early Arab saying

It was written in the time of Ishmael, "if you hear that a bay horse fell from the highest mountain and was safe, believe it." I believe that was my horse. I dreamed of an Arabian horse three days before I met my horse. I still can't explain that. I rarely remember my dreams and although I had loved horses since I was a boy and had always dreamed of having one, this was not the time to acquire a horse, in fact, I couldn't think of a worse time. My life and my heart had been turned inside out. After my mother died following a brief illness during which I nursed her, I moved from Germany with my animals to be near my father, hoping that someday he would relent in his fierce independence and agree to live with my wife and me. The position with a newspaper that I had accepted before my move did not work out – the editor had totally misrepresented the job duties and pay. My wife continued the agony of selling our farmhouse in Germany, and everything that could go wrong with that process did. Then her father died and after she got her mother settled, had sold our house, shipped our belongings, moved to the US and found a job, her mother was diagnosed with cancer and she had to return to care for her mother until her death, and then settle the estate.

The house in America that I had arranged to lease and then buy as soon as the sale of our property in Germany was closed, and the property I had already fenced at enormous cost for the sake of our animals, was being sold by a criminal. All that came to light late one evening when his real estate agent and a bank officer came to my door to tell me the man had undisclosed judgments against him and had used the house as collateral to secure a loan he had defaulted on, and the bank was seizing the property before any of the other creditors could. Literally overnight, I had to find a rural property to rent with enough room for my animals. No, it was not a good time to add a horse to my life and my father and my wife both met the announcement with "you bought a *what*?!" But I could not deny what was meant to be and like the grandmother I had not known, I had learned to trust my feelings. I was also beginning to wonder if I could trust any human other than my father and my wife.

I needed a release from the stress of my life, worries over my dad and angst about the future. I had too much pride to ask anyone for help and I learned the painful truth that even those I'd known for years could be blind and selfish. Some meant well when they suggested that since my life had taken a severe turn for the worse, perhaps I should give up all or some of the animals. Never! I was insulted that they should understand so little about me and what I had been preaching for decades to even suggest that.

When I saw an advertisement in a local newspaper for a saddle club, I called and the woman who owned the stable said that, no, I didn't need to have a horse to join and, yes, she had some horses I could ride. She didn't mention that she had a boarded horse, an Arabian mare, who she was trying to sell for her owner.

It was a dreary, drizzly November day when I saw the horse in the company of the woman who owned the barn and a lady friend of hers who boarded a horse there. The mud-splattered bay mare was at the far end of the pasture and her mane and tail had been cut off. The woman explained they had been such a knotted mess when the mare arrived that she had no choice but to cut them. The horse was owned by a man who hadn't seen her in a couple of years and she'd been moved from boarding stable to stable. The mare looked depressed, she kept her head low and stayed in a corner of the pasture away from the other horses. She looked up at us and began walking in our direction. She focused on me, approached, and laid her head on my shoulder. I wrapped an arm around her neck and inhaled the smell I had missed for years, the sweet grassy smell of horse. I hoped the stinging November wind and rain would be a plausible explanation to these strangers for the tears in my eyes and when I turned toward the women they both had tears in their eyes.

"She never does that with anyone," the stable owner said and then told me how the horse came to be there.

I wasn't just anyone and in me the horse had seen what she had never had in the first ten years of her life, someone who would love her, spoil her, put aromatic cedar chips in her stall in summer and bring her warm oats with maple syrup and apple slices in winter, someone who still gets misty eyed when he watches her outrun the other horses in the pasture, as fast as the south wind, and who would hug and kiss her for all the rest of her life. A man who would marvel that such slender, elegant legs could turn and weave at high speed and that she was so surefooted she could climb the rockiest, steepest ascents. There was an instant recognition between us as if two pieces of life's puzzle had just snapped into place and I will never be able to explain the feeling that I knew this horse, that I had always known this horse and that we belonged together.

Her owner accepted a payment plan for a fraction of her value. It wasn't until I'd made contact with him and then the mare's former trainer, and then received her pedigree and registration that I learned she wasn't just any horse. She had sold for a sinful sum of money as a yearling to an investment partnership and she was a granddaughter of the legendary Khemosabi. She had been shown and worked hard until she fell ill and had been taken to a university equine clinic where the cost of treatment had been in the thousands. When the partnership disbanded the last partner, who knew nothing about and cared little for horses, was the one who ended up with her. She had blue blood, she had won blue ribbons, but she had ended up blue with loneliness until she became my horse. Her registered name didn't make a good call-name and I named her "Cynnamon." Her head carriage came up, her mane and tail grew back, she glowed with good health and daily grooming, she became herd mare at her new stable, and now she is a regal Queen of Arabia.

My father not only didn't criticize my decision to add a horse to my life, beyond his initial surprise, he accumulated treats for her. When his friend who had an orchard gave him peaches, he pitted and sliced any bruised ones into a plastic container for me to bring to Cynnamon. She has a habit of smacking her lips when she wants a treat and she smacked her lips furiously over the peaches. The first time I brought my dad to meet Cynnamon he stood in front of her stall and rubbed her muzzle, calling her a "dumb hoozer," one of his terms of endearment I never quite understood. When I looked at him, I saw the tears in his eyes and told him I'd be back in a moment. *Does everyone who meets this horse cry? Shit, I'm going to start crying myself.*

I promised myself that I would find a way to put him on a calm horse, and that was not Cynnamon. I figured out how many people it would take to lift him into the saddle, and tried to think of whose horse I would appropriate. I regret I was never able to manage that. I did take him to the largest equine exhibition in the east, and pushed him around the exposition center in a wheelchair for the entire day, until I thought my arms would fall off. He fell in love with a white miniature horse, saw the Icelandic horses that fascinated him perform, and we talked about horses during the whole four-hour drive home.

———

When I was an infant, my parents lived with his father and stepmother and the bedrooms were upstairs. My father would stick me into a carpetbag-type conveyance, hold the handles as he used his crutches, and carry me upstairs. It apparently had no lasting ill effects on me.

My mother was beautiful and also a polio victim. I was more than a baby, I was proof that my parents were just like "normal" people. I was the coddled first born and did not gracefully accept a brother when he came along sixteen months later. As I grew, my relationship with my father deteriorated. I feared him and his temper, and I rebelled against his authoritarian way. That peaked when I was a teenager and I couldn't wait to escape my parents' house, to grow my hair long, to wear blue jeans. I was a *bon vivant* disguised as a bookish straight-A student, I was an apostle of the arts and humanities and the world was waiting for me. I was a confusion of hormonal, religious, philosophical and idealistic influences. My father was the steady rock I would cling to in his last years, but in my youth, he was the stone who held me back, who kept me from being me. I would show him, I would be somebody important and I would hide my humble beginnings. What a fool I was, but no more a fool than many unappreciative sons.

I argued most with my mother, because there was no arguing with my father, and I had grown up being told by everyone that I was the image of my mother; I had her hair, her eyes, her wit. Her lifelong girlfriend told me when I was a teenager, "of course you can't get along with her, you are exactly like her." My brother was said to be a copy of our father; everyone said that we were as different as night from day, and it didn't help our relationship. When I look in a mirror today, when I watch some of my mannerisms, I see bits of my father in me that I never recognized before.

The company my father worked for as a watchmaker went out of business when my brother and I were very young. He walked all over the city trying to find a job and in those days the physically handicapped were discriminated against in the employment market, and buildings, parking and curbs weren't handicapped accessible. He refused to ask for help, to go on the dole, or accept public assistance. My mother took two buses to work all night at a hospital as a bookkeeper. He repaired watches at home and among his papers recently, I found tax returns where he reported what he earned then to the Internal Revenue Service.

He was unstintingly honest.

My father went back to school and became an electrical designer. It seemed that he went to school forever and studied subjects that I still don't know anything about, like "statics." He even took a German class believing that one day he could read German engineering publications. He not only had no aptitude for foreign languages, his teacher made the class sing German nursery rhymes and my father couldn't carry a tune in a wooden bucket. Curious though that he could whistle beautifully.

He was that rare genius who could do almost anything, fix anything, and explain anything to anybody on their level. I once listened as he explained a law of physics to a woman who probably hadn't completed high school and she hung on his every word, one of the flock of family friends who thought he walked on water, on crutches. Every child with a homework question his parents couldn't answer was sent to our house. My mother was the resident language and literature expert, and my father covered all other subjects. He missed his calling and would have made a remarkable teacher, a Joseph Campbell for the working classes. His passion for whatever subject matter interested him was infectious. No matter how busy he was, he always made time to help us with schoolwork and I sometimes dreaded his help. He wouldn't just answer the homework question I couldn't, he had to make sure I understood the entire history and future implications of higher math. Any project he helped me with received the highest mark in the class.

He had been a daredevil in his youth and in middle age usually confined his death-defying stunts to "dangerous" experiments in the cellar. They usually involved vats of acid, electrodes, blowtorches and every tool known to man. We all knew better than to question him. I do not exaggerate when I say he could do almost anything – anything included flying an airplane; hunting small game with a slingshot and bow-hunting; repairing old clocks and watches; engraving by hand; re-plating a friend's antique tea service and adding a rhodium finish so it would not tarnish; extracting the platinum from the heating coils of old clothes dryers, purifying the metal and selling it; sewing suits for himself that looked tailor-made and new, pleated curtains for my mother's kitchen; welding; fashioning a pair of crutches for himself out of a whole log of black cherry wood; machining new parts for his and my mother's leg braces; building hand controls for his and handicapped friends' vehicles; building a stair-climber elevator in his house and a shaft elevator in a handicapped friend's house; converting a treadle sewing machine to electric so he could sew leather; preparing friends' and relatives' income tax returns and counseling them about investments, and in his last years, learning to use a computer.

I came home one weekend from working at a summer camp to find my mother in the kitchen in a high state of anxiety. She made an "oooo" sound when something was upsetting her. She was oooo-ing because my dad was up on the roof painting the trim. He had called a painting contractor for an estimate and when the man quoted nine hundred dollars, my dad said he would do it himself. He'd locked his leg braces in their extended position and gone up the ladder carrying paint and brushes. I climbed the ladder and found him on the far side of the roof.

"What do you think you are doing?!" I asked, trying to sound somewhat respectful.

He made small talk and then said "Get down now before you fall." I went back inside the house and my mother and I oooo-ed together whenever we heard a bump on the roof.

My father was outspoken and didn't exhibit many social graces; he likely occasionally offended people. Then he'd perform some random act of kindness in his selfless way and everyone would forgive him. When he heard that an elderly woman on our street, who we didn't know, was about to lose her rundown house for back taxes, he tried to pay her taxes, but apparently one of her relatives had come to her rescue. I couldn't get five dollars from him if he thought I intended to spend it on something frivolous. He was of the opinion that I couldn't manage money and since he so rarely gave me any, I don't know how he arrived at that and I was deeply offended.

Years later, after college, I had a job that didn't pay very well and I bought my first new car, a Camaro with a three-fifty engine, four barrels. It sucked gas from gas pumps as I drove by. I was so poor that I ate three-for-a-dollar boxed macaroni-and-cheese about six nights a week. Among the things I brooded about in those days was the low opinion my father had of my ability to manage money. I hardly had any money to manage and what I did earn, I spent...foolishly, but he still had no right to his opinion when I hid as much about my life from him as possible!

I moved around the country after school, trying this job and that. I had a brief stint as a merchant marine, ran the art department of an office supply store, worked for newspapers and interviewed famous people. I wrote for magazines, became an editor of a horse-sport magazine, and partied with royalty and rock stars. I went to the Arctic, to England, to Jamaica. At various times, I had a dog, a parrot, a cat who moved with me. I rescued broken down animals, patched them up, and found them homes. I broke hearts and had my heart broken. I never told anyone, not even myself, how much I missed my parents. If I had a problem, my father was the last person I'd turn to. There might as well have been a sign on the front door of his house, "This family does not have problems."

I moved to Germany, I learned German, I got a good job as a book editor. I married a German woman who my parents adored and who, in some respects, has my mother's temperament. I can't explain the coincidence that her surname is Valentin, my mother's first name is Valentina, and that her father and my mother were born on the same day. I bought an old house and turned it into a work of art. I became responsible. I became punctual and reliable, steady and focused. I paid my bills on time and used any extra money for worthy endeavors. I remembered all the people from my past who had been good to my family and I sent them birthday cards and Christmas presents. I called my parents several times a week and bought them a telefax machine to save us all money. My mother would call to make sure I received her fax and we'd talk for twenty minutes.

The supreme example of my reliability was when I arrived from Germany to care for my mother during her final illness. My father was in a state of shock and he hardly talked, definitely not about how it would feel to lose the woman who worshipped the ground he walked on. He rarely left her side and sat on the bed holding her hand while I battled an insurance company and doctors, consoled friends and relatives, and exhausted myself trying to save us all from a loss we didn't think we could endure. My mother lost her fight and I stayed up all night before her memorial service and wrote and gave the eulogy at her service. My father saw in me someone he could count on if he had to and it must have surprised the hell out of him. He became generous toward me and helped me through the worst of the financial crisis that would follow after I moved home to help him.

My father could be painfully unsentimental. Within weeks after my mother died he gave away all of her clothes to a charity, including handmade things I had sent her from Europe. He could be touchingly loyal. After she died he never changed a thing about their home down to buying only the brands of household cleaners she bought, and he placed the urn with her ashes on the dresser next to their bed. He could be impossibly proud. When friends and relatives gave him jewelry and watches to repair near the end of his life, he wouldn't admit that near blindness and the palsy in his hands did not allow him to do what he once could. He sent their pieces to a downtown jeweler to be fixed and returned the repaired items to their owners without a word.

My fantasy that nothing bad would happen to my parents because of the disease that lamed them in childhood, that they had already paid a high price, that they would live forever, well cared for by some phenomenal neighbors and friends, while I lived the life I'd dreamed of in Europe, died with my mother. I was glad to come home again to be with my father, glad to be writing again professionally. My father had always admired writers, writing was one of the few things he couldn't do, and he read voraciously. He had a file of newspaper columns I'd written twenty years earlier and he still photocopied and distributed them, to my chagrin. No writer can bear to read what he wrote in his youth. Following a bit of sparkling repartee between characters in the movies we watched together every week, he'd turn to me and ask, "Can you write dialogue like that?"

"I try, Dad," I'd reply.

He knew what I did for a living, but not a lot about who I am, how I think, how I feel, what I believe in. True, I'd changed some of that as I matured and he would have needed a scorecard to keep track, and I didn't talk to him about anything outside his sphere of interest. One subject we could always talk about easily was horses. We were both guilty of taking at face value what we saw in each other and not having the courage or desire to delve deeper, to get to the core of the person. That would have seemed too much like "psychoanalysis" to him and he thought only the weak needed soul-searching conversations, and we were not weak people.

What had it felt like to be him, to be left behind when the

able-bodied boys went off to play, went off to war, including his brother? To lose the mother he worshipped in the prime of her life? To have a failed first marriage and to have experienced the death of their infant? To be reunited late in life with the daughter they had adopted before the marriage ended? To lose a job through no fault of his own and not have enough money to buy Christmas presents for his wife and sons? To later have his father develop senile dementia and not know him? To have me as a son during my capricious years? He suffered it all in stoic silence. He did not believe in God, but his whole life was proof that God believed in him.

My father didn't know how torn I was between the desire to capture a feeling of home, nearly impossible without my mother, and how sorry I'd been to leave Europe. Home, the feeling of having a hometown that I liked was important to me. The reality of being home again after a long absence, as so many others had found, was a disappointment. You cannot recapture a time passed or bring back the people and events that made a home, and it was a high-stakes gamble because I loved him more now than I had at any time in my life.

In Thomas Mann's novel *Tonio Kröger*, Tonio is the son of a highly responsible man. He has an artistic temperament and feels unfulfilled in his hometown and leaves to join a bohemian group of literati in Munich. Their cynicism about life soon makes him feel uncomfortable and he leaves there to return to his father. From there he writes back to a literary friend, "I admire those cold, proud beings who adventure upon the paths of great and daemonic beauty and despise 'mankind,' but I do not envy them. For if anything is capable of making a poet of a literary man, it is my hometown love of the human, the living and the ordinary. All warmth derives from this love, all kindness and humor. Indeed, to me it even seems that this must be that love of which it is written that one may 'speak with the tongues of men and of angels,' and yet, lacking love, be 'as sounding brass or a tinkling cymbal.'" He also wrote, "The writer must be true to truth."

I knew that after my father was gone, I would leave again and return to where I felt most at home, Europe, but I would take the feeling of having had a hometown, the kindness and the humor with me. I would never lose my appreciation for the ordinary. Whatever I wrote, including about the man I loved most, would be the truth, and my father, the most non-gushing admirer of my talent and the most honest person I ever knew, would approve.

———

Grave men, near death, who see with blinding sight
Blind eyes could blaze like meteors and be gay,
Rage, rage against the dying of the light.

And you, my father, there on the sad height,
Curse, bless me now with your fierce tears, I pray,
Do not go gentle into that good night.
Rage, rage against the dying of the light.
— Dylan Thomas from "Do Not Go Gentle into That Good Night"

It was a beautiful May day, the sort of day that elevates your spirit, that assures you life is good, the kind of day that lulls you with a sincere promise that nothing bad can happen on such a day. When my father didn't answer his phone at six in the evening, I decided to go to the barn and take care of Cynnamon, and try to call him again later. I asked my wife to try to call him while I was gone. I had spoken to him twice the day before and was concerned that he was in bed when I called and had complained his arm was bothering him. I asked if I should bring him anything, if I should take him to the doctor for another shot of cortisone and he replied, "It won't do any good, I'm just wearing out." *Damn it.*

I came back from the barn and Nicole said there still was no answer. I tried again and then called my dad's neighbor who had a key to my dad's house and he said he would check on my dad and call me back. I told myself that my dad had probably gone out to dinner with a friend and had forgotten to tell me – that had happened in the past. When my phone rang five minutes later it startled me and I hoped it was my dad calling to chastise me for worrying. When the neighbor said "You'd better come immediately and bring Nicole with you," I asked, "Did my father shoot himself?" and he said yes. The secret fear I'd carried for years had come to pass. I knew my father had a gun, I didn't know where he kept it, I knew if I found and removed it he would never speak to me again, and he, the master of ingenuity, would find another way.

I told the neighbor to lock the house, I would be there in forty-five minutes and we'd call the police after I arrived. I hung up the phone and *"WHY?!"* came out of me. It wasn't a human cry, it was a primal scream of anguish from the soul. I not only knew why, I despised the reasons.

I insisted that Nicole stay home – it was feeding time for the animals and they had to eat on time, and I didn't want her to see what I was about to see. I drove mechanically, through tears, and pounded my fist on the steering wheel.

"I can't do this! I shouldn't have to do this! Why? How could you do this to me, Dad? I even baked homemade muffins for you..." I sobbed as I drove.

The neighbor and his wife met me at the bottom of the driveway when I pulled in.

"Are you sure you want to go in?" he asked. I nodded my head yes, red-eyed and tight-lipped. We went in through the garage and up the cellar steps, and the longest walk I've ever made was down the short hallway to my father's bedroom. I wasn't prepared – how could anyone ever be prepared? I felt like I had a lead corset around my chest and I had to remind myself to breathe. I laid my hand on my father's hand. It was cold. The ivory-handled revolver I hadn't seen since I was a child was still clutched in his other hand. The neighbor held my elbow and turned to lead me from the room. My legs felt like rubber, I thought I would fall. I waved his hand away and walked back into the kitchen, the room in which my parents had lived most. Eerily empty was my father's chair at the kitchen table where I had seen him sitting for years, watching TV with his failing vision and reading the stacks of books and science magazines by the magnifying light I had given him. The neighbor reached for the phone and dialed 911. I took the receiver and instructed the emergency operator that they should send one police car, I didn't want all my dad's elderly, ill friends on his street upset by an invasion of emergency vehicles when my father was obviously beyond help.

I sat in a chair in the living room and waited, not really there. This was a bad dream and I was still a child, clinging to my father's back as he swam out to the middle of Clinton Lake...I was terrified, but knew better than to let on I was frightened. Within twenty minutes the street was filled with blaring sirens and flashing blue lights, and the house was swarming with police, emergency medical personnel, detectives and coroner. They asked me the same questions over and over and I answered woodenly until I couldn't take anymore.

"GET OUT! Just get out and leave us alone!"

"You're upset, understandably; we're just doing our jobs; can you account for your whereabouts today? we have to take your father's body to the morgue; did he leave a suicide note? was he depressed? was he ill? about noon, we think, he's been dead about six hours; after we're done with it would you like to have the gun back?"

Please...just leave me alone.

They gave me their business cards, expressed their regrets, and carried my father in a zippered blue vinyl bag past me and out the front door. The neighbors followed and I was left alone, more alone than I've ever been. I made some phone calls. I got out a bucket and sponge and my mother's favorite cleaner. I went into the bedroom and cleaned up the crime scene. I stripped the bed and put the sheets into the washer with my mother's favorite laundry detergent.

You were right, Mom. They do remove stains. Even precious, irreplaceable, never to be equaled in my life again blood.

I turned over a piece of paper on the kitchen table and it was his suicide note with checks attached. It was mostly practical instructions about his estate. It said that his last good arm had quit working and this was as far as he wished to go. It said he didn't want a funeral service and he hoped this would all be forgotten within six weeks, in time for my brother's wedding. He told me to have a good life. Signed "Dad." Not "Love, Dad"...just "Dad."

Damn it, Dad! What about all the things we should have said to each other? I always sign my notes to you, "Love, Jim." You couldn't write "Love, Dad"?

It was well after midnight when I drove home. The shock and emotional exhaustion were beginning to be replaced by a seething anger.

I hate you, God. I hate what you do to innocent people. You robbed my mother and father of the full use of their legs and arms and waited until I loved them best and needed them most and you killed them. My wife doesn't deserve what you did to her and you took all of our parents in four years' time. I believed in you. You killed some of my friends. I tried to be good, I tried to do good! And this is the thanks I get? Who needs you? From now on, just stay the hell out of my life.

Nicole met me at the door with a stricken look. She hugged me and we cried. What little liquor we usually have in the house is for baking and I drained all of it, trying to deaden the pain, trying to knock myself out so that I could sleep. I knew the next days would be difficult. The alcohol had no effect.

I went to the barn the next morning to see Cynnamon. I was glad nobody else was around. She nickered when she saw me and I entered her stall and gave her an apple.

"Your grandpap is gone now, Cynnamon. No more peaches."

I buried my face in her mane and hugged her and bawled. I felt a glimmer of comfort that I hadn't felt since the terrible events of the evening before.

———

I learned what it meant to be a surviving suicide victim. Awake and asleep, I relived that final scene. I went through the mental list of things I had done for my father, all the times I'd been there for him, how I cared for my mother twenty-four hours a day for three and a half weeks at home until her death and managed everything about that ordeal, when he could not. How he knew without question that I would have been there for him in thirty-eight minutes' drive time if he needed me. How I knew everything he liked to eat and my wife and I cooked his meals in advance. The places I took him when he agreed to go. How I took care of everything as best I could and had people secretly checking up on him and reporting back to me. How I protected his dignity. How I cursed the unfairness of it all that the last of his physical strength was leaving and that if anyone in the world had ever deserved the eyesight he needed to continue a lifelong pursuit of educating himself, he did, and I hated his impending blindness as much as he did. I had given up my house and well-paid job, and my secure existence to be here for him. *Then why in the hell do I feel guilty?* That is the curse of a suicide.

I learned that people don't know what to say to you after a suicide so they often say the wrong thing. I learned that "if you need anything, let us know" is as meaningless as "how are you?" And even when it is sincere, you will not let anyone know. I hid in my rural existence. I avoided people, especially people who brought up the subject of my parents. After his house was sold, I never returned to that neighborhood. Other than my wife, who felt for me but knew she couldn't feel the same things I was feeling, the only relationships I still felt competent in were with animals. I didn't talk much at all, not even to my wife, my soulmate. I judged people, what they did or didn't do, by the sincerity of their words, how they made their living and how damaging it was to our world. I cherished the people who had stayed in my father's life after my mother's death, who had helped him, who visited him, and I resented the ones who had let him down, left him alone. *I cannot be all things to all people and I am sick of being the one who tries while everyone else goes about their self-serving ways!* More than ever, I needed animals because they never betrayed my trust and they never disappointed me. My daily time with Cynnamon was usually the only time of the day when I did not grieve the loss of my father.

I learned that it is easy to fool people. Though I was rarely in the company of people, when I was, I could be witty and charming, even humorous at times, and they never suspected that inside I was spiraling down, down, to the depths of despair. I was almost jealous of people who could turn to drink or prescribed medications to numb the pain...I couldn't do that for reasons of aversion and too many reminders of lives destroyed by them. I was jealous of people who could announce they were having a nervous breakdown and were checking out of life for a while. I had too many responsibilities. I had a wife, a lot of animals, an animal rescue effort, financial burdens, and especially elderly friends who depended on me. *Curse the blood of my father that runs in my veins and dictates that I can never quit, that I have to keep going no matter what, that I have to succeed.* I wanted so badly to quit, only I didn't know how.

I learned that suicide survivors have the right to "get over it" in their own time and in their own way, and nobody, not even those who love you, has the right to expect you to meet their timeline. *Do you know what it's like to have that final scene wake you in terror when you are fighting exhaustion, to make you afraid of going to sleep? Do you know what it's like to hear a documentary announced on his favorite PBS station and think, "I have to remember to tell Dad"? Or to look at the clock at six p.m. every day, the time you always called him, and remember the day he didn't answer his phone? Or to have the phone ring and hope it is him?* Damn him for being so important to me that by "getting over it," by having the good life he wished for me, I would be disrespectful if I stopped showing that his was a loss I can never get over.

I learned that you cannot continue hating God, because God is the personification of Love, and Love was what I believed in most and the reason I suffered so. I learned that you eventually have to forgive yourself and other people, and you have to get on with putting back together a life that is good, in testimony and remembrance to the ones you lost, the ones who taught you well. I learned you have to forgive the one who wounded you by the act of suicide, that rather than it being the burning hole in your heart of a loved one's slow death from illness, or the jagged, gaping hole in your heart of their death by tragedy, it is a sudden, savage slash through your heart that heals slowly and the wound will seep for a long time. The heart will heal eventually, scarred over, but fully functional.

I learned that animals are the greatest healers and among the greatest is my horse, Cynnamon. I had rescued her and she, in turn, had rescued me.

It has been a year and a half since my father's death and I have survived, as my father knew I would, and I am getting on with life. I had walked along a precipice, dangerously close to the edge, and I had stepped back onto solid ground. I had stumbled, nearly fallen, but I regained my legs and now there will be no stopping me. I will succeed in my way, on my terms, and with many of the values my father taught me by his example. I will continue doing the things I believe in and I will continue doing that which my father appreciated most in me, I will write. I am confident about all that because I am my father's son.

Dedicated to the memory of my father, Earl Willis.

"CYNNAMON"

My blessed companion and friend of my Creator,
thou wilt never fail me.
~ THE PROPHET MOHAMMED
❖

LETTING JUDAS BE

The blue and pink streaks of the evening Montana sky ran together like a watercolor painting and washed over the steep rock bluffs as deepening shadows oozed into the canyon below. The stakes of the capture pen were visible on the canyon floor and it would be finished before dawn with the help of some contract workers. Jake raised his binoculars and searched the rocks dotted with islands of pine and the grass meadow of the plateau rimmed by purple lupine. The corona of the setting sun hung just above the crest of the hill directly opposite from Jake and silhouetted the band of grazing mustangs. He counted seventeen, the band stallion, some yearlings, and three mares with foals. Even though it was for their own good, he regretted taking them out of God's country.

Jake shoved the rest of a strip of beef jerky into his mouth and stood up, waving to the boy sitting on the crest of the adjacent hill. The boy waved back. Jake sat back down and began scribbling in his notebook as he waited for Ned to pick his way over the rocks and through the brush. Ned was half his age and moved twice as slow, but he was a good kid and a hard worker.

They were both employed by the federal Bureau of Land Management, the agency mandated by Congress to protect and manage the wild mustangs and burros. About forty thousand of the wild mustangs remained in a handful of western states. The BLM annually captured some of the younger horses to keep regional populations low. If they were allowed to breed unchecked, herds could increase by as much as twenty percent per year. The mountain lion was the mustang's only potential predator, and not a very successful one at that, and the horses shared some range lands overgrazed by cattle and were threatened by starvation in severe winters. A cruel winter thirty years ago had wiped out whole populations of the horses.

Most of the captured horses were adopted out to private horse-lovers, and some of them were first gentled and trained at programs staffed by volunteers and prisoners at penitentiaries.

That was where Jake had his first experience with the mustangs. By the time he was eighteen, he'd accumulated enough juvenile offender convictions to land himself in the "big house" for a year. It had been enough to turn him around and make him appreciate freedom, and he drew a lot of similarities between the wild nature of the mustangs and his own. Like him, Ned came from a broken home and poverty, and had been headed down that same path until Jake saw something of himself in the boy and had taken him under his wing. The horses had done as much to curb the boy's wild streak as they had done for Jake. The boy didn't communicate much, but he had an easy, gentle nature that the horses responded to. In the almost two years that Jake had known him, the boy had gone from scrawny with pasty complexion to windburned, tan and muscular, and he had lost the haunted look in his eyes.

Jake closed the notebook and stood up to stretch. He could hear the band stallion calling to his herd and heard another band of young stallions answering from a hill on the other side of the narrow canyon. Ned came crashing through the brush and made his way over to Jake.

"How many bachelors?" Jake asked him.

"Seven...but they won't get in the way. They can't even get down into the canyon without going all the way around the ridge, the old river bed is the only route into it."

"Good," Jake nodded. "If any of the mares in this band are stragglers they can join up with the boys club later. Let's get back to camp...we gotta be up by 0-dark-30. I told everyone to be here by five a.m. Just make sure Jude has fresh water and a flake of hay before you turn in."

———

The sound of a Jeep pulling up to the camp woke both men before the alarm clock went off. Jude began whinnying and pawing in his trailer, demanding breakfast before Jake even had time to start a pot of coffee. He motioned to Ned, who crawled out of his sleeping bag with a groan, pulled his boots on and set off toward the trailer with a bucket of water.

A well-weathered looking woman and seasoned veteran of numerous round-ups was the first to climb out from behind the steering wheel of the Jeep, followed by three young men, yawning and stretching, and sipping on travel cups of coffee.

"How ya been, Mustang Sally?" Jake asked.

"You're the only one who calls me that who I let live," the woman answered. "Been fine, Jake, how 'bout yourself?"

"Real good, Beatrice" Jake replied. "Soon as Ned is done stretching Jude's legs, you all can finish stringing up the burlap to the posts and putting up the gates. We already got the pens in place. I'm going up on the hill to see what the ponies are up to. At least this time they've only got one escape route and that's right into the canyon...not like the last round-up."

"I hear ya," the woman nodded, "scattered like billiard balls last time."

Jake poured coffee into a thermos and shoved it inside his jacket, and slung the binoculars around his neck.

"See ya in a bit then. Make them boys do some work."

He followed the dry river bed, bisected in the middle by only a shallow stream, and skipped from stepping stone to stone until he was at the base of the foothills. It was a steep ascent to his vantage point, but there was plenty of growth for handholds. The horses would have an easier time of it, after making it down one steep embankment their path into the canyon was wide and well-worn by erosion. The sun was climbing fast and lent a rosy hue to the sandstone and granite cliffs. Jake made his way to his perch of the day before and leaned back against a rock. He unscrewed the cap of the thermos and took a long drink of the strong brew.

The mustangs were already visible. The foals were kicking up their heels in mock battle and the adults looked up tolerantly from their grazing. The stallion patrolled the perimeter of the band and Jake raised his binoculars to get a better look at him. He was a handsome blue-black with a white star on his forehead. He had a few raking scars on his hip and withers, probably testaments to battles with other stallions to achieve his present rank, maybe even from a run-in with a mountain lion. Jake couldn't judge his age from a distance, but thought he was young enough to be included in the BLM adoption program – horses over the age of five weren't considered adoptable and were released. You could take the mustang out of the wild, but after a certain age, it was nearly impossible to take the wild out of the mustang.

A dappled gray yearling approached and circled the stallion, clicking his teeth so loudly Jake could hear the clatter. It was the young horse's signal of submission, a "please don't hurt me" plea in mustang language. The stallion nuzzled him affectionately and moved past him to greet the mares. The foals also made play lunges at the stallion as their mothers nickered in admonishment, but the stallion was a benevolent ruler. They were a striking band of palomino, dark bay, dappled gray, blue roan, dun, and one foal was white. The colorful landscape offered no camouflage for a white horse and Jake thought he'd enjoy a longer life in captivity than he would in the wild.

It wasn't always easy for Jake to help take these symbols of American freedom out of their natural habitat and the BLM program had long been the target of criticism. But he also thought the BLM had been responsive to concerns and he was of the opinion that the fact the mustangs were thriving with management of the populations was proof of the pudding. He also thought that some of the armchair critics of the program might do well to sit up high on a bluff some morning, freezing their asses off, and watching the mustangs who might not be there at all if it wasn't for the management efforts.

He took another swig of coffee and looked toward the canyon floor. Beatrice was waving her arms and barking orders to the boys and even had Ned moving quicker than usual. They had most of the burlap and plastic fencing in place and the boys were mounting the double gates at the entrance of the shoot. The configuration was like a funnel, long and narrow at the entrance, and the end enclosure was wide, where several pens had been erected. When everything was in place, Jake would radio the helicopter pilot who would drive the mustangs off the plateau, down the hillside and across the riverbed. The helpers on the ground would hide behind the burlap screening and once the horses had entered the wide enclosure the boys would scurry under the burlap waving white flags on sticks, and following Beatrice's orders, would attempt to cut the horses into pens according to type – yearlings in one, mares with foals into another, and the stallion in a separate pen. Easier said than done, Jake well realized.

It was Jude, the dun colored gelding now pacing back and forth in a round pen, who was the quarterback of the operation. He was tall for a mustang and had an obstinate nature which hadn't made him a good candidate in the adoption program. Horses who were adopted and didn't work out were often rehomed. Jude hadn't worked out in his first home and had been retained as an important member of Jake's staff. During a round-up the mustangs might balk at entering the enclosure and would likely turn and stampede in the opposite direction. Jude was a "Judas horse," a mustang who had been trained to run ahead of the horses into the entrance of the enclosure. He would be released at the critical moment and the panicked wild horses would follow him out of instinct. Once they were all in, Jake and Ned would slam the gates shut behind them.

Jake often wondered if Jude suffered any guilt over his role in betraying his own kind. He liked Jude, who did his job well, he just didn't feel bonded to the horse the way he had with most of the horses he'd worked with. There was something stand-offish about Jude. Jake thought that losing most of his tail hadn't helped the gelding's self-esteem. He'd had a long flowing tail until Ned accidentally shut the horse trailer door on it and during a long drive the sawing action of metal against metal had sheared off most of Jude's tail. From the back end, Jude looked like a big foal.

After the captured mustangs had calmed down a little, Jake would make a quick assessment of them for health and age. Horses who appeared older than five years were released, as were young horses of unusual colors or particularly fine examples of health and stamina. The goal was not to reduce the gene pool in any way, but to allow the wild populations to be robust and representative of the species. The horses who would be enrolled in the adoption program would be moved to a holding center where they would be checked by veterinarians, vaccinated, and the yearling males gelded. A freeze brand would be placed on their necks, which was the one part of the indoctrination process that Jake held a grudge against, but he kept his opinion to himself. He realized it was necessary for identification purposes, but he also thought it spoiled their wild beauty and it reminded him too much of the numbers prisoners wore on their uniforms.

Beatrice started waving at him from in front of the erected gates and Jake stood up and waved back. He turned and took one last look at the band of horses playing and pawing on top of paradise, oblivious to the fact that their lives of unbridled freedom were about to change forever.

What must be, must be, he thought as he made his way down the hillside.

———

Ned met him at the edge of the riverbed with a pout, kicking loose rocks as Jake approached. Jake gave him an inquisitive look.

"What did that woman do before this...drill sergeant?" Ned asked. Jake chuckled.

"Beatrice has a mouth on her, but she's all bark and no bite. Couldn't count the number of mustangs she's gentled that anyone else would have given up on. Come on, let's get this show on the road," Jake said.

The two of them walked toward the gates of the enclosure.

"Your boys ready, Bea?" Jake asked.

"Ready as they'll ever be, if they haven't crawled off for a nap somewhere," she said and pulled an unfiltered cigarette out of her shirt pocket. "You calling Billy?" she asked.

Jake nodded.

"Okay, Ned, go get Jude and keep him behind the right gate."

Jake walked over to the radio and motioned to Beatrice to get into position.

"Look alive boys!" she yelled as she marched along the outside wall of burlap.

Jake scanned the horizon and saw the small chopper zigzagging back and forth in the distance. He picked up the radio microphone.

"You there, Billy? You're up next," he said.

"That's a ten-four," a crackly voice came back. "I'm on my way and I got ten bucks riding on Sea Biscuit."

———

The stallion looked up and snorted as the helicopter's drone approached the plateau. He whinnied nervously and the mares instinctively surrounded the three foals. The helicopter slowed to a hover at the far edge of the crest and hung like an ominous dragonfly.

"Get ready 'cause here we come," the pilot said into the radio and Jake gave a thumbs-up signal to Beatrice and her boys. He took Jude's lead rope from Ned and as the boy walked off to take up his post behind the left wing of the gate, Jake undid Jude's halter, dropped it to the ground and loosely wrapped the lead rope around the gelding's neck.

Billy pressed down on the throttle and the main rotor picked up speed. He nosed down the helicopter and the blades began sending waves across the grasses as the band of mustangs collected in a huddle. The band of bachelor stallions on the next hill trumpeted a warning. The foals bleated in fright and every member of the band turned to face the approaching helicopter as the stallion paced back and forth in front of them. The stallion realized this wasn't a foe he could fight and flight was their only option. He screamed once and broke into a run through the middle of the herd and they turned on their heels and followed. He made it to the near edge of the plateau and turned to make sure his band was all accounted for. The whites of his eyes showed in fear, but he screamed again in encouragement, and leapt off the lip of the plateau onto the rocky ribbon of path that led down to the riverbed. The foals screamed in fear as their mothers nudged them forward. The stallion attempted to choose the easiest path around the rocks. The pilot held back. Now that the horses were to the point of no return he didn't want to unduly frighten them, the footing was tricky enough at their current speed.

Jake licked his lips nervously and waved again toward Beatrice. Jude flared his nostrils in excitement. The thunder of pounding hooves could be heard as the helicopter appeared over the lip of the plateau and began descending, driving the mustangs across the riverbed. The stallion was the first horse across and he turned once again to face the airborne threat as the other members of the band ran past him and kept running. Jake hoped Billy could spur the stallion to catch up with the rest of his band, but understood that the stallion thought by bringing up the rear he was protecting the herd from the most imminent danger. The draft from the helicopter began to kick up dust from the canyon floor as the horses broke through a wall of dust, headed right for the gates. Jake could no longer see the stallion, but he moved to the outside edge of the gate and positioned Jude.

"Now!" he yelled as he let the lead rope drop and Jude bolted in front of the approaching mustangs and ran straight into the enclosure. A wave of colors, dust and flashing hooves rushed by Jake and Ned, and Jake turned to see the stallion a hundred yards away as the helicopter banked sharply. The pilot waved once, circled around the ridge and disappeared over it. The stallion's sides heaved as he ran in circles. He was lathered in sweat and his eyes flashed as he reared and screamed in rage, his nostrils flared and bloodred. Ned hung on his side of the gate waiting for Jake to move forward with his side.

"Now, Ned! – forget him, he's not going to go in!" Jake yelled and began to rush forward with his wing of the gate, but the bolts holding the top hinge to the post tore loose, sending the gate cockeyed and causing Jake to trip and fall.

"Shit!" he yelled. "Ned, close yours and come help me."

Ned slammed his side shut and raced across the entrance, grabbing Jake's elbow with one hand to help him to his feet and trying to tug the lopsided gate vertical with the other hand. Jake looked up just as Beatrice and her boys popped under the burlap screening like groundhogs, just ahead of the mustangs who had slowed and were milling about frantically in the enclosure. But as one boy came up from under the burlap, his shoulder tore loose one end of the screening and it fluttered in front of the Judas horse. Jude reared in fright and whinnied, and the stallion answered with a scream. Jude's reply was to turn and begin racing back toward the entrance of the shoot and the other mustangs followed.

"Holy shit!" Jake yelled and before he could stop him, Ned picked up one of the white flags on a stick and ran into the enclosure. Jake knew that no horse will run down a man on purpose and he hoped for Ned's sake that someone had informed this band of mustangs about that behavioral tidbit.

He stood behind the twisted and useless gate as an explosion of dust, screaming horses, and Ned yelling something unintelligible came rocketing through the narrow opening. One mustang hit the left wing of the gate and sent it flying open as the horses came pouring through it with a dust-caked Ned in hot pursuit. With Jude in the lead the band of horses reached the stallion and passed him. The stallion whirled toward his enemy and reared, focusing on the boy still waving the flag on the stick, and he lowered his head and charged.

Jake was too surprised to move as the stallion slid to a stop just feet from Ned and reared again, pawing the air in defiance.

"Whoa! Whoa!" Ned yelled, afraid the stallion was going to strike him with his fore hooves, but the stallion spun instead and his flank grazed Ned and knocked him to the ground. Ned lay there for a minute trying to get his breath back as Jake watched the horses thundering up the dry riverbed and splashing mightily as they crossed the shallow stream. Ned got up with a groan, picked up his hat and slapped it against the torn knee of his blue jeans.

"Damn it!" he said. He looked over at Jake who was doubled up with laughter.

"What's so damn funny?" he asked disgustedly.

"I'd say old Jude just out-Judassed our asses!" Jake said with a grin. Ned would wince whenever Jake told the story later, saying the two of them waving their silly white flags looked like two old ladies trying to flag down a taxi with their hankies and calling Ned's stampede control efforts as "useless as teats on a boar-hog."

Jake and Ned watched Jude lead the band up the rocky hillside like he knew where he was going. The stallion hadn't caught up to the other horses yet and he turned frequently, prancing and snorting, staying between danger and his band.

"What are we going to do...call back the helicopter?" Ned asked, pointing toward the radio.

Jake rubbed his chin.

"Nope. We're just going to let him and his friends be."

"Think the BLM will agree?" Ned asked.

"Yep. This is the last round-up of the season and this is one of the smaller populations, they ain't in any real danger. Beside, Jude is over five years old, he ain't adoptable anyway and we can train a new Judas horse."

"Think the stallion will leave him alone?" Ned asked.

"If he has any sense, he'll be grateful...he has Jude to thank for getting his mares back. And when he notices Jude is lacking some critical equipment, he won't think him much competition. Jude can always take up with the band of bachelor stallions if he wants, they'll accept him."

They stood there watching as the dust settled and the horses slowed their pace high up on the hillside. The stallion turned to face in their direction a final time, pawed the ground twice and snorted one last threat before the horses disappeared over the crest of the hill, onto the grassy plateau. They broke into a run of celebration and the staccato of their hoofbeats echoed through the canyon.

"But don't you think – " Ned started to ask, but Jake silenced him by clapping his hand on his shoulder.

"Let it be, boy. The important thing is that he's free again and there ain't nothin' in this life more important than being free.

Nothin'."

He turned and started kicking loose the stakes of the capture shoot and dropping them to the ground. Ned picked them up one at a time and stacked them. Jake let Beatrice and her boys go at noon since he'd have a hard time justifying paying them for a full day for a failed round-up. It was near dusk when he and Ned finished loading the stakes and rolls of burlap and fencing into the back of the truck.

As Jake slid into the driver's side of the pick-up, he looked up toward the hilltop. One horse stood on the crest, silhouetted against the sun sinking like a hot coal. From his unusually short tail Jake knew it was Jude. He gave the mustang a farewell salute as he slammed the truck door shut and drove off, the empty horse trailer swaying and bouncing behind the truck.

———

Your destiny is a mystery to us.
What will happen when the buffalo are all slaughtered? The wild horses
tamed? What will happen when the secret corners of the forest are heavy
with the scent of many men and the view of the ripe hills is blotted by
talking wires? Where will the thicket be? Gone!
Where will the eagle be? Gone! And what is it to say goodbye
to the swift pony and the hunt?
The end of living and the beginning of survival.
~ CHIEF SEATTLE
❖

LISTEN, CHILD

Listen to their calls, child,
listen to their hearts,
appreciate their nature, child,
the beauty they impart.

A world without them, child,
would be barren, cold and gray,
and we must work to save them, child,
since only humans have a say.

They have much to teach us, child,
of lives devoid of sin,
one more interesting than the next,
and all of them our kin.

They were intended as a gift, child,
which some choose to ignore,
be thankful that we have them, child,
for their sake, I implore.

There are those who'd kill them, child,
spurred on by human greed,
but kind spirits will prevail, child,
because we understand their needs.

Your questions all have merit, child,
your concerns are all well placed,
they do not deserve to die, child,
only you can insure their fate.

LIKE SNOW ON ROSES

There are things in this world that do not make sense –
that we should chance upon a fawn, aquiver with fragile beauty
and hear gunshots in the distance.
That we could stand on a mountain peak
and survey pristine splendor,
return to our valley below and deny the existence of a Creator.
That we should choose to not recognize that Love in all its forms
is still Love,
or that Humanity in all its colors and faiths is still Humanity.
That we could ignore the cries of children,
the wails of animals,
the prayers of people yearning to breathe free.

There are things in this world which are unfathomable –
that we would hurt the ones who love us best,
or not recognize the difference between lust and Love,
or know that the greatest and most enduring Love is Friendship.
That we would value physical beauty over the purity of the soul.
That we could choose to ignore simple pleasures
and live in the hum of technology,
or silence the song of birds with our poisons,
or cover habitats with concrete,
or take the animals that symbolize freedom for us
and confine them.
That in the sizzle and aroma of meat on our grills
we do not hear the screams
and smell the stench of the slaughterhouse.
That we would not forgive.

There are things in this world I do not understand –
that we would fail to nurture our children or appreciate our elders.
That education and healthcare are not available to all.
That we would glide through shopping malls
in a quest for things we do not need,
while we know there are people in this world
who do not have enough to eat.
That we would fail to recognize that challenged people have
something to teach us about facing challenges.
That we do not all know that Art and Poetry and Music transcend
the physical and take us to a higher level,
and that books open windows to other worlds.

There are things in this world that are incomprehensible –
that we would fail to tell those we love, how much we love them
and tell them often.
Or that we would wait until it is too late.
That we could look into the eyes of an innocent creature
and harm him,
or attempt to profit from his suffering.
That we would choose to look outward for the answers to
mysteries whose answers lie in our hearts.
That we would not recognize that all religion is based in Love,
and that we would conduct acts of aggression religiously.
That we can ignore problems
and not choose to be a part of solutions.
That we would choose to live lives of quiet desperation
instead of aspiring to greatness.
That we would not hold truth as dear as life itself.

There are things in this world that do not make sense...
like snow on roses.

A KILLING FROST

There is an emptiness of spirit,
a taint upon our souls,
a coveting of the material,
yet all that glitters is not gold.

It was not inborn in us,
we put it there with greed,
an ignorance of suffering,
a deaf ear to those in need.

We covered it in concrete,
reinforcing it with steel,
and in our building fever,
removed the capacity to feel.

Our lives we rule with timeclocks,
appointments, financial goals,
we've welcomed in the devils,
and paid the price in souls.

Can you not hear Nature calling?
"Come lose yourself in me,
forsake your modern madness,
in forests, mountains, sea."

We don't know where we're going,
or understand yet where we've been,
or know the price of sacrifice,
until we pay the wages of our sin.

Salvation is in the doing,
we each must do our part,
to give something back or suffer yet
a killing frost of the human heart.

❖

PRAYER FOR THE ONE I LOST

A moment of distraction, a forgotten lock,
a poor decision, a breach of trust,
a thief, and you were gone.

You are the first one I think of when I wake,
and the last one I pray for before I sleep.
Where are you little one?
I've done everything humanly possible
to bring you back,
and now your return will require a higher grace.

May the angels keep you safe from harm, warm and dry.
May white light surround you
and lead you to someone you can trust.
May you feel my love searching for you in the darkness.
May my tears pay the bail for your release from fear.
May my heart beat a beacon you can follow.
May my suffering mean that you will not.
May you be found.
If not for me, then for another who will love you well.

I am here and you are there,
and that in no way separates us.
Not even loss can break this bond we share,
and whether in this world or the next,
oh, what a reunion that will be!

May I someday find the comfort I cannot find now.
May I learn to not blame myself,
because I know you do not blame me.
May I find the strength to accept tragic news.
May I learn to love another in your stead,
if you do not return.
May you know I loved you then, I love you now,
I'll love you forever.

Be safe, little one, I miss you so.

❖

CHRISTINE'S MAGIC BOX

From the moment Miss Wells walked into the classroom, Christine suspected something was wrong. Miss Wells looked rather sad and serious, and even perhaps as if she'd been crying.

"Good morning, children," Miss Wells began.

"Good morning, Miss Wells," the class answered routinely.

"Children, I'm afraid that I have some sad news this morning," Miss Wells said, managing a weak smile. "Our friend Jennifer will not be returning to school. She misses us very much and we miss her, and she wanted me to tell you that she likes the cards we've made for her, and especially the coloring book we made. Her mother and father also wanted me to thank you and they want to visit us some day to thank you in person."

Miss Wells walked a bit up the row of desks and stopped at Jennifer's empty desk.

"You know that Jennifer has been very sick and now her doctor has said that she must not return to school, and that she must rest in bed."

"Will Jennifer die, Miss Wells?" asked Roberta.

Miss Wells looked toward the ceiling and swallowed hard.

"I don't know," she answered thoughtfully.

But Christine thought that Miss Wells did know and was only trying to be nice. Christine looked down at her desk.

"Children, I am very sorry to have to start our morning on such a sad note. I promised Jennifer that I would tell you why she has been away so long, and to tell you how much fun she had with us and how much she learned."

Christine could believe that. She had known Jennifer since the first grade and Jennifer had always been one of the smartest, prettiest and nicest girls in the school. She wished now that she could have been a closer friend of Jennifer's or had had the chance to know her better. Christine had been too busy. She always hurried home after school so that she could finish her homework and then help her mother and grandmother. Her father had died when Christine was a baby and now she was filling in for him. Her thoughts were interrupted by Miss Wells.

"Children, I must confess, I really don't know how I should explain to you. Jennifer doesn't want us to be sad and she wants us to understand. She worries about us and her family. Well, we are going to have to be very brave – brave like Jennifer."

Christine watched Miss Wells' bottom lip quiver and somebody a few seats away sniffled.

"There is a very bad sickness that you probably have heard of. It is a disease and it has many different kinds. We call all of them 'cancer,' and Jennifer has cancer."

"But Miss Wells," James blurted out without raising his hand, "don't only old people get cancer? My grandfather had it and he died last year. He was old though."

"Yes, old people often get cancer, but so do people my age (and Christine waited for her to say her age, but she did not), and sometimes very young people get cancer. Sometimes even babies.

"That is why your parents and teachers, and the school nurse want you to see a doctor when you don't feel well. And that is why the doctor asks you questions, and feels, and asks you if things hurt, or sometimes the doctors will make a test. There are excellent chances that you can be healthy again with the doctor's help, but sometimes you have to do something that you don't like very much..."

"Like drinking something that tastes awful!" James blurted out again.

"Exactly. Unfortunately, sometimes the doctors can't help us as much as they'd like to."

Christine couldn't imagine why. She thought her own doctor must know everything, because each time Christine got sick, her doctor helped to make her better. Christine's doctor was an Indian, and maybe she knew some special medicine that could make Jennifer better. (Christine didn't understand that her doctor was another kind of Indian from New Delhi, and that a lot of doctors had already tried very hard to make Jennifer get well.)

"Children, I am not a doctor and I can't explain to you very much about cancer or why Jennifer has gotten so sick. I think it would be a good idea if you would talk to your mothers and fathers this evening about Jennifer. I think they would like to help you to understand. We all have a sadness about Jennifer being sick that we need to talk about, especially with our families.

"I'd also like to ask that your parents contact me if they have any questions," Miss Wells added. "I think we may be able to help one another and perhaps some of your parents would like to help Jennifer's parents. Perhaps we could even ask the school nurse, or a doctor, to come talk to our class."

Most of the children brightened at the suggestion, because anytime someone came to talk to the class the children usually had no homework that evening.

"We will have more to talk about later. We'll continue sending Jennifer cards and surprises to show her that we love her. For now though, please open your books to page eighty."

———

Christine walked home from school more quickly than usual, forgetting even to sneak a peek at her baby birds in their nest near the end of the path. She burst in the kitchen door and plopped her books on the table, which brought a "*Shhh*, Chrissie, your grandmother is taking a nap," from her mother.

Her mother slowly stirred the saucepan on the stove as Christine told her about her day at school, being especially careful to remember everything Miss Wells had said.

"Chrissie, I'm very sorry, for Jennifer and for her parents. I'd heard recently that Jennifer was very sick. I think maybe we should have talked about this sooner. I'm going to call Miss Wells tomorrow and thank her for talking to you and the other children. I think some other parents will call her as well."

(Many parents did call Miss Wells, but some said that she had scared the children and that she should not talk about such things to a class of nine-year-olds.)

"Mom, why does Jennifer have to die?" Christine asked. "It's not fair – she's just my age!"

"I wish I could tell you," her mother said, wiping her hands on a dishtowel and sitting down at the table. "Come here," she said, pulling Christine into a hug and smoothing her hair.

"You see, Chrissie, we all have to die because it is the end of the circle. Being born is the beginning of the circle and dying is the end. Some people, like Jennifer, get very sick or have an accident, like your father, and the circle finishes faster than we think it should. One day your father was here and the next day he wasn't.

"We can only accept that and do the best we can. It is what he wanted for us. He didn't want to leave us and we didn't want him to ever leave, but we couldn't change it. We've had to live with it as best we could and to be the best we could be."

Christine was very quiet.

"Life should be a lot of fun, Chrissie, especially when one is your age. But as wonderful as life can be, there are some hard things, some rough spots. Some things hurt very much, things a kiss cannot make all better. It is never easy to get through the bad times – they hurt. As we grow up, we learn to accept things better, to make some good of everything.

"You don't understand all of this now, but you'll understand more later. Maybe I don't understand as much as I should. As much as we'd like to, we cannot stop what is happening to Jennifer, but we can show her and her family that we care, and show them that we'd like to help."

"Like making her cards?" Christine asked.

"Of course. And I think her mother is very busy and very sad. I'm sure she doesn't always feel like cooking, so I'm going to cook things and take them to her.

"Now, I'm going to finish our dinner," Christine's mother said, dabbing the dishtowel to her eye. "I'd like you to do your homework and after dinner why don't you talk to your grandmother about Jennifer? Your grandmother is very wise and when I was a little girl she always gave me very good answers to my questions. Still does!"

Christine nodded. She loved talking to her grandmother and she only half minded doing homework.

"One more thing, Chrissie. I know it is going to be hard for everyone who loves Jennifer, hardest of all for her mother and father. It is so hard to watch someone you love be sick, but it is a very special time, because we have a chance to show Jennifer how important she is to us."

Even though her mother's back was turned, Christine saw the dishtowel go up to her mother's cheek.

"We didn't have a chance to tell your father how much we loved him, or needed him, or would miss him. I hope he knows," and she began to cry.

"Don't cry, Mommy," Christine rushed to her mother. "Daddy knows! I tell him every night before I go to sleep."

"I do, too," her mother said and hugged her back. "It's okay to cry – if you are sad or hurt, or you miss somebody very much, it's good to cry."

———

Both Christine and her mother were unusually quiet during dinner, but her grandmother didn't seem to notice. She was a bit hard of hearing and she seemed to be lost in her own thoughts.

After the supper dishes were washed by her mother, dried by her grandmother, and stacked by Christine, who expertly dragged a kitchen chair this way and that so that she could reach the cupboards, Christine followed her grandmother back to her bedroom.

She was fascinated by "Oma's" room – which is what she called her grandmother, "Oma" meaning grandmother in German, and her grandmother having come from Germany many years ago. Christine sometimes sat with her grandmother after dinner, admiring the lace-curtained window or the pastel-colored mints in the cut-glass dish next to Oma's chair. Most of all she loved listening to Oma's stories about when she was a girl and had her own pony and cart.

Christine told Oma about Jennifer and everything Miss Wells had said. Oma listened quietly, only asking once for Christine to repeat something.

"Oma, are you going to die?" Christine asked suddenly.

"Yes, child, I surely will. I've lived a long time and one day I'll be too old to live."

"But why, Oma? Why can't everybody keep living? Why do people have to die, or get sick, especially nice people like you and Jennifer, and Daddy?"

"Hmmm," Oma sighed and thought for a moment.

"Chrissie, we are like boxes. Each of us, the outer part, is a box. These boxes come in all sizes and shapes, and all colors. Some of them are very beautiful boxes. Some of them are brown cardboard. Some of them are tin and painted to look like real gold – some of them are real gold. But they are only boxes. No matter how big the box, or how pretty it is, or how strong, the only thing that is important is what is in the box.

"These boxes get moved around, they get wet, they have heavy things sat upon them, they get torn and worn out. They get dented, they get punctured, and sometimes a part of their contents leak out, but – usually for a long time – they are still a box. Their purpose is to protect and move around what is inside them."

"But, Oma, if the boxes get hurt, won't the things inside get hurt, too?"

"Usually not. Most of the things in the boxes are things that cannot be hurt. They are things that have no shape, so you can't chip them, or crack them, or break them.

"Inside the boxes are the most beautiful things! – all snuggled together and glowing and jingling, and it is they and never the box that has worth. We simply keep our boxes polished out of respect for what's in them. Sometimes we must even try very hard to not see the box and to only see what is inside."

"What happens when the box breaks, or gets old and falls apart, Oma?"

"Then, first of all, most us miss the box, because it was always around before and now it's not. Instead of remembering the things in the box and seeing them, we miss the box. That is when we have to remind ourselves that the important things that were in the box stay behind. They are our treasures and we must be thankful for however long we've had them and for however long we can hold onto them. The box was only what brought the treasures to us, and those treasures stay with us, box or not!"

"Won't we forget about what's in the box when we can't see the box anymore? What's in my box, Oma?"

"Chrissie, so many questions! Why, you know better than anyone about what is in your box. Think! Be quiet for a moment, sit still and think. Feel. Listen. What *is* in your box?"

Christine did as Oma suggested. She sat and listened and felt. She wrinkled her brow and felt some more, way down deep in herself. She scrunched up her nose and then she smiled.

"There!" said Oma with a pleased nod of her head. "Now, what's in your box?"

"Such a lot of things, Oma. Good things. Maybe a bad thing or two, but many, many good things!"

She and her grandmother talked a long time about the kinds of things that can be in boxes, with Oma occasionally exclaiming "Yes!" until Christine's mother stood in the doorway for a moment and then silently backed away. She smiled at the sight of an old woman and a little girl understanding one another perfectly.

"A curious thing about these boxes," Oma continued, " is that you can never fill them too full. They'll always hold more. But some boxes, I'm sorry to say, are rather empty. Some people do not care enough about filling their box. You must always be careful about what you put in your box. Some people fill them with the wrong things – too much of one thing, or not enough of another, one's just as bad as the other. You must be very clever and know the difference between a real treasure and something that only looks like a treasure."

Then Oma stood up with a clap of her hands and motioned to Christine.

"Come here, child, help me."

She walked toward the open closet door and bent to pull out a stool. She stood and rested a moment, and using Christine's shoulder for support, she stepped up and rummaged around on the top shelf.

"Ah!" she exclaimed as she stepped down with a package.

"This is for you," she said, unwrapping the tissue paper from around a beautiful metal box, locked with a small gold lock. "It's nearly as old as I am."

The box sparkled in the light of the lamp, all red and gold with a stamped design around its edges, and a painting of a castle, or maybe a cathedral – Christine wasn't sure which – on its lid, and tiny, handpainted people in fine clothes, standing around horsedrawn carriages. It looked like a fairytale box – like a magic box!

"It's beautiful, Oma! What's in it?"

"Probably nothing, as far as I remember. At least nothing that could break," she said with a wink. "I lost the key a long time ago. I'd like you to have this box as a reminder of what we talked about. I hope you will keep it to remind you that it isn't the box, what the box looks like, or what country it is from, or what color it is, or even if the box is there or gone – it is always only what is in the box. They are our treasures."

"Thank you, Oma," Christine said, taking the box and kissing her grandmother. "I will always remember," and she turned to leave Oma's room.

"Oma," she said, pausing at the doorway. "I know what is in your box."

"Do you, Christine? Well, good. It would make me happy if

you'd remember when the box is gone."

"I will, Oma. I love you. Good night."

———

Christine carried the box to school with her the next day. Each time someone asked her what was in it, she just smiled and said "Everything."

Some of the children were a little jealous over the pretty box, not even knowing or caring what was in it. Many of the children thought that because the box was beautiful it must contain spectacular things. Some children began to make fun of the box, because they thought it looked so strange to carry around a box such as this.

"I know," one boy told Christine, "you only have your peanut butter and jelly sandwiches in that old box!"

Christine just smiled and thought about what her grandmother had said. She spent the day trying not to see the other "boxes" around her, but to see what was in them. She was quiet, and listened, and felt. Then she had a wonderful idea.

"I think that's a wonderful idea," her mother said after Christine told her that evening. "I'm sure Jennifer would enjoy a visit from you, but I must call her mother first and we'll see if Jennifer is feeling up to having a visitor. And I would like to take a cake to her mother."

But Christine was already on her way to Oma's room to ask her a very important question.

Christine was glad when her mother told her that she had phoned Jennifer's mother, who had said that Jennifer would like to see Christine on Saturday afternoon. Her mother explained that they must only stay a short time, because Jennifer tired very easily and had to sleep much of the time.

Christine nodded her head. She felt a little afraid down deep in the bottom of her stomach. Her mother told her that Jennifer had lost most of her hair because of the medicine that the doctors gave her and that Christine must be very brave and not make Jennifer uncomfortable by acting surprised.

"Someone's always telling me to be brave," Christine thought, *"but it doesn't seem to get any easier."*

———

She spent the next two days practicing being brave, until Saturday came. She was very quiet on the drive to Jennifer's house and she sat clutching a bag in her lap.

"What's in the bag, Chrissie?" her mother asked.

"Something for Jennifer," Christine answered, looking out the side window.

Her mother wanted to ask another question, but she knew that sometimes mothers must be quiet, too.

"How nice to see you both," Jennifer's mother said as she opened the door. She accepted the cake with a grateful smile.

"Christine, your mother and I are going to have a nice visit in the living room, but first I'll take you back to Jennifer's room. She's more comfortable there."

Jennifer was tucked into an overstuffed chair next to the bedroom window when Christine and their mothers walked in. She smiled.

"We're glad you and your mother could..." but then she began to cough hard and her mother rushed over, patted her on the back and plumped up the pillows behind her.

Christine wore a worried look and glanced up at her own mother for reassurance. Her mother nodded an *it's okay*, but she looked very serious.

"We'll leave the two of you alone for awhile," Jennifer's mother said after Jennifer had stopped coughing and she led Christine's mother to the hall.

It was awhile before either Jennifer or Christine spoke. Christine smiled and Jennifer smiled, and then both of them looked out the window.

"I haven't seen you in a long time," Jennifer said. "How is everyone at school?"

"Okay," Christine answered. "We're making a globe of the world out of paper maché that's taller than me! Miss Wells told us that she had been to visit you and we're making you something special in art class, but I can't tell you what it is 'cause it's a surprise."

Then she wondered if she had already spoiled the surprise and she looked down at her feet.

"I don't look like I used to," Jennifer said. "Sometimes it makes people feel sad, because they remember me before I got sick, when I had long hair. The medicine made me lose my hair, but it's growing back some."

Christine looked up at Jennifer, who looked so small tucked into her chair. As brave as Christine was trying to be she felt the tears welling up in her eyes and her voice came out in a gurgle.

"It doesn't matter what you look like, or what anybody looks like. It only matters what you look like inside."

She looked out the window again and angrily wiped at the tears rolling down her cheeks. She had told herself during the drive to Jennifer's that she would not cry, and here she was breaking her promise.

"Here's a tissue," Jennifer offered and leaned back into her pillows. "We've used a lot of tissues."

Christine blew her nose loudly. "I'm better now," she said. "I'm sorry – I came to cheer you up today!"

"It's alright, you have. We all cry, especially my mother. Most of all, I worry about my mother. I keep telling her she has to be strong and go on after I'm not here to take care of her. She'll have to be strong for my father and he'll have to be strong for her."

"Does it hurt? Does it hurt to..." but Christine could not say the word.

"To die? Sometimes. Sometimes it hurts very bad, but the doctors give you something to take away the pain. But the medicine makes me sleep too much. Sometimes I want to stay awake, even when it hurts. Mostly it hurts in your heart, because of all the people you love who love you back. Sometimes the love and the pain are so mixed up together!"

"Are you scared?" Christine asked. She knew she was.

"At first, I was very scared, and my mom and dad, too. They tried to act so brave, so I'd be brave. But then, I accepted it and mostly it's just peaceful now. Soon the pain will be over with and I know that's the hardest thing for the people who love me to watch."

Jennifer closed her eyes for a moment.

"I just wish I could leave them something," she said quietly. "If I were older, or stronger, maybe I could. I just haven't thought of anything yet, but I don't have much time. That makes me sad."

Christine thought about that, then she remembered what she had brought for Jennifer. She reached down and picked up her bag, and pulled out Oma's red and gold enameled box.

"It's beautiful!" Jennifer exclaimed. "What's in it? Is it a box for something?"

And Christine told her. She told her all about boxes and their treasures, and everything exactly the way Oma had explained it. Not only did Jennifer understand, but she had some wonderful ideas of the kinds of things that boxes can hold. Christine saw that Jennifer knew very well what was in her own box.

Soon the two of them were talking and laughing and remembering, and before they knew it, it was time for Christine's mother to take her home.

"Thank you so much, Chrissie," Jennifer whispered, holding the box tightly to her chest. "Now I know what I'm leaving behind for everyone!"

Christine beamed because the tickle of happiness insider her felt stronger than ever before. She leaned over and gave Jennifer a gentle hug and a kiss on top of her head.

"Will I see you again, Jennifer?" she asked hopefully. But Jennifer didn't answer because she had fallen asleep.

"I'm sure I will," Christine said softly, "box or not."

―――――

Christine answered the door when Jennifer's mother came to visit several weeks later. She brought her into the living room where her mother sat looking at the family photo album.

"I'm sorry I must make this a short visit," Jennifer's mother said. "My husband and I are leaving for a few weeks and, well, I have so many things to do."

She explained that since Jennifer's death, Jennifer's father had urged her to come away for awhile to some quiet, special place where they could collect themselves.

"I'm sure that's a very good idea," Christine's mother agreed.

"Christine," Jennifer's mother turned to her, "we want to thank you and the other children, and Miss Wells, for making this time a little easier for us and for Jennifer. It has been a very difficult time for us and we appreciate that we had Jennifer for as long as we did, and that we were able to show her that we loved her."

Christine's mother reached over and took Jennifer's mother's hand and gave it a firm squeeze.

"I also came by to return this to you, Christine," she said, and feeling inside the bag she'd brought with her, she pulled out Oma's pretty box.

"For the last several weeks, this box was very special to Jennifer, and she even asked that it be next to her in the hospital. It was very sweet of you to lend it to her, and I'm curious about what is in it. After Jennifer was gone, we looked for what must have been in the box, but we only found everything that Jennifer had before."

Christine accepted the box and held it on her lap before answering.

"This is a magic box that my grandmother gave to me," she said, tracing her finger around its gilded edges. "But it's only one of many, many magic boxes. And like all of them it is full of the most wonderful things, especially now that it has been with Jennifer."

"But I don't understand," Jennifer's mother said. "We asked her what was in the box and she just said 'everything,' but later – well, the box was locked and we couldn't find the key, so we shook it gently – it felt quite empty."

"What was in the box, Chrissie?" her mother asked.

Christine began slowly at first, eyes closed tightly, and she tried hard to include everything Oma had said, and the list of things she and Jennifer had thought of.

"Mostly they are the things we are made of. Not just things that you can see, but also things you can feel. Like when a parade passes by and you can feel the drums in your stomach and your toes won't keep still. The way music can make a tingle down the back of your neck. The way the air smells when the leaves begin to fall and the different way it smells when the flowers are blooming, or after it rains.

"The way you feel when you help somebody because you want to, and not because you have to. The way the sun makes someone's hair shine. The different sounds of people's laughter – some in little hiccups, some like bells tinkling, some like big bursts from their bellies!

"The way you feel when you make something special for someone. The smell of cookies baking and the feeling of sliding into a warm bath. Or making yourself pretty just for yourself, that feeling, too.

"The feeling you have when you finish something you didn't

think you could finish, or did something you didn't think you could do. Or just the feeling of trying.

"The sound of rain dribbling down the window, or the feeling of wooshing down a hill in the snow. Making someone smile who looks like they could use a smile. Saying 'good morning' to someone because it *is* a good morning.

"The feeling you have when you think of all the people you love and all the people who love you.

"The feeling of appreciation for everything you do have, instead of feeling sorry about what you don't have, or about what you've lost. The feeling of caring, really caring, about all those people who aren't as strong as you, or as smart, or as healthy or happy. The feeling you have when you teach someone to do something, or when they teach you.

"Keeping promises even when they are very hard to keep.

"Singing just because you feel like singing! Making up the words and the tune as you go along.

"The feeling of a hug when you need one and of having someone wipe away your tears. Saying 'thank you' every time for everything and meaning it.

"The way the sun sparkles across the water like millions of diamonds and the way it sets at dusk like a big red balloon.

"Forgiving somebody and hoping that when you need it, you'll be forgiven, too.

"Respecting the truth enough to never lie. Knowing the difference between speaking the truth and keeping silent so that the truth doesn't hurt someone. Always being willing to consider somebody else's feelings instead of only thinking of yourself.

"The way it tickles when a bird walks along your finger, or when a puppy kisses you, or when a cat 'kneads dough' on your lap.

"Sharing when you have enough and understanding that sometimes enough is really too much. Most importantly, sharing yourself.

"Promising yourself that no matter how old you'll get, or how many cares and worries you have, you'll never let the child in you stray too far away (*that was one of Oma's*).

"Remember on every Christmas morning forever, those first Christmas mornings, and how big and bright the tree was, and how the packages shone, and the way the pine smelled (*and that had been one of Jennifer's*).

"Being thankful for having enough to eat, because some people don't, and being thankful for being warm and dry indoors when it's cold and wet outdoors.

"Laughing at the 'bad' things you did, or someone else did, because they really weren't that bad and they really didn't matter. Not compared to the important things, they didn't.

"Always caring about what is right and saying you're sorry when you'd done the wrong thing.

"Thinking twice before you complain. Oma said it is better to use your breath to say what you plan to do about it, instead of complaining about the way it is.

"Patting somebody on the back. Always remembering to encourage them and to tell them they have a friend and that you care.

"Not closing your eyes to the bad, but trying to do something to make it better. Making the world a better place – Oma said if you pick up a piece of paper off the sidewalk or plant a flower where there didn't use to be one, then you can sleep better at night.

"And seeing, *really* seeing, like waking up and seeing everything for the first time. And hearing, *really* hearing. Hearing every instrument in the orchestra and letting them carry you up and up until you're flying! And *really* smelling and *really* tasting...doing everything with feeling. Knowing the way wet dirt feels between your fingers and the way you shudder when there's a worm in it. The way the wave feels when it washes over your feet and the way it feels like it's pulling a sand rug out from under your feet when it runs back to the sea.

"Doing something nice for yourself and looking around for somebody to be nice to.

"Knowing all the colors of the sky and being able, every day, to say 'There's the purple, there's the gray – oh, there's a new pink!'

"Running just because you can and helping somebody who can't to not mind that they can't. Be their legs for them. Being able to ask for help when you need it and understanding that you are often doing the other person a favor. Oma said everyone needs to be needed.

"Always looking for a way to be helpful. Opening a door, carrying someone's package, giving up your seat.

Christine stopped and took a deep breath before continuing.

"Crying when you miss somebody. Crying from happiness for them.

"The way someone's cheek felt so soft, or their eyes crinkled up when they smiled, or their arm felt so strong, or the way their hair smelled. The way you feel like you love someone so much that you just want to crawl up inside them.

"And getting back up again after you fall down, or get knocked down. Dusting yourself off, taking a deep breath and going on. For yourself and for them."

Christine covered her face with her hands for a moment, then she looked up with a smile and with a tear glistening on each cheek.

"Such a lot of wisdom in such a little box," Christine's mother said softly, looking at her with pride.

"Chrissie," Jennifer's mother reached over and laid her hand on the box. "Jennifer told me before she died that I must not miss the box, that I must hold onto what was in the box. Now I understand what she meant and I hope that she will be proud of me. I want very much to hold onto what is in the box and I thank you so much for helping me to remember.

"Where is your grandmother, Chrissie? I'd like to also thank her for sharing her beautiful box."

Christine looked at her mother and then back to Jennifer's mother.

"I'm sure she knows," Christine said, "but my grandmother died last week."

"Oh dear!" Jennifer's mother looked startled. "I'm so sorry...I didn't know."

"We're doing okay," Christine's mother said. "It's not easy. We loved her very much and we miss her, but as she said, only the box is gone."

Christine picked up the box and kissed it, and then placed it on Jennifer's mother's lap.

"I have many things to remember Oma by and I know she also would want you to have this. Nothing can ever replace Jennifer in your life, but sometimes, when it's hard, I hope you'll remember."

"I will, Chrissie," Jennifer's mother promised. "Thank you."

They gave each other a strong hug at the door and Christine's magic box sparkled in the sunlight as Jennifer's mother carried it to her car. And from then on, they all remembered.

The End – but not *really*

Dedicated to the memory of my friend, Christine Michel.

I expect to pass through this world but once;
any good thing therefore that I can do,
or any kindness that I can show to any fellow creature,
let me do it now, let me not defer or neglect it,
for I shall not pass this way again.
~ ERIENNE DE GRELLET
❖

PLAY!

Of work we have enough,
of worries too often,
of sorrows too many.
Play!

Play with your dog,
play with your mate,
play alone,
play to spite the fates.

Dance and sing,
ring bells!
A jump, a kick, a cabriole,
forget all that's dull and droll,
play!

Play music, bang a drum, toot a flute,
play away the clouds,
play away the bills,
play away the tears.

Play king o' the hill,
play hide-and-seek,
play blindman's bluff,
show you are tough enough,
to play.

The grim, the gray are there each day,
standing watch, taking advantage,
nagging, pleading, reminding you of responsibilities,
worrying you to death.

The somber, the serious be damned.
Laugh in their faces and play!

ON FRIENDS

Friends whet our thirst and then quench it.

We have our "lemonade" friends, the ones who sweeten life when it hands us a lemon. Our "coffee" friends who give us a wake-up call when we need it. Our "tea" friends, comfortable as an old bathrobe in need of darning.

We have our "beer" friends, the salt-of-the-earth types with whom we might share an off-color joke and then laugh too loudly. There are the "cognac" friends, an acquired taste with a hint of melancholy and a lot of depth. There are the "wine" friends, as necessary for communion as they are to conviviality, they help to numb the pain while remaining good for the heart, and the "elderberry wine" friends in whose presence you can take off your shoes.

We have our "mint julep" friends, smooth, easy and a comfort to be around, and our "champagne" friends, witty, sparkling and a pleasure to celebrate with. The "scotch" friends who are terribly correct and proper, and a little stiff at first. The "whiskey" friends who have a kick and bite to them, who are fun to spar with and worth quoting.

There may be exotic friends – amaretto, ouzo, schnapps, grand marnier, tequila, sangria and sake – the ones who take us beyond the ordinary and excite us with their differences. The "cordials," who are on the periphery, but would still be missed. The "spiked punch" friends, those colorful confusions of tastes who we can't quite figure out, but they intrigue us. And the "milk" friends with whom we can share a cookie and a giggle.

Water, the elixir of life, the clear and ever-present friends without whom life might be unbearable and with whom we can be ourselves. And finally, the cocktails that we mix with them, some times too much of this, too little of that, but always a surprise, a joy, a "Cheers!" for the soul.

What the angels are to Heaven, friends are to this world.

THE BASSET CHRONICLES:
Driving Over Miss Daisy

We filed down the walkway on the way to the new truck. A new vehicle had been a necessity because my wife had recently swerved to miss a cat in the road and had totaled our sport utility vehicle. Nicole clutched the truck keys, the dogs jumped with glee over the chance to slobber on a different vehicle, and I lagged behind with a case of terminal dread.

"Dead man walking!" Alexis cried as I shot her a dirty look.

"Okay, you guys in the back," I said, lifting each of the Bassets onto the tailgate. The Mommy and I got into the cab of the truck.

"HEY!" Alexis yelled in my ear as she popped her head through the cab's back window. "We need more pillows back here."

"Goshdarn it," I grumbled, getting out of the truck and going back inside for an armload of bedding. I opened the back window of the truck topper and dropped in a load of blankets and pillows before returning to my co-pilot's seat.

"AND SOME POPCORN," Alexis announced.

"Alexis, this is not an entertainment outing. We are doing a dry run so your Mommy can get some experience before she has to drive to the college tonight to teach. In the dark. On windy country roads. Full of deer and other varmints."

Nicole began to bite her bottom lip.

"Lights, clutch, shift, emergency blinkers, windshield wipers," I ticked off as I pointed out the location of all the pertinent equipment.

"TUNES," a familiar brown muzzle blared in my ear again. "And none of your Baby Boomer stuff...Barbra Streisand makes my gums bleed."

"ALEXIS! Would you please make yourself comfortable and quiet. We are *not* having music."

"Why not? It would drown out the screams of terror," Alexis said.

"Ready?" I asked Nicole and wondered how long it takes Saint John's Wort to kick in.

"Tower to Daddy, tower to Daddy, we have you cleared for take-off," Alexis droned in the background.

"Alexis! Shhhhh!" I said, my hand white-knuckled on the armrest.

Nicole successfully backed the truck down the driveway and ground it into first gear as we proceeded down our lane. We stopped at the edge of the road. She looked left, she looked right, gently eased off the clutch and began to give the truck some gas...

"STOP!" Alexis shrieked.

...and popped the clutch, stalling the truck with a lurch.

"WHAT?!" we both screamed and turned around.

"I want to check the mailbox," Alexis said. "I'm expecting a letter."

"Alexis, of all the stupid stunts..."

Just then a stampeding herd of the neighbor's perpetually escaping cattle came thundering down the road at exactly where we would have been had Alexis not interrupted lift-off.

Alexis stuck her head back through the cab window and spat my cell phone into my lap.

"It's your insurance agent and she said you owe me a LOT of treats."

"I believe I have the hang of this now," Nicole announced weakly. "Shall we go home?"

"YES, PLEASE!" everyone in the truck yelled in unison. The Mommy navigated back up the lane and driveway in reverse, in a truly expert manner.

If a dog will not come to you after having looked you in the face,
you should go home and examine your conscience.
~ WOODROW WILSON
❖

CAN ANYONE HELP MY COUSIN SADIE?

I'm addressing this to all humans. I need help! My name is Stella and I'm a purebred dog – what you'd call a "breeder." I live in a huge high-volume kennel in Missouri. There are a couple thousand dogs here. I've been here about eight years (that's human years) and I figure I've had at least two hundred puppies. At least.

Oh, I don't want to give you the wrong idea...I'm not in any danger, or anything like that. There are people here who take care of us. They probably each have about a hundred dogs with litters of puppies to take care of, but they eventually get around to each of us. I know I get at least one pat on the head per day. I have a stainless steel cage and there's room enough to lie down and turn around. We get two meals a day, just dry kibble, and at least the water is clean. They even have veterinarians who work here. At first it struck us as odd that they could find people who studied to be doctors and took an oath about compassionate care of animals to work here, but they did.

But enough about me, it's my cousin Sadie I'm worried about. You see, I haven't seen her since we were puppies. We can't write or call of course, but I hear things occasionally through the "grapevine." Some of the delivery trucks that take all the puppies from where I am to pet shops also stop at the place where Sadie is, in Kansas. I hear things...and they worry me.

I've heard Sadie lives in a cold and drafty barn. That's how it is in the winter, in the summer time the barn is an oven. The man who runs the place hardly has any help and Sadie's in there with a couple hundred dogs. They have their cages up off the floor with wire bottoms, so that they're easy to hose down, dogs and all (although I hear they rarely clean them), and I'm afraid that wire must hurt Sadie's paws. I've also heard the dogs get moldy food once a day, that their water, if they have it at all, is days old and dirty. Sadie has had even more puppies than I've had and I've heard about half of them have died.

Poor Sadie! I'm just heartsick over this and I don't think there's a thing I can do about it. I expect I'll be here over the next couple of years and after that, who knows? But I'd at least like to know how Sadie is and I know if she were here with me living in luxury, she'd join me in asking:

If you all have enough puppies now, do you think we might go home sometime soon? I'm not really sure what a "home" is, but I hear the people here talk about going "home" at the end of the day, and they tell me my puppies have all gone to "homes." I figure me and Sadie might like to try out a "home" someday and see if it's to our liking.

Any help you can provide will be greatly appreciated!

Sincerely,
Your friend, Stella

...if one person is unkind to an animal, it is considered to be cruelty, but where a lot of people are unkind to animals, especially in the name of commerce, the cruelty is condoned and, once sums of money are at stake, will be defended to the last by otherwise intelligent people.
~ RUTH HARRISON
❖

RAGE OF ANGELS

The Archangel Gabriel was in a snit and everyone who worked in the west wing of the Ivory Palace was avoiding him. It had gotten so bad that his personal assistant had called in and said she was taking a "personal day." When Abacus the bookkeeper was told that he'd been tasked to be Gabriel's replacement assistant, he wasn't happy in the least. He tried calling the Department of Divine Intervention to see if they could spare an angel or two, but their line was constantly busy. He next tried Paradise Lost & Found and they promised to look into the request, but Abacus didn't think they sounded as sincere as was usual among the heavenly host. He trudged down the corridor toward Gabriel's office with his wings drooping and hesitantly knocked on the door.

"Go away! Come in! Don't just stand there – who are you and what do you want?!" the Archangel boomed.

"It's me, your Excellence," he replied nervously, "Abacus – you sent for me."

"I did? I did! Yes, well don't lollygag, get in here, we have work to do."

Gabriel went back to shuffling around piles of paper on his desk, occasionally picking up a piece of paper, then wadding it up in disgust and tossing it in the corner.

"Look at this!" he fumed and waved a newspaper clipping. "Are they all idiots?!"

"Who, sir?" Abacus asked timidly.

"THEM!" Gabriel spat and pointed earthward. "Humans. I tried to warn Him on Day One that He was making the wrong choice for a superior species, but would He listen? No! For God's sake, what was he thinking?"

Abacus winced at the language even though it was impossible to take the Lord's name "in vain" in Heaven – in fact, hardly a sentence was uttered there that didn't contain at least one reference to the Chief Executive Deity.

"What have they done now, your Lordship?" Abacus asked.

"They've started drilling for oil in the Arctic wilderness,

that's what they've done. How dare they! That's God's country and they'd do well to leave it alone, or so help me, I'll..." but instead of finishing the threat, he got up from behind the desk.

"Come here, Amos, and I'll show you what I mean."

"Abacus, your Holiness."

"No thanks, I've got a calculator," Gabriel replied and used his clipboard to part the clouds.

"Now there's an example," he said, waving his hand to create a close-up view of a woman sitting on a park bench, heavily made up with lacquered hair, tight clothing, and long fingernails.

"She's got God-given natural beauty, why in the world does she think she needs all that paint?"

Abacus stared at the image of the woman and surmised the paint was probably good for business, but he kept his opinion to himself.

"And look over there," Gabriel pointed and brought the front yard of a small home into view. All Abacus saw was a lot of human clutter mixed in between the flowers and grass.

"I'm sorry, your Splendiferousness, but I don't see anything wrong."

"A truck tire painted white and used as a flower planter – and you don't see anything wrong?! Plastic flamingoes and fake wild geese? If that's their idea of taste then it's no wonder they're such a sorry lot."

"It might not be my place to say so, sir, but we have to remember they *are* His favorites," Abacus said.

"You don't have to remind me of that! How else could they get away with everything they do? Even the religious ones are at each other's throats – Presbyterians don't like Southern Baptists..."

"Why is that, sir?" Abacus asked.

"...because at any moment a Baptist might break out singing and dancing and testifying, that's why. The Presbyterians think they are almost as reprehensible as the Pentecostals."

"They don't like Pentecostals, sir?"

"They don't trust them. It's impossible to argue with someone who is speaking in tongues. Still, they think Pentecostals are one step up from an Episcopalian."

"What's wrong with Episcopalians, sir?" Abacus asked politely.

"Why hush my mouf'," Gabriel said in a poor imitation of a sarcastic southern drawl, "if them 'piscopalians ain't ordaining gay people."

"But if you love the Lord aren't you supposed to be carefree and gay, sir?" Abacus asked innocently. Gabriel gave him a long-suffering look and continued.

"Give me some old-time Mormons...now there were some brave men," Gabriel said.

"Brave, sir? How so?" Abacus asked.

"Had more than one wife, they did. Now that's brave!" Gabriel replied.

"Well, if everyone is so unhappy with all the different denominations, why don't they just pick one and be that. Maybe Lutheran?" Abacus suggested.

"Lutheran? Ha!" Gabriel said. "Lutherans think it's sinful if you put tiny marshmallows in the jello salad you're bringing to the church social! For the love of God, I don't know what to do about these people."

Abacus shrugged and busied himself with inspecting the landscape down below.

"Look there!" Gabriel pointed, his voice seething with disdain. "Not there – there!" he said and smacked Abacus on the back of the head. "Look what that man is doing!"

Abacus held his head and squinted into the cloud portal as a scene came into view of a factory worker dumping a putrid green chemical mix into a river.

"Can you believe it?!" Gabriel ranted, jumping up and down. "Just wait until I find his file..."

Gabriel flipped through the ream of papers on his clipboard.

"Aha! Here it is. 'Future cause of death: Chemical poisoning.' Good! He'll get what he deserves later."

Abacus smiled weakly and nodded. He had to admit it was unbelievable what humans did to their planet.

"I'll tell you, Abdula, the problems caused by humans are more complicated than Madonna's lovelife," Gabriel said and then noticed his assistant's shocked look.

"Not THE Madonna, Adolph! Madonna the singer."

"I see, sir," Abacus croaked and began patting his pockets for a roll of antacid tablets. Gabriel took a step sideways, suspecting Abacus had fleas.

"Think that one was bad, Albatross? – take a look at this." Gabriel waved his hand in a circular motion and the scene changed to a collection of buildings that resembled a factory. The sound of barking dogs was deafening and the stench was incredible. Abacus sniffed and put a hand to his nose.

"That is a puppy mill," Gabriel explained, "a factory that breeds misery."

Just then a shiny black car pulled up in front of the headquarters building below and a cocky looking man chomping a cigar got out of the passenger door. Gabriel scowled. The man looked around at the concrete compound surrounded by chainlink fence and beamed with pride. Gabriel scowled deeper. Thunder began to rumble in the heavens and the man looked up and held out his hand to feel for raindrops. The last thing he saw before the delivery truck barreled down on him in the sudden blinding rain was the painted smiling face of a huge puppy on the grillwork of the truck.

"Good Lord!" Abacus shrieked and then covered his mouth in horror as the man's cigar arced through the air and landed with a hiss in a puddle. Gabriel wore a self-satisfied look.

"Your Excellence, that was...I mean surely...I don't mean to question your judgment, but really..." he stammered.

"Relax, Adolpho, it's all right here," Gabriel said as he stabbed his finger onto the clipboard. "Alfred J. Hunter, puppy mill owner. Future cause of death: Run over by 'Heaven Help Us Puppy Farm' delivery truck."

Abacus peered at the paper in disbelief and shook his head.

"It does, indeed, sir...but look at the date. It says 'December 24, 2023.'"

"Really?" Gabriel said and stared down at the notation. "What a pity," he said and smiled slightly. "Put that one down as 'clerical error.' And always remember: 'Dog spelled backward is God.'"

"As you wish, your Worshipfulness," Abacus squeaked.

Gabriel waved his arm and the scene below changed to a pastoral setting. Swallows swooped, butterflies flitted, and a doe with twin fawns came skipping across the meadow. Gabriel smiled sweetly – deer were one of his favorite species. Abacus kept looking from the scene below to Gabriel smiling and wondered if this was real or a Walt Disney film. He was about to say something appreciative when a hunter popped out from behind the bushes and shot the doe dead. Her babies fawned over each other for a millisecond and then went scampering into the woods.

"SWEET JESUS!" Gabriel bellowed and before Abacus could collect his wits the Archangel threw a lightning bolt at the hunter with such force that he nearly toppled off the cloud. The bolt missed the hunter, exploding the tree next to him into a million splinters of smoking wood. The hunter was unscathed, although he was in desperate need of a change of underwear.

Abacus felt himself swoon with fright when from behind Gabriel a golden arch appeared. Abacus decided he wasn't just faint, now he felt half hungry.

"Yes, Gabriel – what is it?" a celestial voice echoed from within the arch as a beautiful man with long flowing hair, white robes and comfortable sandals appeared.

"My Lord!" Gabriel stammered. "To what do I owe this honor?" he said as he squirmed. He took a step backward and nearly toppled over Abacus who was shaking and genuflecting.

"You tell me," the Son of God replied. "You called."

"Ah yes...that..." Gabriel said and mopped his brow. "Well, I've been thinking that we don't get much of a chance to chat anymore...what with your schedule and all...and I thought perhaps we could have lunch."

Abacus made a strangling noise as Christ pursed his lips. Out of consideration for Gabriel's millennia of outstanding service, He could overlook an "inaccuracy."

"Thank you, but no. Perhaps some other time," He said. "Speaking of schedules, shouldn't you be down there trying to clean up that mess?" He asked as He pointed toward Earth.

"I was just saying so to Alexander a moment ago," Gabriel replied and finally took his hand off of Abacus's head, which he'd been using to steady himself.

"I'm on my way."

He gave Abacus a warning look as he fanned his wings and then floated down through the opening in the clouds. When Abacus had finally regained his composure enough to focus his eyes he saw that he was alone on a patch of cloud.

"Goodness gracious!" he exclaimed. He decided that even if there was Hell to pay later, tomorrow he was calling in sick.

Gabriel floated down through the Earth's atmosphere wearing

an expression that resembled a constipated crow. It might take an Eternity to process, but he vowed that one day he was going to submit his resignation.

Animals do feel like us,
also joy, love, fear and pain
but they cannot grasp the spoken word.
It is our obligation to take their part
and continue to resist the people who profit by them,
who slaughter them and who torture them.
~ DENIS DE ROUGEMENT
❖

We have enslaved the rest of the animal creation,
and have treated our distant cousins in fur and feathers so badly that
beyond doubt, if they were able to formulate a religion,
they would depict the devil in human form.
~ WILLIAM RALPH INAGE
❖

THE BASSET CHRONICLES:
Yes, Virginia, There Is an Alexis

In between lords-a-leaping and maids-a-milking, we were trying to proceed to Christmas in some kind of orderly fashion. My wife, Nicole, being German, was insistent on observing every Christmas tradition throughout the Advent Season. She prepared refreshments for the last Advent Sunday before Christmas and we and the entire furred family gathered in the living room. The group eyed a large bowl of eggnog, Christmas cookies, and special puppy and kitty treats with a glint in their eyes.

"Dad, can Alexis tell us another Christmas story this year?" Sassy and Hercules asked in unison, and from the look on Alexis's face, I knew she'd put them up to it.

"Oh, what a lovely idea," Nicole answered before I had a chance to stop her. She had missed last year's Christmas tale.

"Be glad to," Alexis volunteered, trying to avoid my gaze. "I'm going to tell you the story of Santa Claus, or Saint Nikolaus, as he is known in Germany."

"Where's Germany?" Winston wondered.

"It's a tiny country on the other side of Pittsburgh with no parking spaces," Alexis answered. Nicole, Winnie and Flash, and the German contingent of my family raised their eyebrows.

"Mommy and Daddy were married on St. Nikolaus Day in Germany," Amadeus remembered.

"*Lovedaddy, lovedaddy, lovedaddy,*" Daphne sighed.

"Oh, for crying out loud, why don't you go back to wandering from room to room?" Alexis said to our oldest Basset girl.

"Dad, tell Alexis to be nicer," Sadie requested.

"I'll try to be nicer if you'll try to be smarter," Alexis answered. "Now, if I may continue…this is the story of Santa Claus and his worst Christmas ever."

Now my eyebrows went up and I sensed trouble on the horizon. The rest of the group gave Alexis their rapt attention and even Bamboo the Siamese ceased his shredding of the carpeted cat tree and hung by one claw while attempting to look inscrutable.

"Once upon a time, at the Santa compound in the North Pole, Santa Claus was in a very bad mood," Alexis began. "Not only was Christmas just days away, but he was very behind on his Christmas orders with no hope of catching up, because he had only that morning discovered that the Siamese kittens had chewed through his computer cables and thrown up a large hairball into his computer printer."

Alexis smirked at the kittens Bamboo, Oscar and Lucinda, and I glanced nervously at my computer, but suppressed the urge to go look. Nicole just wore a look of confusion.

"Where was Mrs. Santa Claus?" Gabriel asked.

"She'd gone to the islands with their hunky Puerto Rican pool boy to visit his sick mother," Alexis said. Nicole's look of confusion now became a gaping stare.

"And to make matter's worse," Alexis continued, "Santa couldn't get any of the parts he needed to finish his Christmas orders, because the UPS delivery truck couldn't get to Santa's workshop."

"Because of all the snow?" Tina asked.

"No! Because the whole place was surrounded by wolves – big, ugly, slobbery, rude, *vicious* wolves," Alexis said emphatically while staring at our resident wolf, who narrowed her amber eyes to slits and began to raise her hackles.

"Alright, Alexis," I intervened, "that's enough editorializing – let's get back to Santa."

"Hmmph. Well, and if that wasn't bad enough, most of Santa's reindeer were laid up and unfit for their long Christmas Eve mission," Alexis said.

"Vat vas wrong wiz zem?" Winnie asked.

"Bloat!" Alexis answered to gasps. "Tummy aches, little reindeer hooves flailing in the air, moaning and groaning – bloat."

"Bean-O! Gas-X! Turn 'em upside down and shake 'em till they burp!" the suggestions came as a litany from the crowd. I restored order as best I could and bid Alexis to continue.

"With each passing day, Santa was in an increasingly foul mood. He went to the liquor cabinet for something to steady his nerves and discovered the elves had drained everything except a bottle of Mad Dog 20-20."

"The Daddy has a funny story about Mad Dog 20-20, a

cheerleader in high school and an empty football stadium..."
Frazier began until I slapped a hand over his muzzle. Nicole gave
me her "we'll discuss this later" look.

"Didn't the reindeer have a mommy?" one of the Beagle
Boys asked, looking at Nicole with adoration.

"What am I – flypaper for idiots?" Alexis replied and just
then Daphne began to cough and wheeze. She squinted her eyes,
began chomping her jowls and contorting her mouth.

"Oh dear," Nicole said, concerned. "What's wrong Daphne?"

"Ohmygosh – she's seizing!" Alexis screamed. "Quick – I
need a crash cart, STAT! And a defibrillator. Everyone move...we
need room – and 50 cc's of lidocaine..."

"Alexis!" I interrupted. "You've been watching too much
'E.R.' – keep quiet, I think she's trying to say something."

Daphne pulled herself up to a sitting position, opened her
eyes wide, pointed her muzzle upwards and crooned
"LOVEMOMMY!"

"YAY!" the crowd cheered, except for Alexis. "Daphne has a
new word!"

"Okay, okay," I calmed the throng. "We seem to be getting
off track here. Alexis, how about continuing?"

"Now where was I?" Alexis tossed an ear over her shoulder
arrogantly. "Ah yes...so Santa was hungry, slightly inebriated,
aggravated to no end, and just then there was a knock on the
door."

"Come in!" Pongo the deaf Dalmatian barked, having
misunderstood my signing.

Alexis glared anew and continued.

"Santa rose from his easy chair, lurched to the door and threw
it open. There on the doorstep in the freezing cold and blowing
snow stood an adorable angel with golden locks.

"A very merry Christmas to you, dear Santa!" the angel said.
"We know that you have had some trying times lately and to
reward you for all you do, I've brought you this beautiful
Christmas tree!" she said and pointed behind her. Santa looked
over her head and glowered at the sparkling tree laying on the
snow.

"Where would you like me to stick it?" the little angel asked
sweetly.

"And thus," Alexis concluded, "began the tradition of the

little angel on top of the Christmas tree."

"HaHaHaHA!" Sassy and Hercules fell backwards over the couch as Nicole coughed a Christmas cookie halfway across the living room.

"Teeheehee!" the kittens danced around in glee. The Beagle Boys gave each other a "high five" and Bamboo lost his one-claw hold on the cat tree and plummeted into the eggnog. Pandemonium reigned.

"That's enough!" I yelled. "ALEXIS…"

"I'm outta here," she called back over her shoulder as the dog door slapped shut behind her.

Someday we'll remember this moment and politely change the subject.

Dogs are not our whole life,
but they make our lives whole.
~ ROGER CARAS
❖

Odd things animals. All dogs look up to you. All cats look down on you.
Only a pig looks at you as an equal.
~WINSTON CHURCHILL
❖

THE ZEN OF CAT

The Man was very sad. He knew that the Cat's days were numbered. The doctor had said there wasn't anything more that could be done, that he should take the Cat home and make him as comfortable as possible.

The man stroked the Cat on his lap and sighed. The Cat opened his eyes, purred and looked up at the Man. A tear rolled down the Man's cheek and landed on the Cat's forehead. The Cat gave him a slightly annoyed look.

"Why do you cry, Man?" the Cat asked. "Because you can't bear the thought of losing me? Because you think you can never replace me?"

The Man nodded "yes."

"And where do you think I'll be when I leave you?" the Cat asked.

The Man shrugged helplessly.

"Close your eyes, Man," the Cat said. The Man gave him a questioning look, but did as he was told.

"What color are my eyes and fur?" the Cat asked.

"Your eyes are gold and your fur is a rich, warm brown," the Man replied.

"And where is my fur the darkest?" the Cat asked.

"It is darkest along your back, your tail, your legs, nose and ears," the Man said.

"And where is it that you most often see me?" asked the Cat.

"I see you...on the kitchen windowsill watching the birds...on my favorite chair...on my desk lying on the papers I need...on the pillow next to my head at night."

The Cat nodded.

"Can you see me in all of those places now, even though your eyes are shut?" the Cat asked.

"Yes, of course. I've seen you there for years," the Man said.

"Then, whenever you wish to see me, all you must do is close your eyes," said the Cat.

"But you won't really be here," the Man said sadly.

"Oh, really?" said the Cat. "Pick up that piece of string from the floor – there, my 'toy.'"

The Man opened his eyes, then reached over and picked up the string. It was about two feet long and the Cat had been able to entertain himself for hours with it.

"What is it made of?" the Cat asked.

"It appears to be made of cotton," the Man said.

"Which comes from a plant?" the Cat asked.

"Yes," said the Man.

"From just one plant, or from many?"

"From many cotton plants," the Man answered.

"And in the same soil from which grow the cotton plants, it would be possible that other plants and flowers would grow? A rose could grow alongside of the cotton, yes?" asked the Cat.

"Yes, I'm sure it would be possible," the Man said.

"And all of the plants would feed from the same soil and drink the same rain, would they not?" the Cat asked.

"Yes, they would," said the Man.

"Then all of the plants, rose and cotton, would be very similar on the inside, even if they appeared outwardly very different," said the Cat.

The Man nodded his head in agreement, but didn't see what that had to do with the present situation.

"Now, that piece of string," said the Cat, "is that the only piece of string ever made of cotton?"

"No, of course it isn't," said the Man, "it was part of a ball of twine."

"And do you know where all of the other pieces of string are now, and all of the balls of twine?" asked the Cat.

"No, I don't...that would be impossible," said the Man.

"But even though you do not know where they are, you believe they exist. And even though some of the string is with you, and other pieces of string are elsewhere...even though some pieces of string are short and others are long, and even though your ball of twine is not the only one in the world...you would agree that all the string is related?" the Cat asked.

"I've never thought about it, but yes, I guess they would be related," the Man said.

"What would happen if a piece of cotton string fell onto the ground?" the Cat asked.

"Well...it would eventually be covered up and decompose into the soil," the Man said.

"I see," said the Cat. "Then perhaps more cotton would grow above it, or a rose."

"Yes, it would be possible," the Man agreed.

"Then the rose growing on your windowsill might be related to the string you are holding as well as to all the pieces of string you do not know about," said the Cat.

The Man knit his brow in thought.

"Now take each end of the string in one hand," the Cat ordered.

The Man did so.

"The end in your left hand is my birth and the end in your right hand is my death. Now bring the two ends together," the Cat said.

The Man complied.

"You have made a continuous circle," said the cat. "Does any point along the string appear to be different, worse or better than any other part of the string?"

The Man inspected the string and then shook his head "no."

"Does the space inside the circle appear to be different from the space outside of the circle?" the Cat asked.

Again the Man shook his head "no," but he still wasn't sure he understood the Cat's meaning.

"Close your eyes again," the Cat said. "Now lick your hand."

The Man widened his eyes in surprise.

"Just do it," the Cat said. "Lick your hand, think of me in all my familiar places, think about all the pieces of string, think about the cotton and the rose, think about how the inside of the circle is not different from the outside of the circle."

The Man felt foolish, licking his hand, but he did as he was told. He discovered what a cat must know, that licking a paw is very calming and allows one to think more clearly. He continued licking and the corners of his mouth turned upward into the first smile he had shown in days. He waited for the Cat to tell him to stop, and when he didn't he opened his eyes. The Cat's eyes were closed. The Man stroked the warm, brown fur, but the Cat was gone.

The Man shut his eyes hard as the tears poured down his face. He saw the Cat on the windowsill, then in his bed, then lying across his important papers. He saw him on the pillow next to his head, saw his bright gold eyes and darkest brown on his nose and ears. He opened his eyes and through his tears looked over at the rose growing in a pot on the windowsill and then to the circle of string he still held clutched in his hand.

One day, not long after, there was a new Cat on his lap. She was a lovely calico and white...very different from his earlier beloved Cat and very much the same.

———————

If a fish is the movement of water embodied, given shape,
then cat is a diagram and pattern of subtle air.
~ DORIS LESSING
❖

I love cats because I love my home and after a while
they become its visible soul.
~ JEAN COCTEAU
❖

ON LEARNING FROM ANIMALS

Anyone who has ever worked with animals, particularly with formerly abused or neglected animals, has observed their capacity for adaptability, their ability to forget their former lives and to respond to love. Many of these animals come to us with "baggage," and after a certain amount of reliable good care, they display little evidence of their former lives. Most animals even have the capacity to adapt following a medical trauma, such as amputation of a limb, and most throw themselves back into life as successfully on three legs as they once did on four. As they age, they do what they can do until they can't do anymore.

Animals live in the here and now, they live for the moment. They don't spend time brooding about the past, they don't worry about the future, and except in the face of clear and present danger, they aren't concerned about their own mortality.

Animals are honest. When they are happy they make the appropriate noises and they play. A warning growl is a warning to be heeded. A cry of pain means genuine pain. A lick and a caress mean affection and trust. There is no duplicity in their world and what you see is what you get.

Animals nurture their young and their lives and world revolve around their young until their young are able to go out into the world on their own, well prepared for everything they will face. Animals respect seniority and realize that their mature members have much to teach. For many animals, their lifelong relationship with their mate will be the most important relationship they will have.

Animals never ignore their own needs, they achieve balance and pursue nothing to excess. When they are hungry, they hunt or forage and eat, and they always eat what is appropriate. Because they balance nutrition and exercise, they are almost always fit. When they are tired they sleep. They pay attention to their grooming and most help to groom each other, partly for hygiene, partly as a ritual of companionship. Animals divide their day and their activities according to what it must be for them, what is good for each as an individual, what is good for all as a whole. They rebel against confinement, they own the world and they want access to it.

There is no confusion in the animal world. A foe, prey, a friendly fellow species are all immediately apparent and most are able to drink together at a common watering hole.

Animals communicate constantly and effectively. Every member of their group is at all times completely informed about the moods and needs of each member, and their present situation in their environment. When they want company, they seek it; when they want to be alone, they remove themselves from the group. There are no meaningless social graces in the animal world, every movement and action has meaning. There is no insincerity. They have optimized their senses and they drink information from the world around them.

Animals are innocent. They don't ravage the Earth. They don't hate or plot the annihilation of another species. They don't take more than they need of resources. They don't jeopardize their own survival and they accept what they cannot change.

Animals don't agonize over the existence of a Creator, or how the world came to be. How supremely arrogant of imperfect humans to claim that animals, who by their very nature are surely closer to the Creator than we, do not have souls, or that only humans are created "in His image"!

Animals are in this world, they symbolize the best of creation and all of creation beats in their breasts. Creation is for them evidence of a Creator. They are in tune, they each play a part in the rhythm of life and they are each as necessary to the music as is every instrument in a symphony.

One species has risen to the position of conductor – the Human, and like a symphony conductor, we face in the opposite direction from the musicians.

Rather than adapting and surviving, we've filled our vocabulary with "I can't," "I won't." We live lives of regret and bemoan our pasts. We don't live in the present, we exist in a mind-numbing condition of stress and second-hand information. We worry about the future, about dying, to the point that we no longer know how to live. We need outside sources of entertainment because we've forgotten how to entertain ourselves. We create imaginary worlds because we can't cope with the real world. We can hate solely on the basis of appearances without understanding the inner being. We aren't very good at expressing our needs and we are blind to recognizing needs in others. We give confusing signals – we say "yes," when we mean "no." We say "good morning" and we don't mean it. We lie to ourselves and we hide our true feelings from others.

We don't get enough sleep. We either eat too much of everything, or not enough of what our bodies require. We are poisoning ourselves with chemicals, preservatives, antibiotics and hormones hidden in our diets. We are raping the Earth. We spray every square inch of our plots of land with fertilizers and pesticides. We have wiped out whole species of animals intentionally and others through sheer ignorance, and Earth's ecology hangs precariously in the balance. We are cruel to animals.

We don't live by our senses, we've subjugated them to a senseless degree. We don't listen to our instincts, we use prejudicial reasoning. We deny our animal nature, creation is something we control and manipulate, and we don't recognize our relationship with the rest of creation, or that the Creator lives in us, because we've set ourselves apart. We use the excuse that modern life no longer allows us to be who we once were, when we know that we have the power to make life anything we wish it to be.

Perhaps our greatest sin is what we do to our young, who still begin life in innocence. We ignore them, force them to fend for themselves. We don't teach them the lessons they will need to know in order to live successfully. We fill our days and lives with the wrong values, we have no time for ourselves or our children, and we hand the children adult responsibilities before they are prepared for them. We teach greed and selfishness. Drugs and addictions have become our way of dealing with the stress of the lives we create and they've become the lessons we teach our young. We teach them to repeat our mistakes. Odd that we could do that to children and still live in a culture of youthfulness where the aged are not respected for their wisdom, they are forgotten.

It is not too late to learn lessons from the animals. Be good to yourself. Play more. Sleep more. Bask in the sun. Live each day fully and balanced. Be honest and sincere, tell the members of your group what you need and ask them about what they need. Touch...hold a hand, feel a leaf, let the stream run over your fingers. Smell, listen, see the world around you. Arrange your lives around nurturing your young. Respect and love your mate. Learn what the old have to teach. Let go of greed. Protect and stop poisoning your environment. Eat only when you are hungry and only what you should eat. Adapt and survive. Realize that you are not alone and accept that you have something to contribute to the pack. Turn off the artificial noise, the mechanical drone and be here now, in this world. It is a beautiful world and you are a part of creation, and in your heart beats all that the Creator intended.

The world is waiting for us to get back in step with the music, to fearlessly turn our backs to the musicians and to face in the same direction as they. To once again gather at the same watering hole.

———————

Ask the experimenters why they experiment on animals,
and the answer is: 'Because the animals are like us.'
Ask the experimenters why it is morally okay to experiment on animals,
and the answer is: 'Because the animals are not like us.'
Animal experimentation rests on a logical contradiction.
~ PROFESSOR CHARLES R. MAGEL
❖

It's inexcusable for scientists to torture animals;
let them make their experiments on journalists and politicians.
~ HENRIK IBSEN
❖

THE MESSENGER

I dreamed I came upon a meadow
sunlit and fragrant, a small dog at my side.
As we walked on in silence I saw
across the blue ribbon of a river, a field,
where animal spirits licked the morning dew
from brilliant poppies...basked in sunshine...
batted at butterflies.

"Is this Heaven?" I asked.
He nodded yes and as we rounded a bend in the path,
I saw ahead a wondrous garden
surrounded by a halo of mist,
where animals and children lay among the flowers.
Cool breezes rustled leaves
and over all hung an aura of beauty and peace.

"Is this Heaven, too?" I asked.
"An honored place," he said, "for those who lived
a Hell on Earth – who died of neglect, torture,
unloved, unwanted and abandoned."

We walked on until we came to a precipice
that overlooked a dark canyon.
Lightning crashed above the horizon
and illuminated iron prisons on the desert floor.
I heard the wails of captive men,
the screams of women imploring for water,
railing against the absence of Light amidst an acrid smoke.

Before I could ask he answered, "These were their tormentors."

We continued solemnly
until the sound of laughter and music greeted us,
and we came upon a village square,
where carefree women, children and men played at games,
or walked arm in arm.
"They are happy," I said.
He agreed and replied, "These were their rescuers.
They are blessed above all."

I spent time among them until I awoke, bathed in a new peace.
For whatever this Earthly day may bring,
I knew that no wrongful deed goes unpunished,
nor is any saving grace without its reward.

I hugged my small dog closer to my chest
and blessed him as a messenger of truth and love.

We call them dumb animals, and so they are,
for they cannot tell us how they feel,
but they do not suffer less because they have no words.
~ ANNA SEWELL

If you have men who will exclude any of God's creatures
from the shelter of compassion and pity,
you will have men who will deal likewise with their fellow men.
~ SAINT FRANCIS OF ASSISI

WORTH WISDOM

If it costs more than you can afford,
it probably is not worth it.
If it will make someone's life better, it is worth it.
If you feel it is sapping your soul, it is not worth it.
If you feel you are learning something, it is worth it.

If they are never on time,
they might not think you are worth it.
If they forget your birthday,
they definitely do not think you are worth it.
If they give you gifts for no reason,
they think you are more than worth it.
If you are always giving and they are always taking,
it is not worth it.

If they communicate to ask how you are and not just to say how
they are,
if they support your decisions,
even the ones they don't agree with,
or fully understand,
then they are true friends and they are worth it.

If you left them in a better condition than when you found them, it
was worth it.
If you put the earned money to good use,
it is probably worth it.
If it involves killing anything, it is not worth it.
If it involves saving a life, it is always worth it.
If it does not restore quality of life, it may not be worth it.
If it damages your health, it is not worth it.

If you wasted time but it made you feel good,
it was worth it.
If it took courage to do, even though you failed,
it was worth it.
If it made you feel that you were better than you thought you
could be, it was worth it.
If it has turned from a casual pursuit into something that rules your
life, and it does not help others,
it is probably not worth it.
If you helped someone who couldn't help herself,
it was worth it.
If the other person refuses to help herself,
it probably is not worth it.

If it requires saying something unkind, it is not worth it.
If winning the argument is more important than finding out why
the other person believes what he believes,
it is not worth it.
If it improves your environment, it is worth it.
If it damages the environment, it is not worth it.
If it is intended to make a statement of your status,
it is not worth it.

If you had to tell a lie, it probably was not worth it.
If you spared someone hurt feelings,
it probably was worth it.
If you paid someone a compliment,
it was worth it to both.
If you had to talk someone into doing something he did not
consider right, it was not worth it to either.

If it was only for physical gratification,
it probably was not worth it.
No matter how simple, if you found something edifying in it, it
was worth it.
If it improved communication, it was worth it.
If the only reason to do it is financial gain,
it probably is not worth it.
If it makes you feel beautiful, it is worth it.

If you sleep better at night because of doing it,
it is worth it.
If it makes you lie awake at night, it is not worth it.
If it damages your relationship with your partner either it is not
worth it, or your partner is not.
If it is the honorable thing to do, even though it is difficult, it is
worth it.

If anyone tells you that you do not have worth,
they are wrong.
You have worth.

❖

I care not for a man's religion
whose dog and cat are not the better for it.
~ ABRAHAM LINCOLN
❖

Believing as I do that man in the distant future
will be a far more perfect creature than he is now,
it is an intolerable thought that he and all other sentient beings
are doomed to complete annihilation after such long-continued progress.
To those who fully admit the immortality of the human soul,
the destruction of our world will not appear so dreadful.
~ CHARLES DARWIN

WHAT SHALL I CALL YOU?

I'm not sure how I should address you.
Should I call you God? – or Yahweh, Jehovah, The Creator,
The Great Spirit...The Goddess?
I only know that I've been aware of your presence
for most of my life.

I've heard your voice in the howl of the wind,
and the mournful cry of the loon skating across the lake.
I've seen your face etched in snow-capped mountains
in the distance,
and reflected in the rippling pools of mountain streams.
I've seen your shadow pass across gold-tinged clouds
of streaming blue and pink.
I've felt your breath in desert winds and sea breezes.
I've felt your touch in the warmth of the sun
and cold blasts of Arctic air.
I've watched your tears run in rivulets to raging rivers
until the parched ground was steaming.
I've seen your light break into a rainbowed beacon of hope
and illuminate the coast after a storm.
I've seen your artistry in the gnarled hands of an old woman
struggling to perform the tasks of her girlhood,
and your courage in a disabled person succeeding against all odds.
I've felt your absence in the deeds of men.

Only I don't know how to address you.

I've seen your divine intervention at work in our lives,
and felt your presence in the lick of a dog,
the purr of a cat,
the nuzzle of a horse,
and in the cry of the wolf as she pursues her prey.

In a mother's embrace.

I've felt your love on a starry night,
in the lapping of the waves against the shore.

In the birth of a child.

In a father's kiss.

I've smelled you in crisp mountain air tart with pine,
and in the intoxicating perfume of lavender in bloom.
In woodsmoke and mown orchard grass.

In the scent of a woman.
In the sweat of a man.
And in a baby's breath.

I've heard your footstep in the crack of lightning,
in boughs breaking under the weight of snow,
in the thunder of caribou hooves racing across the plains.
In the silence that follows death.
I've felt your passing in the fog that descends on valleys.

While others explain you in lofty terms and weighty tomes,
and search for a relationship with you,
or for clues to your existence,
I wonder why they don't know you are in us all.
I feel you there, deep inside, and know that we are all created by
you, in you, and you in we.
We are one and I know you by heart.
Only I don't know how to address you.

And what of "commandments" and sermons preached by man
about how we should live in harmony with you and your wishes?
How do we sort out your words from theirs?
Perhaps they amuse you...perhaps not as much as our depictions of
you in our art.

What of our temples and cathedrals,
and monuments built in your honor?
...when all you desire is that we construct something honorable in
our hearts.
What of prayers and supplications, rituals and sacrifice?
Life is a prayer, faith is living and not giving up,
and Love is the answer.
Isn't that what you've planted in our hearts?

It's really very simple, isn't it?
Believe.
Love, honor, respect, appreciate,
and leave this world a little better than we found it.
Everything, including these words, is a gift from you.

You exist beyond the confines of time,
and we, with our temporal constraints, struggle to comprehend.
You embody all these things and more,
omniscient and omnipotent.

Only I don't know how to address you.
Forgive me, bless me, heal me, help me.

Regard Heaven as your father,
Earth as your mother, all things as brothers and sisters,
and you will enjoy the divine country that excels all others.
~ TRADITIONAL SHINTO SAYING
❖

THE CREATOR'S LAMENT

Tell them below in the valleys!
Proclaim it now from the hills!
This is the world I created for you,
yet perfection you've sought to kill.

For centuries I've kept silent,
But now the truth must be told,
Your insolence is appalling,
What have you done to my world?

Warn them, your brothers and sisters,
Admonish them for their hate,
You were created from a common seed,
And you share a common fate.

The creatures are your family,
As dear to me as you,
Help them live well, I beg you,
Not one do I wish to lose.

You may not heed me now,
You may think this world you own,
But it was gifted to you by my grace,
Every tree, every stream, every stone.

Appreciate what I've made for you,
Be kind to your fellow man,
Love the wonder of all Creation...
Or reap the whirlwind by my hand.

I AM!

I may have weak moments,
but I am not weak.
I may not always do what is right,
but I am essentially good.
I may not always be lovable,
but I am worth loving.
I may be ignored,
but I have something worth saying.
I may be alone,
but I am never lonely.
I may be surrounded by chaos,
but I will have peace within.
I may not always notice need,
but I care.
I may see need and not have a solution,
but I will make a contribution.
I will accept what I cannot change,
only until I find a way to change it.
I may not have the answer,
but I will help find it.
I may have a problem,
but I will not be a problem.
I may not always know the truth,
but I am honest.
I may encounter evil,
but I believe good shall prevail.
The past is over, today is here,
tomorrow will come,
I know how I should devote my energy.
I may seem infinitesimal,
but I am a child of the universe.
I am an individual,
but I am a part of creation.

In truth, no man is above another,
the pauper and the prince are brothers.
The Creator inhabits the broad expanse,
and also lives in my heart.
My body may be ravaged,
but my soul is invincible.
My earthly days are numbered,
but my soul is eternal.
Time without end, love that survives,
harmony forever...
I am!

My music is best understood by children and animals.
~ IGOR STRAVINSKY

All beings tremble before violence. All fear death, all love life.
See yourself in others. Then whom can you hurt? What harm can you do?
~ THE BUDDHA

ON WRITING

Because I write, people who aspire to the writing life often ask me about how to begin as a writer. The bad news is that there aren't any shortcuts; the good news is that almost anyone intrigued enough about the process to ask the question can write. You begin at the beginning...you write. That's assuming that you've already done the groundwork and that is reading.

Reading is the foundation and framework of the writer. Writers read everything they can lay their hands on, including the backs of cereal boxes and milk cartons. There is even something to be learned from marketing and advertising texts, such as economy of words, simple language and conjuring thoughts and enticing feelings. A supposedly true anecdote is told in publishing circles about the Midwest farmer who mail-ordered a book he had seen advertised in a magazine. After he received his order he wrote to the publisher, "I read your ad and I bought the book. I wish to God that the same man who wrote the ad had written the book!"

You must read the classics, Dickens, Thoreau, Wilde and more. You need to read some contemporary masters, Annie Proulx, Annie Dillard, Terry McMillan, Stephen King, John D. MacDonald, Andre Dubus III and J.K. Rowling. Digest them, analyze them, compare them. What relates those authors is the ability to tell a damn good story and that's *all* we writers are, storytellers. You won't be able to duplicate their language, that belongs exclusively to them, but take heart in the fact that you have an English-language vocabulary of half a million words to decide from about which word to put after which.

Read writings in your areas of interest, more importantly, read outside your usual scope of interest. If you challenge yourself as a reader, you'll be better prepared for the challenges of writing. Read poetry and prose and discover that they take you to places far greater than the sum of words. If you think you won't like prose because it doesn't rhyme, or think that because it doesn't have the constraints of rhyme that it is easy to write, how many who felt the same way were mesmerized by the reading of Auden's haunting prose during the funeral scene in the film "Four Weddings and a Funeral"? Prose and poetry should be read aloud – they don't achieve their full impact when they are allowed to sit static on the printed page. If you love language, experience them.

Read plays and see how dialogue can define the characters, tell the story and move the plot forward. Allow Tennessee Williams's characters to soothe you with honeyed speeches dripping with gardenias – and then he'll stab you in the heart with their words.

Read the inimitable genius, Shakespeare, and watch modern film translations of his work. How *did* he do it? We will never know, but nobody since has done it any better.

Read about the craft of writing and what other writers have to say about it. Read any number of the magazines and books that list resources for writers and explain how to follow the "rules" of publishing. Only after you are very good at following the rules will you be allowed to break some of them...maybe.

Aspiring writers often say, "I've only ever written term papers," – or press releases, or news articles, or whatever. But you have *written*. You have already learned to conquer the fear of the blank page. Writing news or non-fiction or business writing is excellent training for writing fiction. You've already learned how to be disciplined about writing, you now simply add in the components of creativity and imagination, and most of us have more of those than we realize when we first begin.

Before you begin you must forget about being published and commercial success. Many of the best writers never achieved "commercial success" during their lifetimes, yet some of their works can still be found on library shelves hundreds of years later and are required reading in schools. Some of those authors didn't begin writing, or writing for publication, until late in life. The wisdom you've accumulated over years can only help your writing and it's never too late to start. At most, you may be able to supplement your present income and you should listen to the advice of writers who have achieved success, "don't give up your day-job." You'll suffer enough mental turmoil as you wrangle with words without adding insolvency to the mix.

We write because we have to – the problem is not how to begin, but how to turn it off. We recognize each other by the far away looks in our eyes; we hold conversations with ourselves and practice dialogue. We eavesdrop on real people talking. We scribble notes on any available scrap of paper, or chant into mini-cassette recorders. We'll be halfway through a room when a poetic phrase or story idea will pop into our brains and we'll forget why we entered the room in the first place. We will always read another's work and wish we could write like that. We will breeze through ninety-nine percent of a piece and then fret for days over the one sentence we can't whip into shape. We are never happy with our writing, we will never be happy with our writing. In public we'll assure everyone that we are no different than anyone else who works, we're the same as a plumber or an electrician. "It's just a job," we shrug (although most of us live below the poverty level). In secret, we acknowledge that the curse of a writing life is one of our greatest blessings and seeing our name in print is its own reward.

You must write every day...anything at all, a paragraph, a rewrite of an old piece, a letter to your mother, a very creative to-do list.

You must learn to be your own editor. Put away the things you've written for a while in your desk drawer. Take them out some time later and look at them again. Be detached; make the "author" defend every word and phrase. Practice taking out all the adjectives, all the adverbs, and putting them back one at a time and only if you can justify each one. Be ruthless. Look at the structure of the writing – does it flow? Does the lead paragraph suck you in and does the story propel you through it until you arrive breathless at the end? Does it say what you mean? Does the writing answer all the necessary questions of who, what, where, when, how and why, and does it do so in a necessary order? Do the characters live and do they talk like real people? Does their speech create images of them without benefit of descriptions? Will the reader care about them, love them or hate them? Know when to quit editing and how to hold on to the original inspiration that breathed life into the piece.

Keep the language of your writing simple. You had to learn to crawl before you could ride a bicycle. In fact, if you own a thesaurus pick it up now and throw it into a far corner! Read it on occasion and learn some new good words, words that capture exactly the essence of what you might mean sometime, but a thesaurus serves no purpose while you are writing. There are a lot of adjectives and adverbs that describe the act and manner in which we love, and a lot of synonyms that shade the degrees of love, but I'll bet when you are writing about love, you mean "love," and nothing else but "love" will do. Some of your brilliance will suffer if the reader has to look up definitions during the climax of your story.

Stop worrying about your commas and rules of grammar – nobody except a copy editor and your high school English teacher understands them anyway. You can fix those problems later, or a copy editor will before you're published. One editor pointed out that I often use sentence fragments. I *think* in sentence fragments, most people do. People talk in sentence fragments. I know my reader is completely competent in stringing my fragments together and formulating a complete thought. Hemingway built an entire literary career on fragmented thoughts that he wove together beautifully. Note that I'm talking about fiction, where we have the luxury of stylistic vagaries, and I'm not suggesting you violate English grammar. There are classic short books on style and grammar that you can obtain from any bookstore and many word processing programs have language correction functions and tips.

Write for yourself. It has been said that writing is like opening a vein and it is. There will be days when you will extract one precious drop at a time and other days where you'll experience an arterial gush. There is no such time as a day in which you can't write. You must learn to write in and about confusion, frustration, mental paralysis and pain, and impending financial ruin, because that is life and you should not be immune to any of the experiences that you will put your characters through. If you are suffering "writer's block," write about it! I came home from dealing with my father's suicide and wrote an e-mail message to some friends telling them about it. It was a terribly self-indulgent act and therapeutic, and reading it must have been painful for them, but I had to do it. In moments of peace or crisis, I am a writer. If I didn't get it out on paper, I might implode. (E-mail has become the plague of the writer's friends and family, because it allows us to assault them immediately.)

Create in your mind a mental image of your imaginary reader. Who is he or she? What interests her, what makes him angry, what is that person passionate about? Write to them. Achieve a balance – don't insult your reader's intelligence by explaining things she already knows, don't make your reader work too hard to understand what you're writing about. Your reader *enjoys* coming up with her own mental pictures of your characters and settings, don't spoil her fun by describing the character's acne scars and that his coffee table is scratched and chipped unless there is a point to it. Set your stages sparsely and allow your reader to finish decorating them. A beginning writer's common mistake is not allowing enough room for his reader's imagination. A reader's most common mistake is assuming that everything a writer writes about the writer has personally experienced or harbors a desire for. If that were true, Stephen King's neighbors would have burned him at the stake long ago. Readers sometimes don't give writers enough credit for imagination. I wonder how many people have accosted King on the street and told him "You are one sick individual!"?

Most of all, write from the heart. The mind is the technician who strings the words together, who hammers them into place, who blows off the eraser dust. The heart is the soul of the writing, the truth teller, and the inspiration.

Over a decade ago I wrote a story on a difficult subject, death, intended to give children a way of comprehending death and perhaps allow parents an opportunity to discuss the subject with their children. Over thirty publishers declined to publish it and I saved one of the rejection letters. It said, "You have the power to evoke powerful emotions, please don't stop writing. However, this work is not commercial." The editor then asked if she could keep the copy of the manuscript for herself and share it with friends who had experienced a loss. Years later, the journalist wife of a movie star published a children's book on the same theme and it was a commercial success. I have included my story, "Christine's Magic Box," in this book, because I still believe in it and after having experienced some painful human and animal losses over the past decade, it still means something to me. I hope it will mean something to you and that is far more important than "commercial success." (I also include it with a bit of "take that!" attitude toward "commercial" publishing.)

I receive a lot of mail from readers. Most often they write to say something I wrote is "nice," or "beautiful," occasionally they tell me their own interesting stories, and sometimes they tell me about a meaning in one of my works that I didn't recognize is there. Readers will never stop surprising you with their capacity to educate you. That is encouraging because it means the reader is doing her job.

Recently, I received a message from a woman who asked me to please stop publishing "schmultz" and "drivel," and who claimed that my writings give her a stomachache. I printed her message and hung it above my computer, and I'd like to tell her two things: 1) "schmaltz" is spelled with an "a," and 2) thank you. Eliciting any response from a reader, even physical discomfort, means that the writer is doing his job.

Since I often write about animals for animal-people, most of the questions I receive about writing come from that community. I believe animal-people are more in tune, including with their self and their creativity. If there is a common denominator among those who love animals, it is heart, and I can think of no better qualification for a writer. You already have the most essential component, you need only work on your technique, and that you will learn by reading and by doing, and in the doing you will find your "voice." Everyone has a story to tell, probably more than one, so tell it and tell it well. If you are happy with the end result, if your imaginary reader appreciates it and your self-editor has approved it, we readers will, too, even if it's only published on the back of a milk carton.

There is another old saw in publishing that says that two kinds of work always sell, anything written about Abraham Lincoln and dog stories. I've long threatened only half-jokingly that someday I *will* write a story about Abraham Lincoln's dog...that is unless one of you writes it first.

I am in favor of animal rights as well as human rights.
That is the way of the whole human being.
~ ABRAHAM LINCOLN
❖

THE EAGLE
HAS BEEN AWAKENED

The eagle has been awakened,
by the screams of humanity,
by the roar of countless souls sent heavenward,
by the cries of children,
by the sobs, the weeping amidst falling debris.

She has flexed her talons
and spread her wings.
Her golden eyes flicker
as she peers through the billowing smoke and flames.

She is searching for a sign,
a scurry, a rustle, the squeak of fear.
Be very afraid, you who hate democracy,
who are willing to spill the blood of innocents.
Her justice is swift and her retribution is terrible.

Until she perches again, alert,
waiting and watching,
for the peace of a new day.

*Dedicated to the men and women who protect
our safety and freedom. Thank you.*

To Our Redeemers

We had grown complacent,
some had worshipped greed,
some ignored friends and family,
those who suffered, those in need.

We did not know we'd lose you,
one bright September morn,
and now we weep and curse,
the loss that we must mourn.

We wish that we had told you,
how much you meant to us,
as you went to work that day,
to forgive ourselves we must.

Now as we sort through rubble,
in grief and terrible pain,
we want to tell you now,
you did not die in vain.

The next morning we awoke,
a resolve was made anew,
it could have happened to any,
the tragedy that struck you.

Now the world has come together,
against a common sin,
and because of your example,
this war we know we'll win.

The future is uncertain,
but we are unafraid,
we are each a little stronger,
because of the price you paid.

Two thousand years since one man died
to save our eternal souls,
your cross was made of steel and glass,
and you died to make us whole.

*Dedicated to the victims of the
September 11th, 2001 tragedy.
You did not die in vain.*

Who sees with equal eye, as God of all,
A hero perish or a sparrow fall,
Atoms or systems into ruin hurl'd,
And now a bubble burst, and now a world.
~ ALEXANDER POPE FROM "AN ESSAY ON MAN"

THE BASSET CHRONICLES:
It's Not DiGiorno, It's Despicable

I came in the back door carefully carrying the pizza box and savoring the delicious aroma. Alexis, the ever suspicious, met me at the door.

"What's that?" she asked.

"It's a pizza...my dinner. Ever since your mother left for Europe, I've subsisted on salad and macaroni and cheese, and I can't face another meal of it."

"Is that pepperoni I detect?" Alexis asked.

"Err – yes. Now go away."

"Isn't that an unusual menu choice for a vegetarian?" Alexis continued.

"I don't deny it, but pepperoni is my one weakness. I walked by the pizza shop and I couldn't resist. I'm only human, plus I'm half Italian...pepperoni is in my blood."

"So then, Mr. Animal Advocate is going to forsake years of preaching and resort to HYPOCRISY!" Alexis sniffed.

The pizza began to lose some of its delicious aroma.

"I suppose I deserve that snide comment. I'll admit it, I'm weak. I'll light candles or something in retribution."

"It's your reputation." Alexis sighed.

"Alexis, give me a break. It's not like I killed the cow who went into the pepperoni!"

"That argument won't wash. What was it Sir Paul McCartney said?...if slaughterhouses had glass walls, nobody would eat meat?"

The pizza suddenly became a symbol of carnage.

"I...uh...well, perhaps it wasn't as carefully thought out as I..."

"Wait a minute," Alexis paused. "Aren't you the guy who wrote 'How Could You?'"

"You know it," I said.

"Then HOW COULD YOU?!"

"Oh for pity's sake – okay! You win. I guess I'll bury it up on the hill and hold some sort of memorial service," I said and looked sorrowfully at the pizza box. I grumbled as I began rummaging in the refrigerator looking for something to eat. I took out a carton of eggs.

"Are those free-range eggs from happy chickens?" Alexis asked innocently.

"NO, THEY ARE NOT," I said. "The local grocery store only sells factory-produced eggs. I don't like it, but I can't change it."

"I wasn't suggesting you could," Alexis said and acted offended. "I was only thinking of those poor little chickens with their beaks cut off, forced into molting, living out their lifetimes in cramped wire boxes until their tiny little feet are deformed."

I threw open the refrigerator door and it slammed into the kitchen counter. I stuck my head into it and muttered to myself.

"Don't forget my dinner," Alexis reminded.

I extracted a few items and began mixing them in a bowl. I picked up Alexis's food bowl from the floor and shoveled it full, and put it back down with a *plunk*.

"There!" I pointed. "Bon appetit."

Alexis peered into her bowl and glared.

"What *is* this?" she asked.

"It's green beans, tofu and bean sprouts."

"*Ewww*. I thought you believed in biologically appropriate diets for animals?" she said. "Here's a newsflash – I am a CARNIVORE!"

"Not tonight you aren't. You'll eat it or you'll go hungry."

She sat there with a perplexed look and made faces.

"Perhaps I was a little hasty with my comments earlier," she granted. "Look, I'll make a deal with you. We'll split the pizza."

I opened the pizza box and looked longingly at the golden crust, the delicately crisp pepperoni, the puddles of melted cheese. It started to look appetizing again.

"I don't know...it's wrong. It's against my beliefs," I said.

"Well, it's not like you killed the cow yourself," Alexis reminded me. "And don't worry, I'll never breathe a word of it, not even to the Queen of Brussels Sprouts."

"She'll find out when she calls," I said. "She'll hear it in my voice. She can probably smell pepperoni on my breath through the phone lines."

"What are you, a man or a wimp?!" Alexis asked peevishly. "Divvy up that pie and we'll repent later."

"Okay," I decided. "But we're never doing this again as long as we live."

"Fine," Alexis agreed. "If it will ease your conscience, I'll take four slices, you get two."

I have no doubt that it is a part of the destiny of the human race, in its gradual improvement, to leave off eating animals.
~ HENRY DAVID THOREAU
❖

But for the sake of some little mouthful of flesh we deprive a soul of the sun and light, and of that proportion of life and time it had been born into the world to enjoy.
~ PLUTARCH
❖

Killing animals for sport, for pleasure, for adventures, and for hides and furs is a phenomenon which is at once disgusting and distressing. There is no justification in indulging in such acts of brutality.
~ HIS HOLINESS THE XIV DALAI LAMA OF TIBET
❖

THE BASSET CHRONICLES:
Olan Puppy Mills Studios

Watching for our rural mail carrier lately has been both a joyous occasion and a reason for dread. We had signed up for a Basset Hound "Howliday" card exchange and the homemade cards that arrived daily, one cuter than the next, generated a lot of smiles. There were Bassets in holiday costume, groups of Bassets posed in front of fireplaces, impeccably groomed Bassets surrounded by immaculately dressed children...cards with stickers, cards with bows, cards with glitter.

I am a decent photographer, if I can remember where I put my camera. I have a computer and color printer ("Which one of you cats upchucked a hairball in my printer?!"). We have five Bassets in our household and the chance of getting all five into the same photo, in focus, properly lit, well-groomed and without bloodshed, is about the same as the Florida Supreme Court determining that I actually won the election. The chance of five individual photos being acceptable and ready for this Christmas...I wouldn't have time to do the math.

I walked my fingers through the yellow pages looking for a photography studio, found one with a national reputation and made an appointment.

"Darling," I said to my wife, "I have decided to enlist professional help."

"Therapy is nothing to be ashamed of dear," she replied encouragingly.

"No! I'm taking the Bassets to a photo studio for a holiday portrait. Want to come along?"

"No thank you. I think I'll do something fun, like have my wisdom teeth extracted."

I made Flash, Alexis, Hyacinth, Gabriel and Gallagher as presentable as possible, which for a Basset means clean ears and neatly trimmed nails. This is not a quiet enterprise.

"AAAAGH! Murderer! I'm calling the ASPCA. You cut that one too short, I'm bleeding to death. Mama! My ears, my ears, I'm now permanently deaf. HELP! You got ear cleaner in my eyes. I'm blind. I swallowed a Q-tip, I'm choking."

Next, I had to get the truck ready with blankets, pillows, paper towels for accidents, and treats to keep everybody happy.

"Is everybody ready?" I asked as I came back in.

"Here, sign this – all three copies," Alexis answered and laid a sheaf of papers at my feet.

"What is this?" I asked as I flipped through the pages.

"It's from my agent at the William Morris Agency. Photographic model releases."

"Cut the crap, Alexis, and get in the truck."

The dogs and I drove to the studio in a festive mood, making up Christmas carols along the way. The Bassets particularly distinguished themselves on "Bark, the Herald Angels Sing" and "Oh, Howly Night."

A nervous looking photographer wearing a beret met us in the studio's reception area and introduced himself as Monsieur Lentille.

"It eez a plaisure to meet you," he shook my hand lightly. "And thees is zee little doggies – petite chiens!"

Alexis scowled.

"We will go in now. Please make l'arrrrangement of zee dogs on zee pedestal."

Alexis scowled deeper.

"We will take zees first film wizout flash," he explained.

Flash looked utterly dejected. Alexis smiled.

I figured out that Msr. Lentille meant he'd be using natural light. I picked up the dogs, one at a time, and placed them on the different heights of the posing platform, in what I hoped was a suitable "l'arrrrangement." The dogs looked calm and thoughtful, which is always a dangerous sign.

"Eeez everybody ready?" Msr. Lentille asked and I nodded.

"OO-ooo-OOO! Who cut the cheese?" Alexis coughed.

"Gabriel," said Gallagher.

"I did not!" protested Gabriel, "it was Flash."

"Hmmph! It vasn't me," Flash said and looked pointedly at Hyacinth. Hyacinth repeated her mistake.

"ACK! *Gag* Get me down from here, I'm suffocating," Alexis howled.

"What is zee problem?" asked Msr. Lentille, obviously not

able to understand Basset, which doesn't explain his lack of olfactory sense.

"Whew!" I waved my hand in front of my nose. "That'll be enough of that, please. Now let's compose ourselves and take some good photos."

"Ready?" Msr. Lentille asked again, apprehensively. I nodded and Alexis squinted at Hyacinth suspiciously.

"OW!" Hyacinth howled.

"What now?" I asked.

"Somebody nipped me."

"Alexis!" I said accusingly.

"Not me, I – oh great, wake him up before he....LOOK OUT!"

Old Flash had dozed off and leaned against Gallagher, creating a domino effect. Bassets pitched and rolled and toppled off their perches. Umbrella lights swayed and dived. Msr. Lentille sidestepped and got tangled in his tripod, and the crash had an expensive ring to it. The mélange of "petite chiens" resembled British fans at a rugby match.

"OW! My tail! Somebody get off my tail. Arf! Get your big paw off my ear! MOVE. Get your muzzle out of my face, poop breath. How dare you. Dad! She bit my ear."

"ENOUGH!" I hollered.

Msr. Lentille extricated himself from the crash site, wiping his brow and moaning over the state of his equipment.

"Mon Dieu! My equipment, she is ruined!" he wailed, wiping drool off his portrait lens.

"Oh, I am *so* sorry," I apologized.

"Sorry! You will get zee bill for all of zees. I am an arteest – zees is a travesty. You will pleeze remove theez monsters immediately. I am summoning zee gendarmes!"

"Yes sir," I squeaked.

We spent a complicated afternoon and drove home in a subdued mood, too worn out for even one stanza of the "AROOO-lujah Chorus."

"Goodness, you were gone a long time. How did the portraits turn out?" my wife asked as the criminal element filed back into the house.

"They are called 'mugshots.' It was the biggest pawprinting experience the local constabulary has ever seen. I used the holiday postage money to post bail and nobody is going to believe why our Christmas cards are late."

———————

All animals are equal, but some animals are more equal than others.
~ GEORGE ORWELL, "ANIMAL FARM"
❖

I gave my cat a bath the other day...they love it. He sat there, he enjoyed it, it was fun for me. The fur would stick to my tongue, but other than that...
~ STEVE MARTIN

THE BASSET CHRONICLES:
Anyone Want a Kitten for Six Dollars?
(I Have to Make a Profit)

It was nearly dusk when I walked out the front gate with my Sheltie "Sadie" at my side and my arms full of treats and a lightweight blanket for my horse, "Cynnamon."

"How come Sadie always gets to go to the barn with you and not me?" Alexis asked through the fence.

"Because Sadie knows how to behave around horses. You, on the other hand, cause stampedes when you are bored."

"It's not my fault if horses are...," but Alexis was interrupted by a dilapidated car wheezing and gasping up our driveway. The canine early warning system rushed to the fence and began yowling. An old man got out of the car apprehensively.

"You the man who rescues animals?" he asked and I smiled slightly as the menagerie behind me threatened to scale the chainlink.

"I have a kitten in my trunk," he said. "I can't keep him. Mr. Carney down the road wouldn't take him, said he only wants girls and this 'un's a boy. Said maybe you'd take him."

I stared at the rusty metal of the car trunk and thought how my talk with Mr. Carney about his production of kittens had been only half as effective as I'd hoped. The old man unlocked the trunk and lifted out a cardboard box. A tiny meow escaped and he undid the flaps of the box, pulling out a little bit of gray fluff. The about seven-week-old kitten blinked as snow flurries settled on his whiskers.

"I been feeding him milk, but I can't hardly buy groceries for myself," the man said. "I don't want to see him killed. Will you take him? Please, sir."

I gathered the kitten into my shirt and he began purring. I nodded "yes." I looked closer at the man, his worn clothes and his battered car. Maybe he thought I thought he had more means than he had.

"I can't afford to give you no money," he said. "Wish I could, but I can't."

"That's okay," I replied. "We'll take good care of this little guy, have him neutered and find him a good home."

The old man nodded in satisfaction. I wished him a good evening and turned to walk away and bring the kitten into the house. Instead I turned back toward the man and pulled a five-dollar bill out of my shirt pocket and pushed it into his shirt pocket.

"For your trouble. Thanks for looking out for the little guy."

The old man nodded his thanks and got back into his car stiffly. We exchanged a last knowing look, that in this rural area of "real men hate cats," we were both failures. I watched him drive away and felt the kitten nuzzling against my chest. I had a warm feeling and it was one of those moments filled with the milk of human kindness.

Alexis glared at me and took the porch steps in one leap, shooting through the dog door.

"MOM! THE MONEY YOU GAVE THE DADDY TO BUY MILK WITH IS GONE BECAUSE HE JUST BOUGHT A MANGY MUTT KITTEN FROM SOME OLD GEEZER!"

There are no ordinary cats.
~ COLETTE
❖

YOU KNOW YOU ARE
OWNED BY PETS WHEN...

Running out of paper towels is a household crisis.

You not only know all the characteristics of a good "stool," you discuss them at dinner.

You have a mental list of people you'd like to spay or neuter.

Your checks have messages on them like "Subtract Two Testicles for Every Four Feet."

You consider "The Culture Clash" your bible and believe the chairman of Disney Corp. is the anti-Christ.

You have a bumper sticker that reads "My Basset Hound Is Smarter Than Your Graduate Student."

You can compare and contrast the finer elements of different kitty litter brands the way some people talk about wine.

You secretly wonder about such things as how animals can manage without wiping.

You pray they will someday manufacture Teflon furniture.

You have phone calls forwarded to PetsMart.

When your animal projectile vomits, you compare the speed and trajectory with previous incidents, and if the statistics fall short, you worry if the animal is okay.

You absentmindedly pat people on the head or scratch them behind their ears.

Given the choice of having your teeth cleaned or their teeth cleaned, they get their teeth cleaned.

You not only allow pets on the couch, guests have to sit on the floor because the dog has "territorial issues." Your spouse missed the final game of the World Series because the cat wanted to watch his favorite video, "Birds of North America."

Anytime the animal appears lethargic, you go on-line and investigate vetmed websites, pose questions to your address book and on e-lists, and by the time you digest all the information and field the correspondence, the animal has torn out the windowscreens, masticated a couch cushion and left something disgusting in your favorite pair of shoes.

You have a special uniform you wear for "flame wars" on e-lists and know that being told to "get a life" means you have pushed all the right buttons. Your chatroom handle is "Queen of Spayeds."

You and your vet are on a first name basis and he genuflects when you enter the waiting room. His daughter at Harvard refers to you as "Auntie."

You needed a prescription to recover from "Old Yeller."

You've forwarded more warnings about the dangers of chocolate, onions and mistletoe than the National Center for Disease Control has issued about anthrax and smallpox.

You wear white year 'round, not because you are flaunting a fashion law or belong to a religious sect, but because you have a Dalmatian, Great Pyrenees, Samoyed or white Persian at home.

The world would never guess from your "doggie or kittyspeak" posts to e-lists that in reality you are chairman of the IBM corporation.

Vacuum cleaners in your household don't just die, they go out with more smoke and noise than the Taliban.

By the time you investigate different flea control products, their advantages and potential risks, natural versus chemical methods, and study the life cycle of the flea, any fleas have died of old age.

You tell your children to "heel!" in a grocery store.

For relaxation, you went mall hopping with your girlfriends. Your eyes glazed over when you saw a sign in front of a pet shop, "20% Off All Puppies & Kittens," and you slapped three security guards before they got you safely contained in the manager's office. You stopped at a house with a "Free Puppies" sign in the yard to have an educational "chat," and your kids had to post your bail.

You spend eleven months of the year preaching an appreciation and understanding of canine behavior and the nature of the dog, then you stick fake reindeer antlers on the dog and photograph him for your Christmas card. People are still talking about your spay-neuter holiday greeting from last year, "Deck the Halls with Balls of Collies."

Not only do family and friends think you go overboard with doggie holiday decorations, they've never seen a nativity scene where the holy family is depicted by Boxers.

The average dog is a nicer person than the average person.
~ ANDREW A. ROONEY
❖

Animals are such agreeable friends –
they ask no questions, they pass no criticisms.
~ GEORGE ELIOT
❖

La Visitadora
(The Visitor)

Cathy Ferguson yawned widely as she walked down the nursing home corridor. After ten years as the nightshift nursing supervisor, it would take some time to adjust to the day shift.

"Some promotion," she thought, *"a few dollars more for twice the work."*

She entered the first room on the right, clipboard in hand. There was hardly any point in discussing menu preferences with a patient who barely knew where he was, but procedure was procedure.

"Good morning, Mr. Amato," she said cheerfully. "How are you this morning?"

"Dora?" he asked hesitantly, blinking as she drew back the curtain and opened the window a few inches.

"No...Cathy," she replied. "I'm your new day nurse – remember? We met yesterday."

He stared back at her, but no comprehension showed in his eyes. She began busily tidying up, refilling his water pitcher and fluffing up the pillows.

"Am I interrupting?" a voice asked from behind her.

Cathy turned toward the well-dressed elderly woman standing in the doorway, holding a bouquet of roses.

"No, not at all. I was just about to go over next week's menu with him...maybe you can help. He's not very lucid and I don't understand him when he speaks Italian. Are you a relative?"

"An old friend. I'm Mary Bessler. Mr. Amato has lived in the cottage on my property for over thirty-five years."

"I see. The flowers are beautiful. There are some vases in the cupboard next to the sink."

"Thank you. Yes, they are...Mr. Amato's roses. He looked after my garden. I'm afraid it doesn't look the way it used to before he got sick."

Mr. Amato moaned softly and opened his eyes.

"Dora?" he asked.

"She's well," Mary answered. "She misses you very much and I'm taking good care of her."

"Is Dora his wife?" Cathy asked in a whisper. "He keeps asking for her."

"No...his cat. 'Dora' means 'gold.' He said she was his 'golden hope' – '*Speranza d'ora.*'

"Speranza d'ora," Mr. Amato repeated. "Dora."

Mary squeezed his hand as tears welled in her eyes, and she continued in a low voice.

"He loved that cat more than anything in the world. His wife died a few years after they were married, of cancer...no children. He never remarried. He doesn't have any other family – maybe some distant relatives in Italy, but I don't have any way of contacting them.

"He came over as an immigrant worker. My late husband had an interest in the steel mill and he hired Mr. Amato. There was an accident and Vittorio...Mr. Amato, was injured. He couldn't return to the mill, so my husband gave him some light work around our place.

"I've got this big old house...much too big for me now...and after my husband died, I asked Mr. Amato to stay on and look after things."

"That was very kind and very important to him, I'm sure," Cathy said.

"He's been a good friend. It's not the same without him now. My children are grown and spread out. Mr. Amato and Dora were good company. I still expect to see him giving her a lecture in Italian out in the garden. He'd plant flower bulbs and she'd follow along behind him and dig them up! It gave me such pleasure watching the two of them.

"Look...I brought him something," she said as she laid the roses on the foot of the bed and undid the clasp on her purse. She withdrew a blue cat collar with a small bell.

"Dora's collar. I thought it might bring him some comfort. I'm just sorry I don't have a photo of her."

"We do have a pet therapy program," Cathy started to explain until the hallway speaker called *"Miss Ferguson, please come to the payroll office."*

"Duty calls," Cathy said. "If you'll excuse me."

Mary nodded. She pushed the armchair closer to the bed and sat down, taking his hand in hers.

"Dora," he said.

"She's well, Mr. Amato. She's very well."

———

The cat regarded him solemnly from her chair at the small kitchen table as he conducted his morning ritual. He poured a bit of white vinegar into the chipped bowl of water in front of him, then slowly dipped his eyeglasses up and down in the mixture. He polished them with a clean linen dishtowel before holding them up to the light and inspecting them. Then he carefully put them on.

"Why do you watch my every move, cat?" he asked. "Go outside – earn your keep. Va, ciappa on bel rattin per disnà...Go catch a nice little mouse for supper," he laughed. He leaned over and gently rubbed her ears. She playfully batted at his hand and then jumped down and ran to the door.

"Vegni, vegni! I'm coming," he said. "We have work to do."

———

Cathy always started her morning rounds with Mr. Amato. He was the least responsive of her patients. He floated in and out of consciousness, sometimes speaking in Italian, always calling for Dora.

"You're a very lucky man, Mr. Amato," Cathy thought. *"You have two faithful friends in this life, Dora and Mary Bessler, and that's more than some people can count on."*

She and Mary were on a first-name basis now and she enjoyed their brief daily conversations. Mary's stories about Dora the cat's conquests amused her, but she doubted the fading old man understood much. She wondered if what Mary felt for Mr. Amato was undeclared love, or just two souls who had become inseparable due to familiarity, like a pair of old shoes that belonged together.

"It won't be long now, will it?" Mary had asked her yesterday.

"We can't say for sure, of course. But he's rarely conscious and when he is, he's in another place. A happy place. You have to envy him, Mary. He's reliving the wonderful times of his life – maybe he's playing with childhood friends in Italy. Or working in your garden, taking care of the roses, giving Dora a lecture."

"Dora!" Mr. Amato said sternly and rolled over toward the window.

———

Dora playfully nipped the blossom of a cornflower and stared at him defiantly.

"I'ma telling you one thing, cat. You eat another one of my flowers and I'ma gonna splash water on you!"

Dora knew it was an idle threat and was considering which flower to consume next when a dragonfly went flitting by. She jumped into the air and clasped her paws together futilely. Then she immediately began to lick her paw with an unconcerned air.

"You don'ta fool anybody," he chuckled. "T'i ciapparee ona altra volta... you'll catch them some other time."

———

The nightshift nurse walked quietly down the corridor, stopping to pick up magazines from the lounge chairs and neatly arranging them on a coffee table. She stuck her head in each of the patient's rooms as she passed. Mr. Amato groaned in his sleep. She tiptoed past his bed and closed the window. The night had turned unexpectedly chilly.

———

Dora nudged him gently, which only made him roll over and nestle more deeply into his pillows. She patted his cheek with her paw and he mumbled something and waved her away with his hand. She persisted and began to lick his eyelids with her sandpaper tongue.

"Ohhhh," he complained. "Cat! What am I going to do with you?"

He sat up slowly, focused his eyes and stroked her down her back, ending with a gentle tug on her tail. She playfully nipped his hand.

"What would I do without you?...Se te ghe fudesset minga ti, se podaria fà mi?" he said, shaking his head.

———

The traffic crawled past a construction site as Cathy glanced nervously at the clock on the dashboard.

"Late again," she muttered. Adjusting to the new work schedule was taking its toll on her sleep.

She dashed from the employee parking lot at a half-run, and cursed as she fumbled with the security code on the keypad at the back door. Her shoes squeaked a staccato as she arrived breathlessly at the nurse's station.

"You know, the world won't end if you're a few minutes late," Sandra the new nightshift supervisor said as she looked up from the computer terminal.

"I know," Cathy gasped. "I just think I should set a good example."

"Well, it's not working," Sandra replied. "Two of the girls called off sick."

"Great," Cathy answered as she tossed her purse over the counter and onto an empty chair.

"And I've got some sad news," Sandra said. "Mr. Amato passed – he went in his sleep. I just called his friend, Mrs. Bessler. She's on her way. I haven't done anything in his room yet, I've been trying to catch up on this medication list."

"Don't worry about it," Cathy said. "I'll take care of it. You go home – you need your sleep."

———

A familiar stillness greeted her as she entered Mr. Amato's room. She stood next to the bed for a moment. His right hand clutched Dora's collar and he wore a slight smile of contentment. She said a silent prayer, grateful that another suffering soul had been released.

She picked up the collar and the little bell tinkled as she set it on the nightstand. She replaced it with the rosary beads that hung from the lamp and folded his hands over them. Her hand routinely smoothed out the indentation in the pillow next to his head and then she stared at her hand.

"Cathy," a small voice said tentatively from the doorway and Cathy whirled around with her fists clenched.

"Oh! Mary...I'm sorry...you startled me." She sat down in the armchair and took a deep breath as Mary walked to the bedside.

Mary patted her on the hand.

"This must be very hard for you," Mary said. "You have to deal with this sort of thing all the time."

"I don't think you ever get used to it, but you understand that it's the natural conclusion," Cathy answered. "I'm sorry for your loss. Can I get you anything?"

"No, thank you," Mary answered. "It's not as if it was unexpected," she said sadly. "He's in a much prettier garden than mine now." She twisted the handkerchief in her hands.

"Well, I won't keep you. I'll come back later for his things. I have to make the funeral arrangements...just a small private service. You are welcome to come, of course."

"Thank you," Cathy said. "I'd like that. I'm only sorry I didn't get to know him earlier. I know how much you are going to miss him. I've been meaning to ask, will you be keeping Dora?"

"Dora? Oh no, dear," Mrs. Bessler acted surprised by the question. "The cat died a few months ago...about the time Mr. Amato started to go downhill. She was very old. He was too sick to realize and I didn't want to let on. I kept telling him stories about her and how much she missed him because it made him happy."

"I see," Cathy said thoughtfully. "By the way – what color was she?"

"A very pretty cream color," Mary replied. "Almost a gold – maybe that's why he named her Dora. With some red shading...rather unusual looking. He thought she was the most beautiful cat in the world."

"Well, they are together again," Cathy said with certainty. She stood and impulsively gave Mary a hug.

Cathy looked out the open window of Mr. Amato's room at the cloudless blue sky. She inhaled the spring air deeply. She watched as Mary walked slowly down the walkway toward the parking lot. She felt a sense of peace and hoped Mary felt it as well.

She slowly opened her hand and stared at the tuft of cat hair resting on her palm. She had brushed it from Mr. Amato's pillow. The golden cream strands tipped with red glittered in the sunlight. She blew it from her hand and it hung briefly in the air until the breeze carried it skyward.

ON INTERCONNECTEDNESS

"But inquire of the four-footed animals and they will speak to you.
The winged ones will describe to you;
Declare to the earth and it will tell you in great detail,
The fish of the waters will show you the way."
– Job 12: 7-8

There is a common belief among the tribes of Native American people that everything is related – *everything* – all people, all life, our world, and our spiritual connection with our Creator. Had we been able to embrace that philosophy perhaps the ills of our modern world would never have taken root.

How like a prayer it is to stand under a starry sky at night and look up at the full moon. For most of us today, a full moon is just something that occurs once every twenty-eight days and occasionally twice in that period – a "blue moon." But for the Native American people each full moon was symbolic and had a name. Each different, each the same moon.

We are each different. We each have a name and a unique description, and a set of specific beliefs. We are each the same, but how far we have strayed from the path, from a state of interconnectedness and from a spiritual center.

How can we continue to excuse what we do to each other, what we do to our planet, what we do to the other creatures who share this earth with us? How can we misconstrue the basic tenets of our religions – and all religion is based in love – to mean that we should hate, persecute, or as recent events have shown, murder?

If you look into the faces of children walking to school in Belfast, Northern Ireland, can you tell who is Catholic and who is Protestant? Of course not, but they all wear a common look of fear. Do any of them remember the original reasons for their conflict, or care, or do they just want to be children? Are they tired of being taught to fight their fathers' war?

Is there any difference in the way a Palestinian mother or an

Israeli mother loves her children, her husband, her brother? Do people of other colors and heritages and faiths, men who love men, women who love women, have a different Creator than we? Is it not meaningful when they die together in a common tragedy, or rush together to the aid of the victims, or make contributions to help the victims of tragedy? Are we not members of different tribes, but one people? Does your religion teach hate and discrimination...does it allow for revenge?

Can you watch something grow and not appreciate creation, the mystery of life? Can you still douse it with poison? Do you not feel something stir within your soul when you communicate with a member of another species, feel them respond to you, trust you, show you love? Can you, well-fed, watch a deer grazing, leaping, celebrating life and the glory of creation, look into her soulful eyes and shoot her through the heart? Could you endure the cruel transports, the gruesome stench and the screams of a slaughterhouse for the sake of the meat on your plate?

Can you strike your child or betray those who love you best?

We too often talk about "me," in fact, we've called our youth the "me generation." We often feel like it is "me against the world," but we do not often achieve *me in this world, this world in me, me and you sharing this world.*

You may regard the commonality of all people, all life, as a "pie in the sky" view, a utopian ideal. Can you stand under the full moon at night and regard the majesty of the heavens, smell the freshly mown grass of the fields, feel the night breeze against your cheek, know that people and creatures around the world are looking up at the same heavens, and still ignore the teachings of our elders and deny the voice of your Creator?

In the following, I have woven the Zuni Indian name for each of the full moons, combined with the descriptive terms various tribes used for the individual full moons, followed by lines from a Native American prayer most often attributed to the Sioux, followed by a collection of proverbs included in *The Way of the Doctrine* (the *Dhamapada*) which illustrate some of the basic beliefs of Buddhism, and then *The Lord's Prayer* from the Christian faith. You may read them together as a stanza, or as the corresponding lines of each stanza, and I believe they illustrate the commonality of our hearts, our interconnectedness.

We are, indeed, one people, sharing one world by the grace of one Creator. And as the Native Americans taught us: *"The frog does not drink up the pond in which he lives. There can never be peace between nations until it is first known that true peace is within the souls of men. We will be known forever by the tracks we leave."*

———————

The greatness of a nation and its moral progress
can be judged by the way its animals are treated.
~ MOHANDAS GANDHI

We did not weave the web of life; we are merely a strand in it.
Whatever we do to the web, we do to ourselves. All things connect.
~ CHIEF SEATTLE

A MEDITATION OF MOONS

Dayamcho yachunne...Moon of the strong cold and frost in our teepees, when the wolves run together, when the snow blows like spirits in the wind. Joyful Moon.
O Great Spirit, whose voice I hear in the winds,
By thoughtfulness, by restraint and self-control, the wise man may make for himself an island which no flood can overwhelm.
Our Father who art in heaven...

Onon u'la'ukwamme...Moon of the raccoons and the dark red calves, of frost sparkling in the sun. Purification Moon.
And whose breath gives life to all the world, hear me!
If a man's faith is unstable and his peace of mind troubled, his knowledge will not be perfect.
Hallowed be Thy name...

Li'dekwakkya ts'ana...Moon when the buffalo cows drop their calves, of snow blindness and wind-stung eyes. Whispering Wind Moon.
I am small and weak, I need your strength and wisdom.
The thoughtful do not die; the thoughtless are as if dead already.
Thy kingdom come, Thy will be done...

Li'dekwakkya lana...Moon of the greening grass and the red grass appearing, of the ice breaking in the rivers. Wind Breaks Moon.
Let me walk in beauty, and make my eyes behold the red and purple sunset.
All that we are is the result of what we have thought: it is founded on our thoughts and is made up of our thoughts.
On Earth, as it is in Heaven...

Yachun kwa'shi'amme...Moon when the ponies shed their winter pelts, of blossoms and green leaves, of hoeing corn. Waiting Moon.
Make my hands respect the things you have made.
No suffering befalls the man who calls nothing his own.
Give us this day, our daily bread...

Ik'ohbu yachunne...Moon of the time of fattening, of strawberries. Planting Moon.
Make my ears sharp to hear your voice.
Like a beautiful flower full of color but without scent are the fair words of him who himself does not act accordingly.
And forgive us our trespasses as we forgive those who trespass against us...

Dayamcho yachunne...Moon when the cherries are ripe and of the red blooming lilies, when the branches break under the weight of the fruit. Fledgling Raptor Moon.
Make me wise so that I may understand the things you have taught my people.
Without knowledge there is no meditation, without meditation there is no knowledge. He who has knowledge and meditation is near to Nirvana.
And lead us not into temptation...

Onan u'la'ukwamme...Moon when the geese shed their feathers and the cherries turn black. Joyful Moon.
Let me learn the lessons you have hidden in every leaf and rock.
Not to blame, not to strike, to be moderate in eating, to sleep and sit alone, and to dwell on the highest thoughts – this is the teaching of the Awakened.
But deliver us from evil...

Li'dekwakkwya ts'ana...Moon of the drying grass, when the calves grow hair, when the plums are scarlet. Full Harvest Moon.
I seek strength, not to be greater than my brother, but to fight my greatest enemy...myself.
The evildoer mourns in this world and he mourns in the next – he mourns in both. He mourns and suffers when he sees the evil results of his own deeds. One's own self is the most difficult to subdue.
For Thine is the kingdom...

Li'dekwakkwya lana...Moon of the falling leaves and the changing
seasons. Big Wind Moon.
*Make me always ready to come to you with clean hands and
straight eyes.*
He who has tasted the sweetness of solitude and tranquility
becomes free from fear and free from sin.
And the power...

Yachun kwa'shi'amme...Moon of the bare trees and when the rivers
begin to freeze. Frost Moon.
So when life fades, as the fading sunset,
The gift of the Law exceeds all gifts; the sweetness of the Law
exceeds all sweetness; the delight in the Law exceeds all delight;
the extinction of all desire overcomes all suffering.
And the glory forever...

Ik'ohbu yachunne...Moon of the cracking trees, when the deer shed
their horns, when the buffalo cows' bellies swell with their young.
Respect Moon.
My spirit may come to you without shame.
Thoughtfulness is the road to immortality, Nirvana;
thoughtlessness, the road to death.
Amen

———

*Love the Creator, your God...
with all of your heart,
and with all of your soul,
and with all of your mind,
and with all of your strength.*
~ MARK 12:30
❖

"How Could You?" *was inspired by a nine-year-old Basset Hound adopted by me and my wife on the dog's "last day" at a kill shelter. We named her "Holly Golightly" and I wondered how anyone could betray such a faithful dog by delivering her to an animal shelter where her fate as a senior dog was almost certain.*

In the first year since I wrote and distributed the story it has been published several thousand times in over a dozen languages. It has struck a common chord because it is the composite story of the millions of former pets who die each year in North American shelters. The story has generated mail from around the world and in some countries it is a curiosity because there they have no animal shelters – unwanted animals die in the streets, often cruelly at the hands of the authorities.

One of the best uses of the story to educate the public has been by newspapers that have published it along with photographs taken at local shelters and with related articles on local animal welfare programs and resources. I encourage you to ask your local newspaper to publish it in cooperation with your local humane society or shelter.

―――――――

We ought not to treat living creatures like shoes or household belongings, which when worn with use we throw away.
~ PLUTARCH

How Could You?

When I was a puppy I entertained you with my antics and made you laugh. You called me your child and despite a number of chewed shoes and a couple of murdered throw pillows, I became your best friend. Whenever I was "bad," you'd shake your finger at me and ask "How could you?" – but then you'd relent and roll me over for a bellyrub.

My housetraining took a little longer than expected, because you were terribly busy, but we worked on that together. I remember those nights of nuzzling you in bed, listening to your confidences and secret dreams, and I believed that life could not be any more perfect. We went for long walks and runs in the park, car rides, stops for ice cream (I only got the cone because "ice cream is bad for dogs," you said), and I took long naps in the sun waiting for you to come home at the end of the day.

Gradually, you began spending more time at work and on your career, and more time searching for a human mate. I waited for you patiently, comforted you through heartbreaks and disappointments, never chided you about bad decisions, and romped with glee at your homecomings, and when you fell in love.

She, now your wife, is not a "dog person" – still I welcomed her into our home, tried to show her affection, and obeyed her. I was happy because you were happy. Then the human babies came along and I shared your excitement. I was fascinated by their pinkness, how they smelled, and I wanted to mother them, too. Only she and you worried that I might hurt them, and I spent most of my time banished to another room, or to a dog crate. Oh, how I wanted to love them, but I became a "prisoner of love."

As they began to grow, I became their friend. They clung to my fur and pulled themselves up on wobbly legs, poked fingers in my eyes, investigated my ears and gave me kisses on my nose. I loved everything about them, especially their touch – because your touch was now so infrequent – and I would have defended them with my life if need be.

I would sneak into their beds and listen to their worries and secret dreams. Together we waited for the sound of your car in the driveway. There had been a time, when others asked you if you had a dog, that you produced a photo of me from your wallet and told them stories about me. These past few years, you just answered "yes" and changed the subject. I had gone from being your dog to "just a dog," and you resented every expenditure on my behalf.

Now you have a new career opportunity in another city and you and they will be moving to an apartment that does not allow pets. You've made the right decision for your "family," but there was a time when I *was* your only family.

I was excited about the car ride until we arrived at the animal shelter. It smelled of dogs and cats, of fear, of hopelessness. You filled out the paperwork and said "I know you will find a good home for her." They shrugged and gave you a pained look. They understand the realities facing a middle-aged dog or cat, even one with "papers."

You had to pry your son's fingers loose from my collar as he screamed "No, Daddy! *Please* don't let them take my dog!" And I worried for him and what lessons you had just taught him about friendship and loyalty, about love and responsibility, and about respect for all life. You gave me a goodbye pat on the head, avoided my eyes, and politely refused to take my collar and leash with you. You had a deadline to meet and now I have one, too.

After you left, the two nice ladies said you probably knew about your upcoming move months ago and made no attempt to find me another good home. They shook their heads and asked "How could you?"

They are as attentive to us here in the shelter as their busy schedules allow. They feed us, of course, but I lost my appetite days ago. At first, whenever anyone passed my pen, I rushed to the front, hoping it was you – that you had changed your mind – that this was all a bad dream...or I hoped it would at least be someone who cared, anyone who might save me. When I realized I could not compete with the frolicking for attention of happy puppies, oblivious to their own fate, I retreated to a far corner and waited.

I heard her footsteps as she came for me at the end of the day and I padded along the aisle after her to a separate room. A blissfully quiet room. She placed me on the table, rubbed my ears and told me not to worry. My heart pounded in anticipation of what was to come, but there was also a sense of relief. The prisoner of love had run out of days. As is my nature, I was more concerned about her. The burden which she bears weighs heavily on her and I know that, the same way I knew your every mood.

She gently placed a tourniquet around my foreleg as a tear ran down her cheek. I licked her hand in the same way I used to comfort you so many years ago. She expertly slid the hypodermic needle into my vein. As I felt the sting and the cool liquid coursing through my body, I lay down sleepily, looked into her kind eyes and murmured *"How could you?"*

Perhaps because she understood my dogspeak, she said "I'm *so* sorry." She hugged me and hurriedly explained it was her job to make sure I went to a better place, where I wouldn't be ignored or abused or abandoned, or have to fend for myself – a place of love and light so very different from this earthly place. With my last bit of energy, I tried to convey to her with a thump of my tail that my *"How could you?"* was not meant for her. It was you, My Beloved Master, I was thinking of. I will think of you and wait for you forever.

May everyone in your life continue to show you so much loyalty.

Hear our prayer O Lord...
for animals that are overworked, underfed and cruelly treated:
for all wistful creatures in captivity that beat their wings against bars;
for any that are hunted or lost or deserted or frightened or hungry;
for all that must be put to death...
and for those who deal with them we ask
a heart of compassion and gentle hands and kindly words.
~ ALBERT SCHWEITZER
❖

ON DOING MORE

You obviously love animals and our world, or you wouldn't have made it this far into my book. Are you willing to do more? Will you read the *Appendix* of suggestions and resources that follows and pick at least one thing to do, one area where you can make a difference? Will you educate yourself about the issues and needs? *Please.*

I've been involved with mostly rescued animals for over three decades and with some of the issues surrounding them. I've learned a lot in the process and I still have much to learn. A lot of what I have to learn will be taught to me by animals and it is their purrs and licks and nuzzles that are all the thanks I'll ever need.

Whenever I have stumbled or felt like a failure, it has been many of you and your efforts that have picked me up and inspired me to go on. During the darkest period of my life, after a series of losses of some of the people I loved most and of some wonderful animal friends, it was my own animals who provided the most natural comfort and it was the animal-people in my life who shone their own lights onto the path ahead and urged me to keep going. Being able to concentrate on helping animals, to have a purpose, helped me recover from the deaths by cancer and a suicide of my loved ones, and the financial burdens that resulted. For me, anything else I do is repaying a debt of gratitude.

Being able to give something back, to work for change, especially as a volunteer – even when the work is exhausting, frustrating and financially draining – offers the greatest rewards. The thrill of watching the animal you didn't think would make it live happily. Hearing back from an adoptive guardian about the animal who came from terrible circumstances now thriving in his new home. Watching an animal change a human life for the better. Getting help from the most unlikely sources. Being in awe of volunteers who give their all for the causes they believe in. Working with staff members in the animal welfare system, those who work "in the trenches" and deal with the animal holocaust on a daily basis, those who are so underpaid and under-appreciated.

Following the tragedies of September 11th 2001, when an already overwhelmed American shelter system was flooded with owner-relinquished animals and donations to shelters and rescues suddenly dried up, many of those workers took a cut in pay and paid for food for the animals out of their own pockets. Some of the bankrupt privately funded shelters had to close their doors with little media attention, unsaved by a society that has more than it needs of material wealth.

I have seen some improvements on behalf of animals such as the recent interest in a no-kill shelter system (which could result in the "warehousing" of animals if we don't back it up with a change in public perception and make people realize that a pet is a lifetime commitment). I've observed and admired the well-funded, no-kill shelter systems of most western European nations and how animals are regarded in their society, their animal legislation, sometimes at a constitutional level, and the fact that they don't allow pet shop sales of furred animals. After a long effort by advocates the US postal service has finally approved stamps with a spay/neuter message. There have been some court victories and legal precedents set that regard animals to be more than "property," and have shown that the federally funded inspection system in the USA for those who deal in animals is ineffective, understaffed and underfunded, and that the manner in which animals are transported to slaughter needs to be closely regulated. Two decades ago there were about a hundred organizations worldwide devoted to animals and today there are about five thousand.

How much it pains me after thirty years of watching these developments and participating where I could to know that the same gas chamber that upset me as a teenager when I worked in an animal shelter is still churning out tons of dead bodies in shelters across the richest nation in the world. And to know that at some shelters animals are not humanely "euthanized," they are shot. That their brief lives in some shelters are a hell on earth for the animals. That "shelter" is a misnomer in some states that allow animals to be turned over to Class B animal dealers who then sell them for research. That despicable people called "bunchers" scan free-to-good-home advertisements and collect animals to sell to laboratories for research, or that others do the same and also steal pets to use as live bait to train fighting pit bull dogs. That breed-specific legislation and breed bans can result in the deaths of innocent animals and do not take into account that people are the problem, not the dogs. To realize that every local and state government does not have a low-cost spay/neuter and vaccination program, and that in some communities laws for animals are poorly enforced and "animal control" is nothing but an immediate death sentence. And to hear that some university veterinary medical programs destroy young, healthy animals after they've fulfilled their teaching purpose, and to read that the results obtained from much animal research cannot be extrapolated for human benefit.

How disturbing, after all of our education efforts, to hear on the news that pet shop sales of puppies are up one hundred percent since September 11th and to read that America's largest commercial breeder is spewing out nearly a thousand puppies a week to pet shops. To know that horses are sold for meat in this country – a country that exports all of it, because we don't eat horsemeat, and to see how mares suffer to produce an unnecessary drug, Premarin. To see how we imprison and kill off even those animals we regard as symbols of "wild and free." That a "canned hunt" could be regarded as sport. Or that we could commit such atrocities against our closest animal cousins, the non-human primates, who we've learned can communicate in our sign-language and who have a sense of self. Or to ignore the growing body of scientific work that shows animals to be sentient beings.

A past American First Lady wrote a book about her family's White House pets and donated the proceeds to veterans, a group that certainly deserves help from the government that sent them to war, but she missed a good opportunity to make a statement for animals. She and many others had forgotten about the dogs, mules and horses of war, many who gave their lives in service to our country, many of them destroyed under a policy that didn't even allow them to be adopted by their handlers who loved them after they were retired from service.

As a developed nation our record on animal issues is far better than what exists in the less developed countries of the world. In response to my essay "How Could You?" a professor in Russia wrote to me, "I wish we had animal shelters. Here the animals starve or freeze to death in the streets." A woman in Greece wrote to tell me that the authorities were spreading around poisoned meat laced with shards of broken glass in order to kill the stray dogs, and a man in Turkey wrote to tell me that he believed his life was in danger for protesting to the authorities about their treatment of strays in his village. There are some glimmers of hope though. After the mayor of Bucharest, Romania, announced that seven hundred thousand stray dogs would be captured and destroyed, animal lovers around the world reacted and some animals were saved.

America needs to set an example and stop ignoring the secret sins of what happens to animals here. It doesn't make sense to have a pet food industry worth over eleven billion dollars annually, with over one-hundred-twenty million owned pets, and still have millions of companion animals dying in our shelters while the aftermath of this holocaust is largely dealt with by volunteers. We kill over ten billion animals a year for food, despite all the evidence that especially factory-farm produced meat, eggs and milk are unhealthy. As a government and as a society we have ignored our responsibilities far too long.

Has the public, the taxpayers who bear the cost of an animal welfare system that is inadequate, become less apathetic and have legislators increased their endeavors to make the world a better place for animals? Do pet owners regard animals as less "disposable" than they did previously? Do people who love their own pets do anything to benefit animals in general? Are those who breed and put more animals into this world any more committed to the welfare of those animals for life than they used to be? In the face of the growing number of animal neglect and cruelty charges in our society, and the millions of unwanted animals being destroyed annually, can we still hope for improvements?

Does it make sense that our churches, temples, and synagogues teach creation and preach compassion for family and community, yet many do not include so much as a mention in their sermons and bulletins about that family member, those community members who can never speak for themselves and often suffer terribly? How many "devout" believers have unspayed/neutered animals at home breeding frequently, or who can blissfully ignore a stray dog, or who can shove a hamburger into their mouth without a thought about the circumstances under which that meat was produced, or who can have a chemical lawn service spray their property with poison? How environmentally friendly will your next church social be? No matter what your faith, can you assure your Creator that you are doing all you can to protect the creation and creatures we've been blessed with?

We often point to an uncaring "public" as being the root cause of the animal welfare and environmental problems. We *are* the public. We elect the legislators, we pass the laws, we establish public opinion. We are each surrounded by opportunities to make a difference: to change our own practices regarding animals; to educate someone; to raise a kinder, gentler next generation; to do something to help...give a dollar, give a damn, donate a book of postage stamps, write a letter to an editor. If you are already involved in this effort, then, like me, you are not surprised that we haven't been able to effect a radical change in the "public," when we can't even get some of the people closest to us to pay attention to the problems, to stop contributing to the problems, and instead make some kind of worthwhile contribution.

As I write this, I am for a time living near my childhood home, near an area that was once farmland and orchards. Today, it is an encroaching expanse of shopping malls and concrete. I've never seen such development in such a short period of time, or such building without reason with the same kinds of stores duplicated many times over. When I drive by that monstrosity of commerce run amok, I fight the urge to become a curbside evangelist and I know the rage Jesus must have felt when he overturned the tables of the money lenders in the temple. I want to scream, "Stop! Stop the building! Leave something for the birds, rabbits and deer. Stop the shopping! Give a dollar to something that matters. Go home to your partners and give them a hug, kiss your children, go out in the fresh air and play with your dog. Just please stop...."

We need to open our eyes to what we are doing, how we are doing it, to the world around us and to what our Creator expects.

Oprah Winfrey tells a story about one of her guests who said something that made an indelible impression on her, as it did on me, because it is something I believe intuitively without being able to explain. It's a matter of faith. Oprah had as a guest on her show the mother of a terminally ill boy. As he lay dying his mother crawled into bed with him and hugged him as he drew his last breath. In the moment before he passed over, he looked into his mother's eyes and said, "Mom, it is *so* simple!"

I believe that it *is* simple. I believe that Love rules. I believe we have an obligation to be happy. I believe we know in our hearts right from wrong.

I believe we know that we shouldn't drive past the stray dog without stopping to help. That we know if we've never visited our local animal shelter we can't fully appreciate the scope of the problems. That we need to say thank you to those who do the hard work. That we shouldn't ignore what our neighbor is doing to animals and that we need to have responsible authorities to call on for help. That it's wrong to let the barnyard and feral cats breed out of control, or allow our dog to have a litter so our children can experience "the miracle of life." I believe we know that pets are good for well-trained children and for old people, and that families with pets shouldn't have a difficult time renting a place to live. I believe we know that factory farms are wrong and that there are few meat-eaters in the world who could stomach the sight of the cruel transports and horrors of the slaughterhouse.

I believe we know that we shouldn't contribute to suffering. That we shouldn't be poisoning our foodstuffs. That the offal of rendering plants shouldn't be included in commercially made pet foods. That wild animals belong in the wild and that we must protect their habitats. That no reason is good enough to betray our animal companions. That raising animals for fur or trapping them is terribly wrong. That hunting except for sustenance is senseless and most of the arguments defending the practice are specious. I believe we know that it's wrong to kill.

I believe we know it is wrong to exploit animals for reasons of vanity, entertainment, or commercial gain. That it's wrong to regard them as creatures meant to do our bidding, to bend to our will. That hating all humans for what they do to animals is wrong and that our best hope is to find a way to work together with all humans on behalf of animals, and that will require reasonability and education, not throwing a tofu pie in their faces.

I believe we know that we shouldn't be contaminating and carelessly manipulating the perfect world our Creator entrusted to us. And that we know that the animals, who have never had a voice and will never be able to speak up for themselves, are counting on us to change things for the better.

All of us who work for the benefit of animals are sometimes asked questions along the lines of "don't you like people?" or "why don't you do something to help people?" Such questions show their lack of understanding of how helping animals helps eradicate the seeds of human problems, or their lack of appreciation for how much animals and people can mean to each other. We also need to point out the vast dichotomy between the number of public and private funded programs for human victims versus what is provided to benefit animals. It is also true that one day the surviving human victims may rise up and make important contributions toward correcting social ills and they will speak poignantly on behalf of their fellow victims. Animals remain mute in their chains.

I had a Japanese friend, a horticulturist, who was killed tragically. One day, a year before his death, he visited me and we went for a walk around the grounds of where I was living and in the woods. He pointed out each plant and told me its medicinal properties, or that it would make a good tea, or that it could be steamed as a vegetable, or that its roots were edible. How wonderful to know such things and I haven't look at a "weed" in the same way since. He also told me that in order to be happy and to live successfully, "each day you must do something for someone, something for yourself, make yourself a good dinner, and do your dishes." I haven't religiously practiced the dishwashing part of that life philosophy, but I've tried to practice the rest. He was also known to many of us as a prolific letter writer. At his memorial service it was revealed by the surprising number of especially elderly people who attended that he had frequently written to all of them and more.

Several years ago I visited my favorite and best teacher, the woman who taught me most about art, and who was a talented artist. She was blind to all but light and shadow by then, but she talked about art in such vivid terms that I could "see" in my mind's eye everything she was describing and I could still feel her passion for beauty...a greater appreciation for beauty blind than some sighted people have.

I have known many physically handicapped people, including my own parents, who accomplished more by getting out of bed, putting on their leg braces or getting into their wheelchairs and going off to work than most of us accomplish in a day. I remember family legends of my father, who because of polio did not have the use of his legs, swimming across rivers, flying airplanes, and jumping the cavalry horses he was supposed to exercise until he fell and broke his pelvis. I remember my mother, also a polio victim who required over thirty operations in her lifetime and had such a sense of humor that hospital nurses and fellow patients regretted when she was sent home and they became lifelong friends. While my mother was on her deathbed I grasped for ways to keep up her spirits. I gave her a canary who she named "Caruso" and I placed his cage on her nightstand. At the exact moment she left us, he sang.

I remember my Italian grandfather at the age of almost one hundred working in his garden. I remember my father-in-law, a well-traveled adventurer and a talented writer. After age and illness had robbed him of vitality, he copiously recorded his life and family history in multiple volumes for his daughter. I remember my mother-in-law who made me feel like royalty with the holiday dinners she served. We surprised my wife's parents with a rescued poodle who in their last years gave them more love and comfort than almost any human could. I know my wife, who loves honestly and reliably, who enables me.

I know a woman in Germany who lost her fiancé in the Second World War. She never married and took care of his parents in their old age as if they were her own. Several years ago, she rescued and raised a starling fledgling, and despite consulting with experts, he never grew feathers on his head. He resembles a miniature vulture and has happily coexisted with cats and dogs, ruling her household and all the while believing himself to be the most beautiful bird in the world.

I knew and loved another elderly woman in Germany, a former neighbor who treated me like a son, and whom I called my "German mother." She was a captivating storyteller and kept me enthralled for hours with the tales of her childhood. She had risked her life under Hitler by smuggling bread inside her coat to the Jews. I gave her a kitten who grew up to never leave her side after she became bedridden from a stroke. When I returned to Germany following my own mother's funeral, my wife broke the news to me that she had died on the same day as my mother. It was appropriate that two such angels should finally meet.

I know volunteer animal rescuers who drive thousands of miles per year to bring animals to their new homes, who spend far more of their own funds for the animals' care than is prudent, who sit up all night nursing a sick animal back to health, and who shed tears for the ones they lose, tears that should have been shed by the people who brought them into this world, or by those who hurt them.

I know people who have learned to use the power of animals to make a difference in the lives of autistic and special children, and to brighten the days of old people.

I have known animals who suffered the most horrific abuse, who healed and responded to love, who learned to trust a human again. I know my own animals and how much we need each other, and how much we mean to each other.

It has been a great privilege and very humbling to have known such giving people, and that includes many who are reading these words at the moment. My life has been filled with loving people, loving animals, and miracles of the human-animal bond. You will have your own heroes, human and animal, and since the events of September 11th, 2001, we have all learned the tender lessons of quiet courage. We each must do what we can so that one day when we stand before our Creator, we can do so unashamedly and know that we caused as little harm as possible, and that we did the best we could. We need to make life simple now so that we won't be so surprised later when we learn that it should have been simple.

I won't pretend that by caring and doing more it will somehow make our lives easier. It won't. But it will make life more joyful and fulfilling. This life and this world are what we have. Pay attention. Use them wisely. This is not a dress rehearsal. The tasks would seem daunting and impossible if we weren't who we are and if there weren't so many of us.

To those of you who work for change and are willing to get involved, you have been an enormous help and inspiration to me, and it is a pleasure to inhabit this wonderful world with you. I thank you for allowing me to share with you these "pieces of my heart." We who share a love of and with other species are already blessed, may our efforts for them be similarly blessed.

BLESSED BE

For all the times I needed courage,
for all the times I cried instead,
for any time I disappointed,
by head instead of heart was led.

For any time I lacked conviction,
when efforts seemed to be in vain,
the truth will out, of that I'm certain,
from sacrifice will come the gain.

When in the quiet of an evening,
when I reflect upon my deeds,
I know I cannot ignore suffering,
or the pitiful plight of those in need.

I am but one caring person,
one tiny voice amidst the din,
then from heavenward I heard the promise,
"Blessed be – the vanquished win!"

APPENDIX

Suggestions for Helping Animals and Organizations

Resources from the World Wide Web

Suggestions for Helping Animals and Organizations

There is no such thing as an animal or advocacy organization, or an animal shelter or rescue that does not need help. Unfortunately, even among pet guardians and animal lovers, there may be a misconception that one has to have expendable income to donate, or the right circumstances to adopt another animal before making a worthwhile contribution. Absolutely not true! Talk with the staff of your local organizations and facilities about their needs, implement some of the following suggestions, and you'll soon be making a difference.

(The following has been written from an American perspective. Most of the countries of Europe, for instance, do not allow pet shop sales of puppies and kittens.)

———

Join up! Chances are if you've never been involved with a related organization, you might have some misconceptions about the kinds of people who are involved ("a bunch of elderly spinsters who live with dozens of cats"), or the kinds of activities pursued ("members dress up in animal costumes and chain themselves to fences around nuclear reactors"). You've probably made some wrong assumptions and you'll be pleasantly surprised after attending a meeting and talking with members in person.

Be resourceful. Quick, name the five largest breed-specific rescues in your area. What do you do if you find an injured box turtle on the road? What local agency is responsible for dealing with animal abuse and neglect complaints? Which veterinarians handle middle-of-the-night emergencies? There are probably rescue-resources, wildlife rehabilitation facilities, animal-related groups and activities in your area that the general public is unaware of. Talk to local veterinarians, state and local agencies, breed clubs, shelters and rescues, and compile a list – then share the wealth and ask your local media to publish it!

Be a copy-cat. Do you have access to a photocopier or discounted reams of paper, toner, or other supplies? Every organization and shelter has literature and lists they need copied. If you have computer word-processing or design skills, you can help prepare a newsletter, adoption lists, and other useful literature for a group.

Be a publicity-hound. Do you have writing skills? You can help a group with newsletter articles and press releases to local media. If you have a busy office, belong to a church or civic group, community center, or any place with a well-viewed bulletin board, obtain permission to post a group or shelter's flyers, especially photos and information about animals available for adoption. If you have more time, you can develop a bulletin-board-route and keep boards current in several locations. For offices/areas where a bulletin board is not available, but a reception area is, fill some three-ring binders with pages of available animals and information. Regularly place something animal related in your church or club bulletin.

Be a shutterbug. Are you a photographer of even the point-and-click variety? Many shelters don't have anyone to regularly take photos of adoptable animals. If your local newspaper doesn't publish photos of animals for adoption on at least a weekly basis, encourage them to do so. (Remember, a picture is worth a thousand words, so some attention to proper lighting and a plain background, or outdoor photos taken with natural light will show off the animal to the best advantage.)

Straight from the horse's mouth. Do you have public speaking skills? Talk to local groups and shelters about the messages and information they need disseminated in the community and offer to address civic groups, school classes and community meetings on their behalf.

It pays to advertise (especially when it's free). Do you have access to free classifieds through internet services, weekly shopper papers, or community papers? Place generic spay/neuter messages, ads warning of the dangers of "free to good home," or messages with info about local programs.

Be a pack-rat. Talk to local groups and shelters about their "wish list," the items they need to perform their function, or for on-line auctions, or fundraising sales. Rummage around, talk to churches and other organizations, and even private yard-salers about donating some of their leftovers for your causes.

Be crafty. Do you knit, crochet, or sew? Animal shelters need bedding and their offices may be in dire need of new curtains. Do you do woodworking? Perhaps your local shelters and sanctuaries need cat-trees, scratching posts, whelping boxes, or outdoor dog houses. Are you a fine artist?...murals for their waiting room. Or handy with a paint roller?...brightening up the shelter walls will make it more inviting to the public. Absolutely no skills?...hmmm. Buy some inexpensive twenty-gallon plastic storage containers with snap-on lids. Using a large coffee can lid as a template trace a circle in the middle of a short (width) side starting about three inches from the bottom of the container. Use a utility knife to cut out the circle, smooth the cut edges of the hole with a round file, and *voila!* you have a kitty den that can be lined with towels and even stacked two or three high. Your local shelter's cats will love them and they are easy to clean.

Foster a good feeling. Do you have room in your home and heart for an animal on a temporary basis? Most shelters and all rescue organizations need foster homes. In most cases, they provide all veterinary care and you may only be responsible for the cost of food. Most animals need foster care for only a short time, from a few days to a few months. Even if you can't personally house an animal, you may be able to assist a group or shelter by being a foster-care coordinator, helping to find new foster homes and providing training to new fosters.

Drive yourself crazy. Do you have a vehicle and a love of the open road? Volunteer drivers are needed by shelters and rescues to drive animals to vet appointments, to run errands, and to participate in "relays" that move animals longer distances to foster care or permanent homes. There are numerous internet lists and message boards devoted to transportation needs.

Walk that dog, bathe that cat *(ouch!)*. Many shelters need volunteer dog walkers (unfortunately, for insurance reasons some don't allow the practice). You don't need to be a professional groomer to help bathe and brush animals who need to look their best for potential adopters. Some shelters can use help doing pet laundry, cleaning, filing, answering the phone and other office tasks.

Rescue a rescuer. Volunteer rescuers are very busy people. They usually have their own animals, children, and a partner they haven't been out to dinner with in a long time. Be an angel – take a rescuer to lunch, help them clean the drool and pet hair out of their van, pet/child sit while they get away for an evening, spend an afternoon running errands for them. (How soon can you be here?)

Be a watchdog. Send local media reports about animal neglect and abuse cases to the Animal Legal Defense Fund, and they can assist local prosecutors and agencies in obtaining maximum sentences. Peruse your local newspaper's classified ads for frequent "puppies/kittens for sale" ads from repeat advertisers and check with local tax authorities and the newspaper's publisher about whether the sellers are in compliance with all ordinances and are reporting sales and income taxes properly. (This is a huge source of abuse and non-compliance, and one that has been virtually ignored by the media, especially newspapers who are earning revenue on the advertising. How many will have the guts to investigate that story?) Visit local pet shops and sellers of live animals and report any infractions you observe to the appropriate authorities.

The gospel truth. Nobody should ever buy a puppy or kitten (or any animal, for that matter) from a pet shop...never, ever! No legitimate, caring breeder will ever provide animals to a pet shop. The majority of animals sold by pet shops are ticking time-bombs of medical, genetic and behavioral problems, as well as being overpriced. Most animals derive from puppy/kitten mills, or large commercial breeders where the breeding animals live a hell on Earth. So what part of that scenario is the public not understanding? Educate your family, friends, and coworkers, and keep hammering away at your local media to tell the truth about pet shop sales of live animals and ask them to report on the issues. Tell everyone you know to not buy *anything* from a pet shop that sells puppies and kittens. If the federal government won't pass a law prohibiting such sales (as many other countries have done), we need to financially cripple the sellers.

"Put to sleep" or murdered, or tortured? It is a sad reality that there are not enough good adoptive homes for all the unwanted animals. Elderly, sick animals and those with behavioral problems often do poorly in the shelter system and are often not considered adoptable. But the *only* acceptable euthanasia method is sedation followed by lethal intravenous injection. (And rather than criticizing those who must perform that thankless job, we should appreciate their kindness until such time as no adoptable animal needs to die.)

Yet some shelters and dog pounds in America are shooting animals, using the gas chamber, or sticking a hypodermic needle directly into the animal's heart. Some shelters are required by state law or voluntarily sell animals for research, and some owners relinquishing animals to shelters actually sign a permission form allowing their animal to be sold for research. Incredibly, the dead bodies of shelter animals are often sent for rendering and some of the "bone meal" and "meat byproducts" used in some commercially made pet foods are actually *made from* dogs and cats!

Find out what euthanasia methods and other practices are being used in your local shelters and ask the media to report on unacceptable practices. Some shelters have a reputation for putting down even young, purebred, adoptable animals, and a few are known for putting down all the animals, every week. Many cite underfunding/understaffing as the reason for unacceptable practices. Head straight for their funding source with an inquiry in hand and enlist the help of the media in resolving the problems.

Of course the goal in every community should be a "no-kill" shelter system supported by education and advocacy efforts, and an effective spay/neuter campaign, but until that can be accomplished, don't allow your tax dollar to support murder.

Just say "no"... to circuses with performing animals, rodeos, cute chimps in costume, roadside zoos, hunting, trapping, fur sales, dissections in classrooms, declawing of cats, docking tails and cropping ears of puppies...anything that doesn't respect the nature of the animal, that is confining, causes fear or pain or disfigurement in the animal, or results in death. No excuses. (*Okay, if humans are willing to cut off their ears, any part of their anatomy that resembles a tail, and the first digit of every finger, we animals might be willing to hear arguments to the contrary.*)

Put your money where your mouth is. Don't buy products tested on animals or patronize companies that conduct animal testing; don't support the economies of countries with cruel animal practices; don't use a credit card or any product from a company that sponsors events, entertainment, or competitions that aren't kind to animals. And don't rely on mainstream media to represent the true picture! Devote some time to going behind-the-scenes and you might be alarmed at how often we lend our financial support to situations that can represent agony for animals. Judge for yourself:

- about the female hormone replacement drug Premarin: *http://www.hsus.org/current/hrtfacts.html*
- about extracting bile from bears in China: *http://www.animalsasia.org/*
- about the practice of killing dogs for meat in Asia: *http://www.aapn.org/fooddogs.html*
- about the premier dogsled race, The Iditarod: *http://www.helpsleddogs.org:/*

Breed some understanding. As apathetic as the public can be, animal people are often just as passionate about their beliefs to the point of division. There should be no discord among "animal welfare" and "animal rights" folk, or between legitimate breeder/exhibitors with caring practices (including accepting back any animal of their breeding) and breed rescuers, or between rescuers and shelter staffs. We need to stop making assumptions and generalizations such as "all breeders are...," "all animal rights people are..." We need to *all* work together for the sake of the animals and we need to run the despicable segment out of Dodge.

After you've compiled a list of all the animal-resources in your community, send them each a letter and ask what kinds of events "we" could all participate in together. (If it's one thing animal people aren't lacking in, it's ideas.) How about a "Dog Days in the Park" event with information booths, fundraisers for rescues, activities for dogs and their people, exhibitions by trainers, and speakers on dealing with common behavior problems? How about a "Cavalcade of Kitties" indoor event in a hotel ballroom with an exhibition of rare breeds, local veterinarians speaking on common feline ailments, discussions on feral cat problems and low-cost spay/neuter programs? You get the idea – now help coordinate it!

Surf with a purpose. Subscribe to some e-lists and newsletters and regularly visit the websites of your favorite national and international organizations. Tap into the wealth of information they offer and request their free literature or modestly priced publications. Become a one-person publicity office and help your local organizations adapt the information to their purposes and to educate their members. Education is the key to eradicating most problems and you can help teach the way to solutions.

The ten-minute advocate. Using the information in mailings from the national organizations and issues outlined on their websites, sign on-line petitions, send e-mails and faxes to legislators, print out information about campaigns and pending legislation for your group members, and urge them to participate. If the issue has a local angle, ask your local media to explore it.

Go wild on the Web. If you have good computer skills, consider creating a website and serving as webmaster for a local shelter or organization. Even if they already have a site, volunteer to place their information, especially about animals in need, on national sites such as Petfinder.com (*http://www.petfinder.org/*), or post messages to all-breed lists such as DogsNeedingHomes, or breed-specific lists.

Be a voice for the voiceless. Get informed about the dangers facing animals advertised "free to a good home," and call some advertisers to politely educate them. Some may hang up on you, but a few may rethink their decision and follow your advice. Collect literature or print up a fact sheet on the issues with local info about low-cost spay/neuter programs and whenever you see signs posted about "free to good home," place the information in the mailbox at the residence. (Naturally, you'll want to be a voice on many other issues as well.)

Signs of the times. Have some T-shirts printed with appropriate messages and contact phone numbers. Order bumper stickers. Talk a local specialty advertising business into providing a discount to the groups in your area. Collect money from local businesses and put up a billboard with a spay/neuter message and list the businesses that contributed. Take advantage of free business card offers from e-print services and order some with appropriate messages and contact information. With any campaign, represent it as a community problem requiring a cooperative solution and not a problem that is exclusively the realm of the local shelter or humane society. (Even taxpayers who don't like animals must pay the costs of an overwhelmed animal welfare system!)

Nickle and dime 'em. With the authorization of the groups you'll be collecting for, make some coin collection boxes or jars and distribute them to local businesses to place near their cash registers. Volunteer to check and empty the receptacles on a regular basis. Ask local grocery stores and any business that deals in pet foods to allow you to place on a shelf hook or rack flyers with your local shelter's "wish list" and where donations can be sent.

Now that you've cleaned out the garage... Some shelters and rescues have to decline donations of bagged food, bedding, etc., because they have no place to store the items. If you have a dry, empty, secure space offer it to them for storage.

Do a reality check-list. How do the practices in your own household and among your family members impact animals and our environment? If you aren't willing to go "totally veggie," are you willing to reduce your consumption of meat, or your purchase of leather goods? Instead of buying factory-farm produced produce, milk, eggs and meat, patronize local farmers and farmers' markets, co-ops, and sellers with organic and compassionate practices. Look beyond the package label and find out if you agree with how the product was produced, and learn about its environmental impact. Recycle! Reduce your consumption of utilities. Help educate your family, workplace, religious and civic organizations about environmentally-friendly consumerism.

You don't have to mow a habitat. Covenants and restrictions in your community aside, some people might like the look of a pristine green lawn that nobody walks on except the chemical-lawn-sprayer, but the monoculture of a manicured lawn offers little for fauna. Plant a hedgerow here, a group of flowering shrubs there, an espalier of fruit trees, a patch of wildflowers, add a birdbath, a decorative pond, and you'll soon have your own Garden of Eden filled with birds and butterflies (which you can enjoy while your neighbors are spending their weekends mowing their acreage).

Charity begins at home. A high percentage of American pets are overweight and many are under-exercised. Behavior problems are exacerbated by boredom, lack of socialization, and too much time spent alone. Many animals crave a same-species companion. Reassess your relationship with your pet and pay careful attention to diet and level of exercise. Get together with other dog guardians for a weekly walk. Join an obedience class, agility, flyball or other dog activity. Make or buy your cat a cat-tree and some new toys. Become involved in an animal-related activity...you'll meet some nice people (maybe find a mate?), and learn things that may benefit your animal friend.

Who will care for them when you're gone? None of us can be assured of how many tomorrows we will enjoy. What if something happened to you and you were unable to care for your pet? Who would you wish to take over that responsibility? Discuss the matter with your family and friends, ask your local humane organization for guidance, and leave clear instructions about your pets in your will.

———————

The worst sin toward our
fellow creatures is not to hate them,
but to be indifferent to them;
that's the essence of inhumanity.
~ GEORGE BERNARD SHAW

I know God will not give me anything I can't handle.
I just wish that He didn't trust me so much.
~ MOTHER TERESA
❖

Resources from the World Wide Web

What follows is a brief selection of resources available on the World Wide Web. I do not necessarily endorse the entire content of any site, or agree with all the views presented, yet they are each valuable for their capacity to educate and inform about issues, and most contain a list of recommended links to other sites. Gone are the days when we could claim to be ill informed about matters that affect animals and our environment – it's all here, at our fingertips, waiting to be explored.

I encourage every animal rescue and shelter with a website to add pages of related articles and links. Only by taking every opportunity to educate the public, especially about behavioral problems, how to wisely choose a pet, all the reasons people use for giving up their pets, and the importance of spaying/neutering, will we ever change the status quo.

Whatever your question or topic of interest, you will also be able to find related material by entering appropriate "key words" with such universal search engines as google.com, metacrawler.com, infozoid.com, or askjeeves.com.

Deserving of special mention is About.com, a collection of over seven hundred topical sites (too many to include in the following) whose guides do a phenomenal job of creating topic-specific communities that include weekly newsletters, discussion, articles and links.

The prefix for all of the following websites is the usual **http://www.**

———

Animal Advocacy, Protection and Welfare/Rights

- African Conservation Foundation
  africanconservation.org
- American Sanctuary Association
  americansanctuary.org/
- American Society for the Prevention of Cruelty to Animals
  aspca.org/
- Animal Legal Defense Fund
  aldf.org/
- Animal Protection Institute
  api4animals.org/
- Animals Australia
  melbourne.net/animals_australia/
- Defenders of Wildlife
  Defenders.org/
- Doris Day Animal League
  ddal.org/
- Ethologists for the Ethical Treatment of Animals/Citizens for Responsible Animal Behavior Studies
  ethologicalethics.org/
- Farm Sanctuary
  farmsanctuary.org/
- In Defense of Animals
  idausa.org/
- International Fund for Animal Welfare
  ifaw.org/
- National Wildlife Federation
  nwf.org/
- People for the Ethical Treatment of Animals
  peta-online.org/
- The Humane Society of the United States
  hsus.org/
- The Jane Goodall Institute
  janegoodall.org/
- The Marine Mammal Center
  tmmc.org/

- The Royal Society for the Prevention of Cruelty to
  Animals – United Kingdom
  rspca.org.uk/
  – Australia
  rspca.org.au/
- United Animal Nations
  uan.org/
- World Wildlife Fund
  worldwildlife.org/

Animal Adoption and Rescue Resources

- Animal Home.com
  animalhome.com/
- Canadian Federation of Humane Societies
  cfhs.ca/
- Can We Help You Keep Your Pet?
  wonderpuppy.net/canwehelp/
- Doginfomat.com
  doginfomat.com/dog04.htm
- DogsNeedingPeopleNeedingDogs.org (publishes one of
  the most useful rescue lists)
  DogsNeedingPeopleNeedingDogs.org/
- Feline Rescue Network
  felinerescue.net/
- "Free To Good Home?"
  parrett.net/animalaid/free.html
- Hugs for Homeless Animals Shelter & Rescue Directory
  h4ha.org/shelters/
- Kyler Laird's Animal Rescue Resources (one of the best
  on the www)
  ecn.purdue.edu/~laird/animal_rescue/
- Petfinder.com/ASPCA (database of over 50,000 animals
  for adoption)
  petfinder.org/
- World Animal Net Directory
  worldanimal.net/wan.htm

Breeding/Not Breeding

- Considerations for Responsible Breeders
  showdogsupersite.com/sdkjour1.html
- No Puppymills.com
  nopuppymills.com/
- Responsible Breeding
  dog-play.com/ethics.html
- Virtual Breeding
  bluegrace.com/virtualbreeding.html

Cats

- Cats at About.com
  cats.about.com/
- Feline WWW Sites
  felinewww.com/
- 21cats.org
  21cats.org/

Conservation and Environment

- American Rivers
  amrivers.org/
- Environmental Defense
  environmentaldefense.org/
- Friends of the Earth
  FOE.org/
- Greenpeace
  greenpeace.org/
- National Parks and Conservation Association
  npca.org/
- National Resources Defense Council
  nrdc.org/
- Rainforest Action Network
  ran.org/
- Sierra Club
  sierraclub.org/
- The Ocean Conservancy
  oceanconservancy.org/

- The Wilderness Society
  wilderness.org/

Diet and Nutrition

- Animal Protection Institute: "What's Really In Pet Food"
  api4animals.org/doc.asp?ID=79
- Hollow's Hound Recipes
  emerge.net.au/~hollow/dogrec~1.htm
- Homemade treats for dogs and cats
  pastrywiz.com/archive/category/pets.htm
- Winnie Wu's Recipe File
  cgocable.net/%7Eblacroix/recipebook.htm

Dogs

- Companion animal (multi-species) behavior links
  users.erols.com/mandtj/behavior/behavior.html
- Dogs at About.com
  dogs.about.com/
- Dog behavior, training, aggression
  groups.yahoo.com/group/agbeh/
- Doginfomat.com
  doginfomat.com/
- Dogomania.com
  dogomania.com/
- Dog-related websites
  k9web.com/dog-faqs/lists/www-list.html
  and related e-mail lists
  k9web.com/dog-faqs/lists/email-list.html
- Guide and Service Dog resources
  ability.org/Guide_Dogs.html
- The Dogplace.com
  thedogplace.com/
- Working Dogs weblinks
  workingdogs.com/links.htm

Fun Stuff and For Kids

- Animaland from The ASPCA
  animaland.org/
- Fluffy Fables
  fluffyfables.com/
- Kid Info (child-safe, multiple topics)
  kidinfo.com/
- Leilah's Laughs (dog humor and more)
  wonderpuppy.net/
- The Snuggles Project (knit, crochet, sew for animals)
  h4ha.org/snuggles/
- Urban Legends at About.com (check those e-mailed warnings before you distribute them further!)
  urbanlegends.about.com/

General Pet

- Acme Pet
  acmepet.petsmart.com/
- Pet Education from Drs. Foster & Smith
  peteducation.com/
- Pet-friendly lodging for travelers
  takeyourpet.com/

Horses

- BLM National Wild Horse and Burro Program
  wildhorseandburro.blm.gov/
- Equine Rescue List & Resources
  equinerescue.info/
- Horses at About.com
  horses.about.com/

Loss and Grief Support

- Death and Dying at About.com
  dying.about.com/
- Petloss.com
  petloss.com/

- Pet memorials, urns, cemeteries, links
  In-Memory-of-Pets.Net/petlinks/home.html

Lost and Stolen Pets Resources

- Links to e-mail lists and website resources
  dogsneedingpeopleneedingdogs.org/lostandfound.html

Vegan/Vegetarian

- International Vegetarian Union
  ivu.org/global/
- Vegetarian Cuisine at About.com
  vegetarian.about.com/

Veterinary Medical

- Allergies, human and animal
  theanimalspirit.com/allergy.html
- Alternative, complementary and holistic vetmed resources
  altvetmed.com/
- Animal disease links from Karolinska Institute (one of the best!)
  mic.ki.se/Diseases/c22.html
- CPR Instructions for use on animals
  members.aol.com/henryhbk/acpr.html
- National (USA) Animal Poison Control Center
  aspca.org/site/PageServer?pagename=apcc
- The Senior Dogs Project
  srdogs.com/
- Veterinary medicine at About.com
  vetmedicine.about.com/

Volunteerism and Job Opportunities

- AnimalConcerns.org
  animalconcerns.netforchange.com/
- HSUS Shelter Employment Listings
  hsus.org/programs/companion/index.html

- Idealist.org
  idealist.org/
- VolunteerMatch
  volunteermatch.org/

Wolves

- International Wolf Center
  wolf.org/
- Wolf and Wolfdog Rescue Network
  wolfsong.org/rescue/
- Wolf Recovery Foundation
  forwolves.org/

Foreign Language Directories

- All Languages (enter the appropriate search term)
  dmoz.org/World/
- German/Companion Animals
  dmoz.org/World/Deutsch/Freizeit/Haustiere/
  (see links at bottom of page for other languages)

I am only one – but still I am one.
I cannot do everything, but still I can do something.
I will not refuse to do the something I can do.
~ HELEN KELLER
❖

THE BASSET CHRONICLES:
Alexis, the Living End

"So, you are finally finished with your book?"
"Yes, Alexis, I am. Finished." I replied.

"You might be. You gonna read the reviews?" her royal sableness asked while slinking up on the couch next to me.

"No, I'm not going to read the reviews. I don't know that there will be any reviews. I don't know if anyone will even read the book."

"You can read it to me," Alexis said and fluttered her Basset eyelashes. "It would be an improvement over having to listen to you talk."

"Alexis, I can always count on you to keep me humble," I sighed.

"Am I in the book?" she asked.

"Of course you are in the book...you are all in the book."

"Even Winston The Incontinent?" she asked. "What *is* he anyway?"

"Be kind, Alexis. Winston is old and can't help himself. And you know he is a Pomeranian-Chihuahua mix."

"He's a bladder on four legs, that's what he is," she said with disgust. "Why do you look so glum?"

"I don't know. I guess it's a bit anticlimactic finishing a book. Rather like sending a child out into the world and not hearing back from him. That's stupid, I suppose. After all, I did finish it. I should be happy."

"I'm happy," Alexis assured me and snuggled her head into my lap. "I'm so happy for you I could just...*sniff*...ooooo, Winston!"

I looked at little Winston, spread-eagled and cross-eyed from his effort in the middle of the living room. I rested my chin in my hand and shook my head. I wondered if James Herriot had to put up with what I put up with.

"CAN WE GET SOME PAPERTOWELS AND AIR FRESHENER IN HERE, PUHLEEESE?" Alexis bellowed.

About the Author

Jim Willis is a writer, artist, and animal advocate. He was born in Pittsburgh, Pennsylvania, and has lived much of his adult life in Europe. In 1990, he and his wife, Nicole Valentin, founded and personally funded a multi-species, all-breed rescue, placement, education and advocacy effort, now The Tiergarten Sanctuary Trust. They have adopted and share their lives with over three dozen rescued animals. Jim is a member of the American Sanctuary Association and the African Conservation Foundation, and is a supporter of other efforts for animals and the environment. His dream is to have a sanctuary with habitat-appropriate facilities for rescued wolves and wolf-hybrids, an expanded adoption program for rescued companion animals, and education programs that promote the human-animal bond. His wife would like a new vacuum cleaner. They may be contacted at *tiergartenjim@yahoo.com*

Sales of *Pieces of My Heart* help further their efforts as well as those of other organizations that sell the book as a fundraiser. Your support is appreciated.

————

About the Illustrator

Christine J. Head was born in Detroit, Michigan and studied fine arts at Western Michigan University. She and her husband Corbett currently live in Massachusetts with their two boxers, Stu and Scully, and a pug, Henry, as well as intermittent foster dogs. Christine is a digital and multi-media figurative artist. She assists animal rescue fundraising and education efforts by offering limited-edition animal portrait prints that are accompanied by each subject's rescue story. She accepts a number of commissions each year; for more examples of her work see: *www.mysketches.com*

Christine has dedicated her illustrations in this book to the memory of her late uncle, the talented painter Richard Jerzy. "He was a phenomenal artist who also loved and appreciated animals. I am continually inspired by his vibrant paintings depicting the extraordinary beauty in our world."

❖

Nullus est liber tam malus ut non aliqua parte prosit.

❖

THE AUTHOR AT A YOUNG AGE DISPLAYING
AN UNCANNY ABILITY TO BOND WITH ANIMALS.

Special Offer for Advocates, Rescues, Shelters and Organizations

Pieces of My Heart – Writings Inspired by Animals and Nature is simultaneously published in the USA and the UK. The author has made a special arrangement with both publishers whereby all advocates and organizations may order the book in quantity (minimum five copies) at the same discount that conventional booksellers receive, in order to benefit their own fundraising efforts. This special offer is not available through the publishers' websites and you must call the respective publisher. (Free shipping is offered for twenty or more copies within the USA or UK, from the respective publishers.) For complete information, please visit the *Pieces of My Heart* website at: *www.crean.com/jimwillis*

Please also note that the two editions of the book have different ISBN numbers, which is particularly important when ordering through on-line or local booksellers. We appreciate your recommending the title to your memberships and to your local bookseller.

The book is available in electronic format worldwide through the UK publisher, AuthorsOnline; refer to their website for details.

A German-language edition of the book is planned. For all reprint or foreign-language rights, please contact the author directly: *tiergartenjim@yahoo.com*

For ordering/shipping in the USA & Canada:
Infinity Publishing.com
ISBN 0-7414-1015-X
(see the Copyright page at the front of the book for contact information)

For ordering/shipping in the UK and to all other countries excluding North America, and for the electronic edition:
AuthorsOnline
ISBN 0-7552-0040-3
www.authorsonline.co.uk
Phone 01992 586788
Fax 01992 586787

❖